LOOTED ART & RESTITUTION

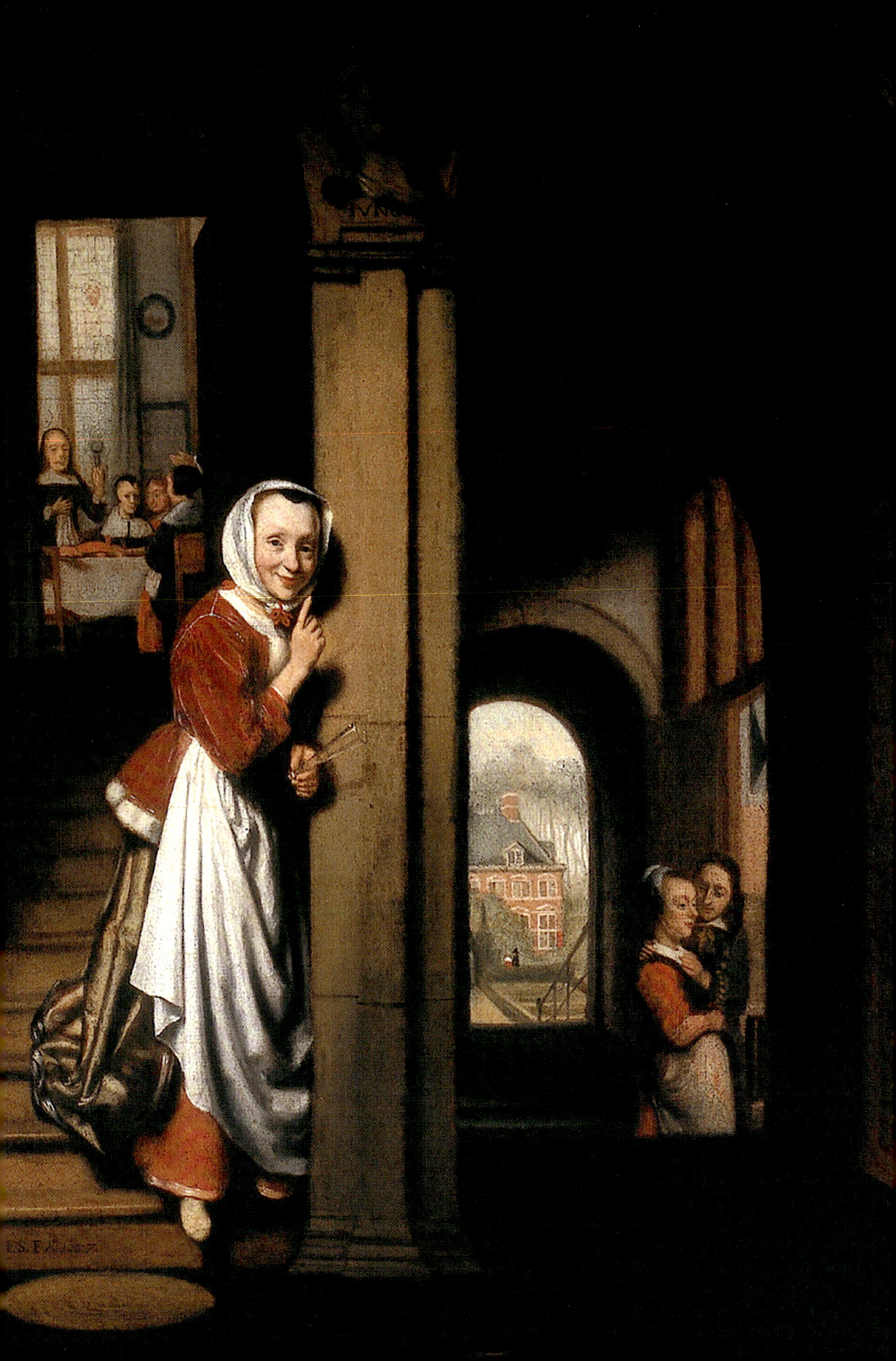

Rudi Ekkart • Eelke Muller

LOOTED ART & RESTITUTION

The Exodus and Partial Return of Dutch Art Property During and After World War II

Waanders Publishers, Zwolle

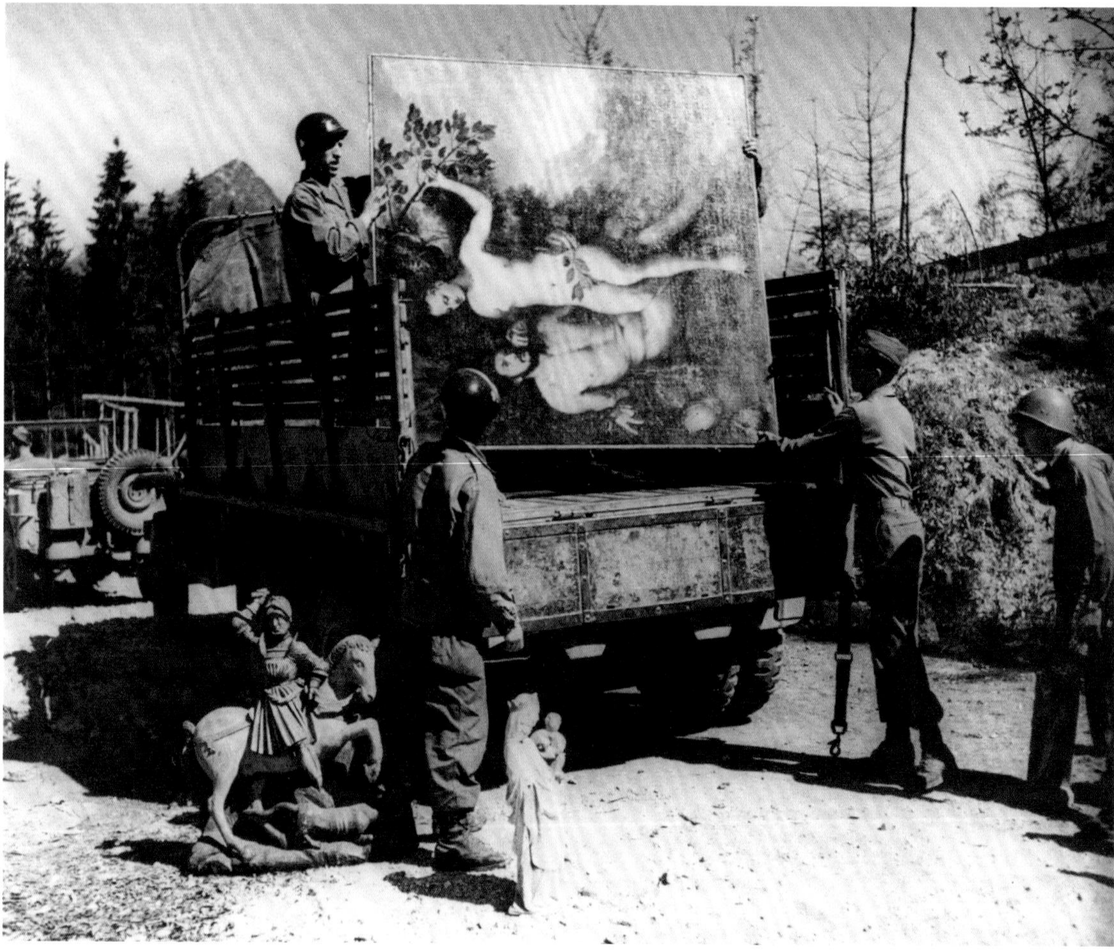

FOREWORD

In 2021, the minister of Education, Culture and Science (OCW) decided to place passive and active informative tasks in the restitution policy for World War II (1933-1945) under ministerial responsibility following the advice in the report *Striving for Justice*. As part of the Ministry of OCW, the National Cultural Heritage Agency (RCE) was thus given an additional task. This task suited well with the RCE's other responsibilities, such as the management of the Netherlands Art Property Collection (NK Collection) and the handling of restitution claims. This concentration of tasks and duties means that potential claimants, collection managers, researchers and other interested parties can now go to one place with their questions.

Information and publications on looting and restitution of cultural goods in the period 1933-1945 are also among the RCE's responsibilities. In this context, a reissue of the publication *Roof & Restitutie* was deemed desirable. This original edition appeared in 2017 at the initiative of the Ter Borch Foundation to accompany the exhibition of the same title in the Bergkerk Church in Deventer. The project was realised in close consultation with the RCE.
Rudi Ekkart and Eelke Muller were the curators for the exhibition and the authors of the book *Roof & Restitutie*. They were willing to extend their original text with a brief update of the developments since 2017. The publisher was also asked to deliver an English edition of the publication as a survey on the subject, covering the pre-war period until the present. In 2023, we commemorate 25 years of restitution policy in the Netherlands and this is an excellent occasion to present the revised edition of *Roof & Restitutie* and introduce the English edition, *Looted Art & Restitution*.

I am very grateful to the authors for their efforts. I would also like to thank Eva Kleeman and Daaf Ledeboer of the Ter Borch Foundation for agreeing to an updated publication and a translation into English.

Susan Lammers, General Director of the National Cultural Heritage Agency (RCE)

INTRODUCTION

There has been an enormous worldwide interest in the issue of art looted during World War II over the past twenty-five years. This interest is continually fuelled by the wide coverage of daily newspapers, radio and television, and, apart from a flood of journalistic publications, has yielded a plethora of books and magazine articles on the subject. Also in the Netherlands, from where many tens of thousands of works of art disappeared to Germany between 1940-1945, much has been written about all kinds of aspects of what, with a certain lack of nuance, is usually referred to as 'looted art'. Moreover, several exhibitions in this context were organised in the country. The first of these was held in 2003 at the Fries Museum in Leeuwarden, the second in 2006-2007 at the Hollandsche Schouwburg in Amsterdam.

In 2017, an exhibition with the title *Roofkunst voor, tijdens en na de Tweede Wereldoorlog* (Looted Art before, during and after the Second World War) was presented in the Bergkerk Church in Deventer. That project not only focused on the exodus of works of art during the years 1940-1945 but also on its prehistory and the destination the objects transported to Germany were given there. It additionally shed light on the post-war return of artworks to the Netherlands, on the restitution of part of this property to original owners and their heirs in the period 1945-1953 and on the renewed restitution policy that had taken form in the previous twenty years. That particular exhibition was complemented by the first edition of the present publication. Eva Kleeman and Daaf Ledeboer of the Ter Borch Foundation were the initiators for the exhibition and the publication. Plans and preparations were carried out in close consultation with the National Cultural Heritage Agency and with the undersigned, the two curators of the exhibition and authors of the publication.

This reissue of the publication in a Dutch and an English edition was the initiative of the National Cultural Heritage Agency. Several necessary changes in text and image were implemented in this new edition. This includes an essential elaboration of Chapter VII, *A new Restitution Policy*, featuring a summary of the developments since 2017. Moreover, it seemed fitting to replace the reproductions of various artworks by images of other objects. In the first edition, we depicted the works of art that were also on display at the temporary exhibition. We have now substituted a number of images by more appropriate and aesthetically superior examples. Naturally, the texts were updated and adapted accordingly. In this manner, this book will optimally represent an extensive general introduction to the Dutch issues of looting and restitution before, during and after the Second World War. It is rewarding that with the publication of an English edition of this book, this story will also be accessible to those who are not fluent in Dutch.

Rudi Ekkart and Eelke Muller

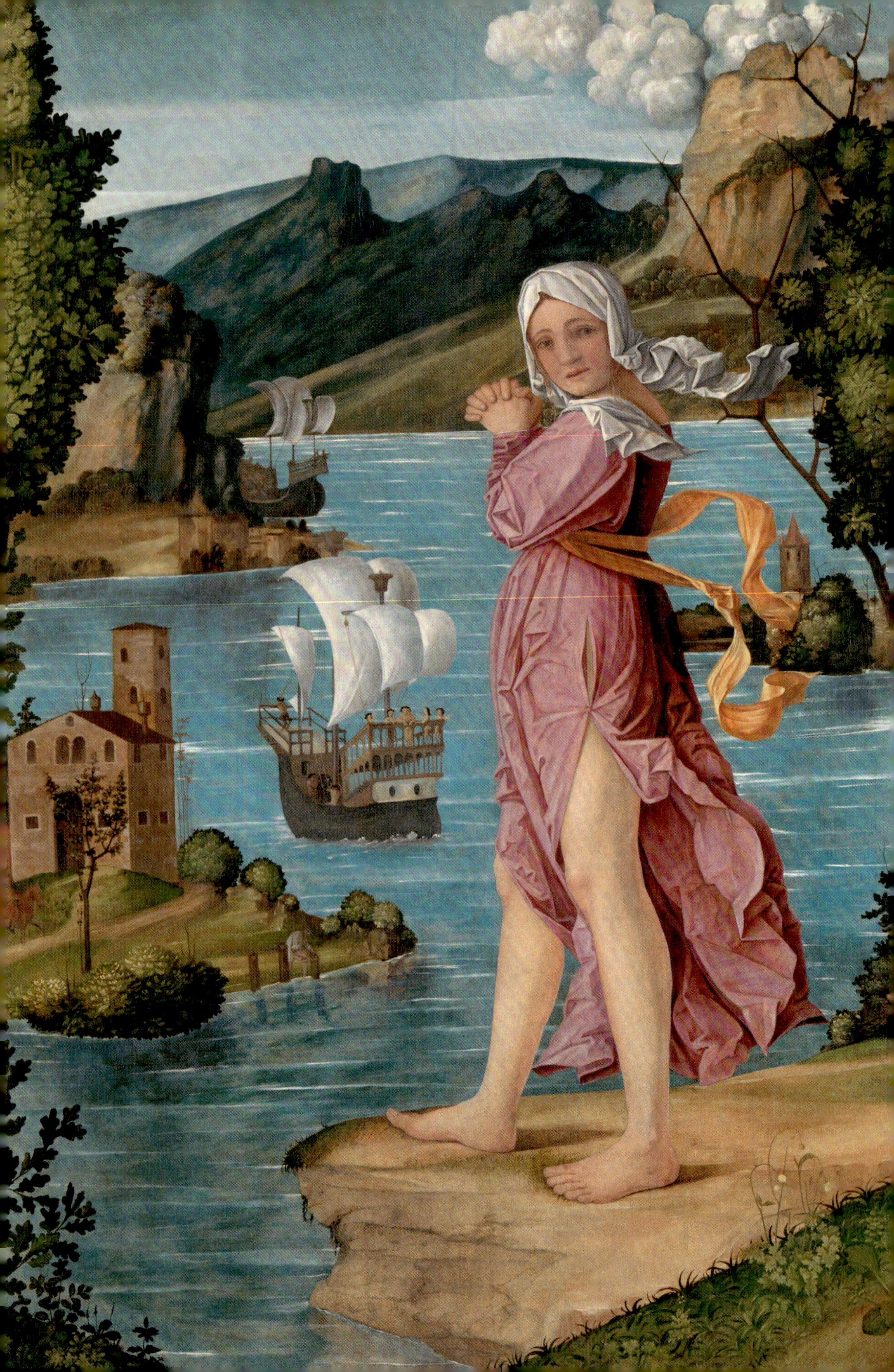

I THE INTERBELLUM

During the period between World War I and World War II, the art trade and collecting thrived in the Netherlands. Current restitution issues are closely related to the extent of flourishing and the share Jewish dealers and collectors had in it. Amsterdam was an art centre of international importance during the interbellum, and many art dealers and collectors of old masters and modern art could also be found outside in the rest of the Netherlands. A large group of dealers and collectors were not exclusively focused on Dutch art but were clearly internationally oriented in their commercial activities. Italian works were particularly popular on the old master market as were French and German paintings in the niche of more recent art. The strong Dutch interest in Italian art was reflected in the major exhibition held at the Stedelijk Museum in Amsterdam in 1934, which included nearly 1300 art objects belonging to Dutch museums, collectors and dealers.

Of these, only about twenty per cent was public property and eighty per cent came from collectors and dealers. Among others, the exposition included over 400 paintings, more than 250 drawings and nearly 140 sculptures. A more general focus on the Dutch art trade was the exposition organised by the Association of Dealers in Old Art in the Netherlands ('Vereniging van Handelaren in Oude Kunst in Nederland' VHOK) at the Rijksmuseum in 1929, featuring more than 1350 works from the property of members of this association or those recently traded by members. By initiative of the same association, a viewing of artworks from the inventory of the international trade was held, again at the Rijksmuseum in 1936. Foreign dealers joined their Dutch colleagues at this event. With its 957 catalogue numbers, it was of a slightly more modest size. The exhibitions mentioned above were only the tip of the iceberg of the undertakings by dozens of dealers in paintings, drawings and applied arts based in Amsterdam and elsewhere in the Netherlands. Not surprisingly, Jacques Goudstikker, who was chairman of the VHOK from 1928 until his death in 1940, was the driving force and protagonist in all three major exhibitions mentioned.

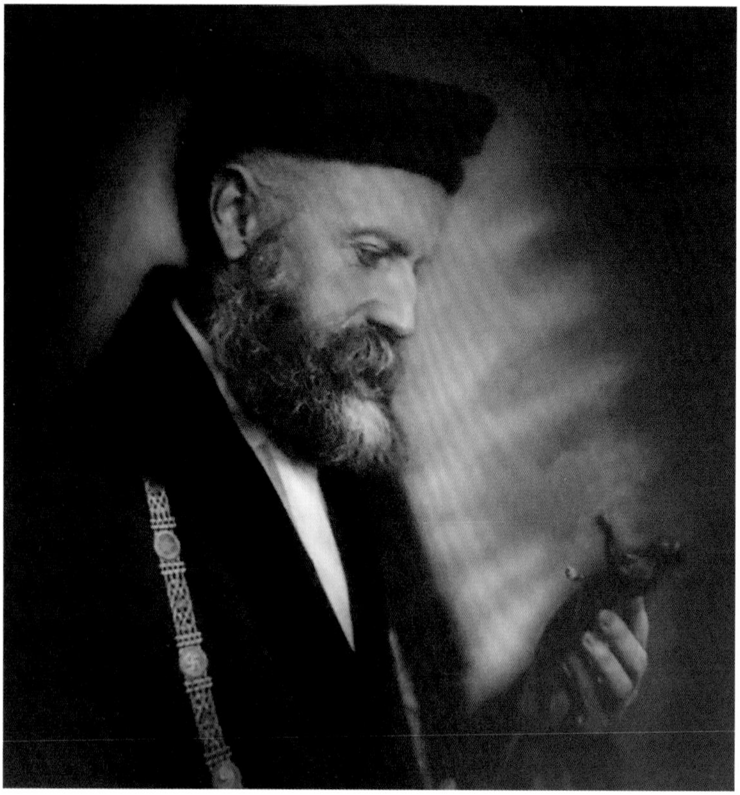

Otto Lanz, 1925

The Swiss surgeon Otto Lanz (1865-1935) settled in the Netherlands after his appointment as professor at the University of Amsterdam in 1902 and lived in the city until his death. Over the course of thirty years, he assembled an all-round collection of more than 400 Italian old master artworks in his home on Museumplein. After his death in 1935, the collection was loaned to the Rijksmuseum. Lanz's widow, however, sold the entire collection to the Führermuseum in 1941. After the war, the collection was returned to the Netherlands. Numerous important pieces were found a place in the Rijksmuseum in Amsterdam, while others are on loan to various Dutch museums, such as the Bonnefantenmuseum in Maastricht. Another part of the recuperated collection was sold at auction in the early 1950s.

The economic crisis that began in 1929 certainly had a major impact on dealers' commercial opportunities. However, the crisis also lowered prices, allowing art dealers with sufficient capital or credit to acquire high-quality objects for relatively low amounts. Moreover, if a dealer could afford to allow ample time to find a buyer for his artworks and also had access to a wide national and international clientele, there were certainly opportunities for success. In the art trade, Jacques Goudstikker (fig. 1) was undoubtedly the most prominent. But there were more important figures who had also established a firm international reputation before the start of World War II, such as the Amsterdam dealers in old master paintings D.A. Hoogendijk (fig. 2) and P. de Boer (fig. 3). D. Katz (fig. 4) in Dieren should also be mentioned. From the early 1920s, foreign dealers had already established themselves in the Netherlands, either by setting up a branch there, such as the Berlin dealer Paul Cassirer (fig. 5), for example. Some, however, established their headquarters in the Netherlands, such as the Austrian dealer Kurt Walter Bachstitz (fig. 6). From 1933 onwards, numerous Jewish traders fled from Germany to the Netherlands. Other colleagues considered it safer to further

he exhibition *Italiaansche kunst* *n Nederlandsch bezit* in the Stedelijk Museum in Amsterdam, 934

he exhibition incorporated 1,293 pieces om more than 100 different lenders, icluding many collectors and art dealers. Among the largest loans were hose by the collectors Otto Lanz (122 pieces), Franz Koenigs (123), Frits Lugt 55), J.C. Bierens de Haan (53) and art dealer Jacques Goudstikker (111). he painting illustrated on p. 10, *Ariadne in Naxos* (c. 1510-1530), hen attributed to Venetian painter Vittore Carpaccio and today to artist ilippo da Verona, hangs above the sofa on the right in the photograph. he work was owned by Otto Lanz panel, 130.5 x 119 cm, Rijksmuseum, Amsterdam, formerly NK2320).

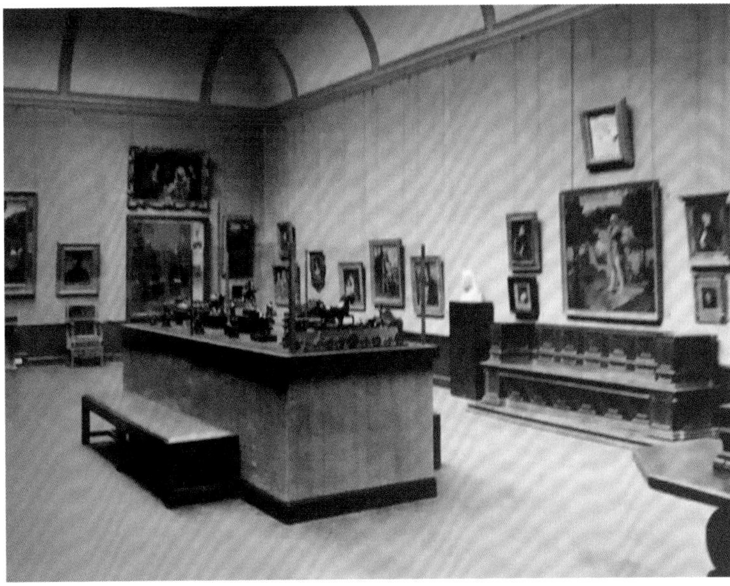

Queen Wilhelmina and Princess uliana at the exhibition *Oude Kunst uit het bezit van den Internationalen Handel*, held at the Rijksmuseum at the initiative of he Association of Dealers in Old Art in the Netherlands (Vereniging van Handelaren in Oude Kunst in Nederland VHOK), 1936

he exhibition was organised on the occasion of the silver jubilee of the association in collaboration with six sister organisations in other European countries. Over 120 dealers from six countries sent in over 950 works of art as loans.

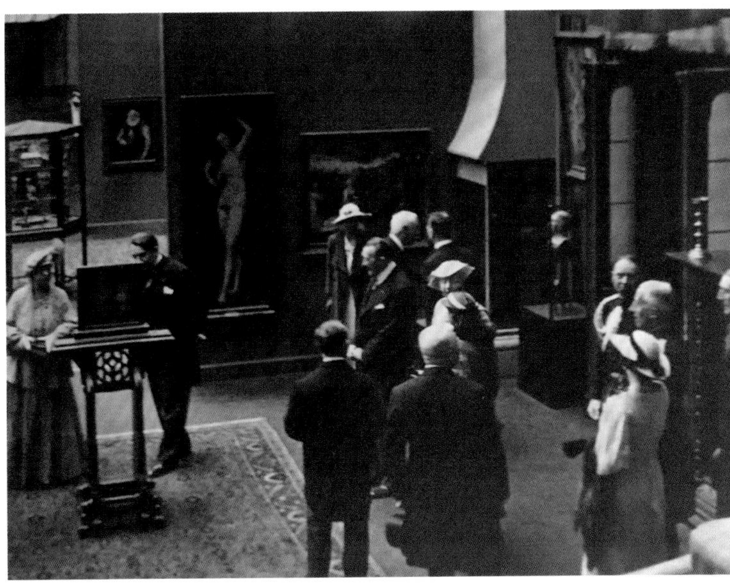

distance themselves from the Nazi regime and emigrated to England or the United States.

The Netherlands also played a major role in the international auction houses during the 1920s and 1930s. The Amsterdam firm Frederik Muller, which was run by Anton Mensing (fig. 7) and later by his son Bernard, was particularly of international stature. There were also various smaller, somewhat less internationally operating auction houses, such as Mak van Waay in Amsterdam, for example.

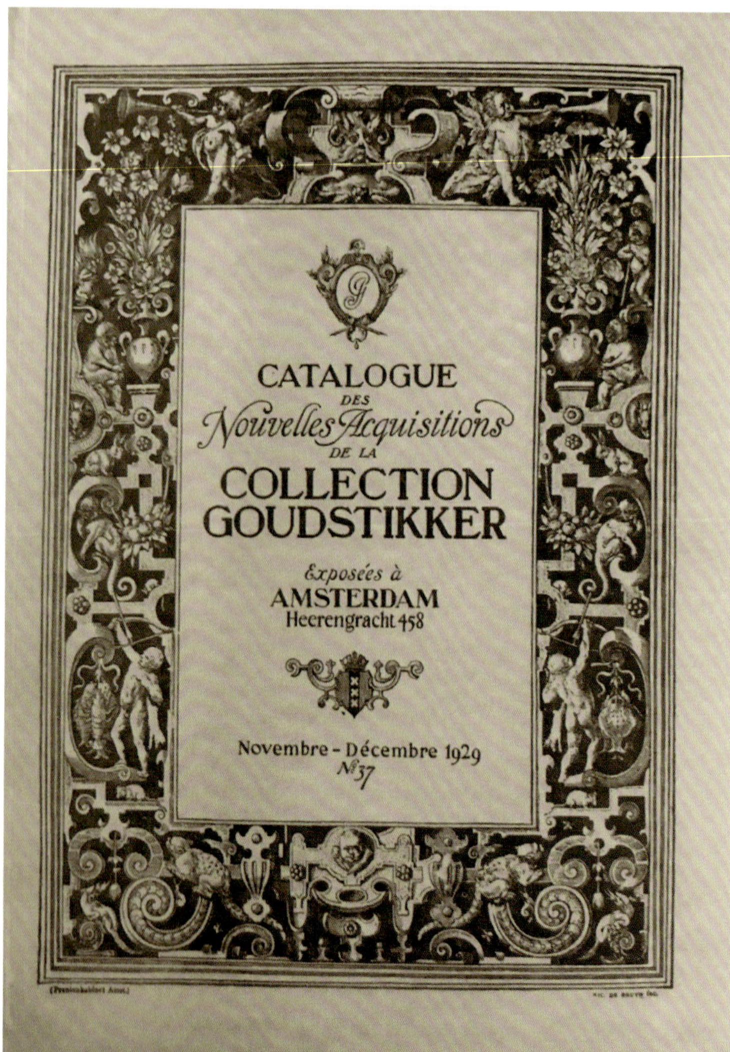

Goudstikker Catalogue, Amsterdam, 1929

In 1915, the art dealer Goudstikker began publishing printed catalogues to accompany exhibitions of artworks for sale held in-house and elsewhere. Initially, the catalogues were modest in size and design. Influenced by Jacques Goudstikker, who joined the firm in 1919 and signed the forewords of the catalogues from that same year, the catalogues became thicker and more luxurious in production. These series of luxurious catalogues, which eventually even ran in editions of 1,000 numbered copies, continued until August 1929, when the 39th volume was published. Apparently, deteriorating economic circumstances forced Jacques Goudstikker to downsize, because after 1929 only publications of a much simpler format appeared, mainly to accompany thematic exhibitions organised by the firm. Catalogues exclusively comprising paintings offered for sale by the firm now appeared only occasionally.

acques Goudstikker at the uction of the Mensing collection, msterdam, 1938

acques Goudstikker (1897-1940) vas the son of Amsterdam art dealer duard Goudstikker, owner of the rt gallery founded by Eduard's ather and uncle in 1845. Although e had probably been involved in is father's business before, Jacques ormally joined the firm in 1919, while lso attending art history classes in eiden and Amsterdam until 1921. In nose years, the art gallery steadily eld annual expositions. Apart from msterdam, Goudstikker also exhibited egularly in The Hague, Rotterdam, New York and Copenhagen. When duard died in 1924, Jacques ook over the entire business and uickly increased its scale, partly by roadening its field of activity. The rm had previously focused almost xclusively on paintings from the Netherlands. However, under Jacques' eadership, foreign art, mainly Italian, ut also German, French and Spanish, lso became part of the stock. The llure he strived to give to his firm was lso reflected in the firm's relocation n 1927. The old premises on the alverstraat were swapped for a rand structure in the Golden Bend of ne Herengracht. Three years later, in 930, Goudstikker purchased the villa Huize Oostermeer in Ouderkerk aan le Amstel, where he resided with his vife. He also acquired the Nijenrode Castle in Breukelen, where he xhibited works of art and organised arties and celebrations. In 1931, the rt firm was converted into a limited ompany with Jacques Goudstikker as s director and largest shareholder. he firm was by far the leading art lealer in the Netherlands during the nterwar period.

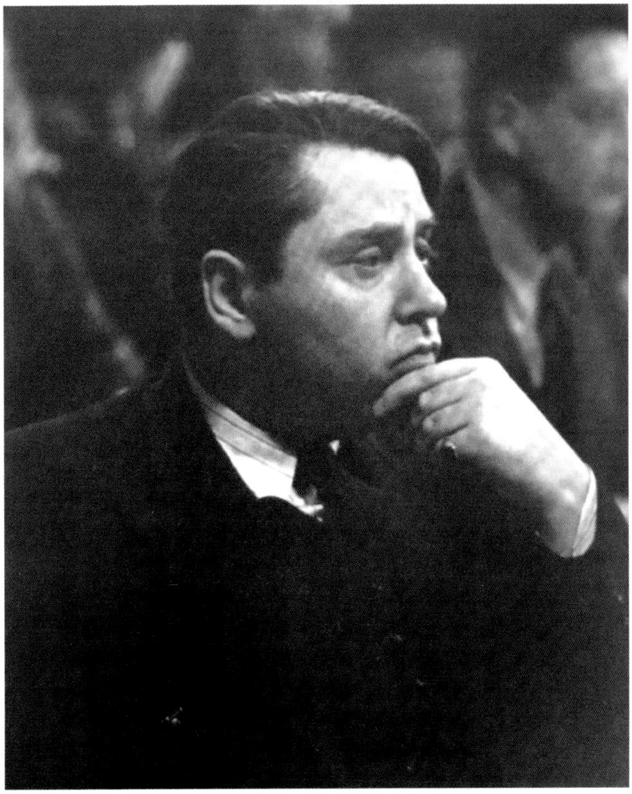

Abundant were the Dutch collectors of art, and many of them managed, even after the economic crisis of 1929, to feed their collecting hunger. The holdings of a few remained together, such as those of H. Kröller-Müller, D.G. van Beuningen, W. van der Vorm, F. Lugt and J.C. Bierens de Haan. Others, sometimes due to war conditions and sometimes by other causes, were later dispersed or divided in parts. Besides prominent collectors, such as those just mentioned, numerous smaller private collections existed. As in the art trade, these included several Germans, some of whom were already living in the Netherlands in the 1920s, such as Fritz Gutmann, Fritz Mannheimer and Franz Koenigs. Gutmann and Mannheimer were of Jewish origin. Other collectors did not leave Germany until after 1933, hoping to find a safe haven in the Netherlands.

The brothers Benjamin and Nathan Katz (1891-1962 and 1893-1949) in their gallery in Dieren, 1936

During the war, the Katz firm went into liquidation. To continue dealing in art, a company was formed in 1941 with non-Jewish business associates of the Katz family as directors. At the beginning of the war, the Katz brothers did business with Germans on a large scale. Moreover, Nathan Katz was to keep an eye on the works on the Dutch art market that could be of interest to Hitler's collection. The Katz brothers' merrits for the Führer collection gave them temporary protection. As the situation for Jews in the Netherlands became more and more critical, the family made plans to flee the country. Nathan Katz received permission to leave for Switzerland in 1942, later followed by the emigration of 25 of his family members via Spain to South America. In exchange, Nathan Katz arranged for a portrait of a man by Rembrandt to be transferred into Posse's hands. After the war, Benjamin Katz continued the art gallery in Dieren until his death in 1962.

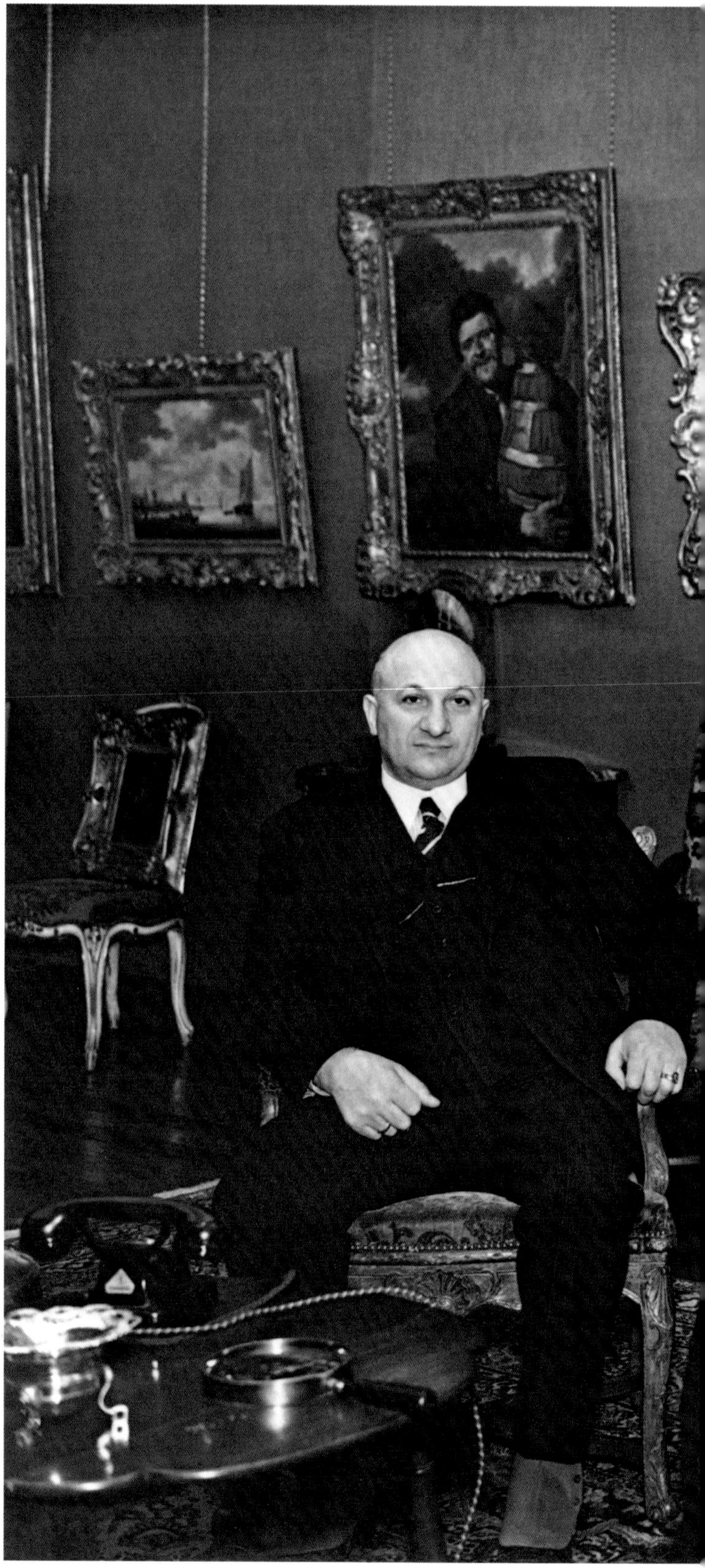

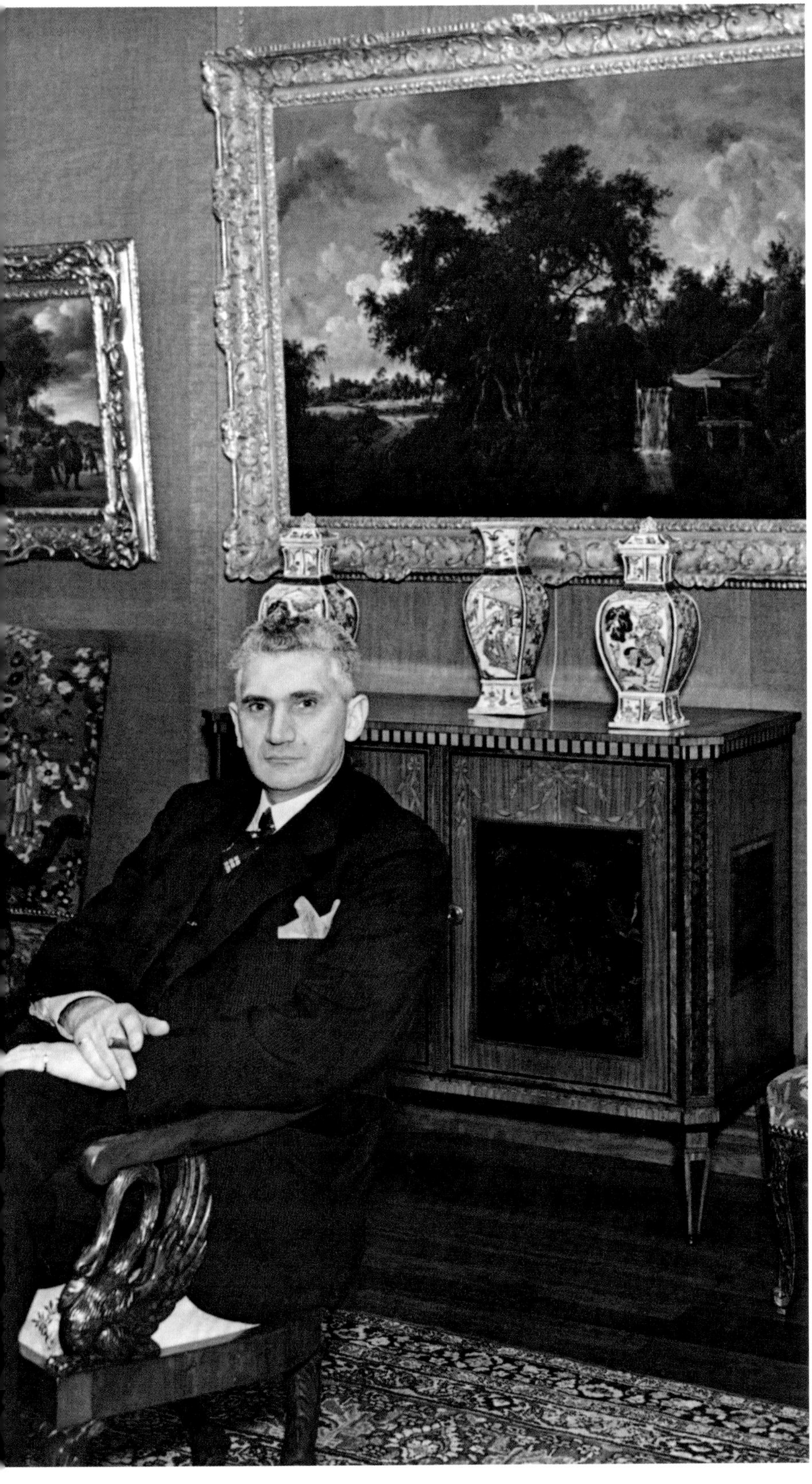

1

The Birth of Christ, c. 1490-1500
FILIPPINO LIPPI (1457-1504) and workshop
Panel, tondo, 86 x 86 cm, Private Collection

This painting was one of the highlights at the 1934 exhibition of Italian art. It belonged to the Amsterdam art dealer Jacques Goudstikker. After the German invasion and Goudstikker's tragic death in 1940, the tondo was acquired by Hermann Göring. It was returned to the Netherlands after the liberation and came into the custody of the Dutch State. In 2006, the panel was restituted to the Goudstikker heirs, along with a large quantity of other works of art from the gallery's old trading stock.

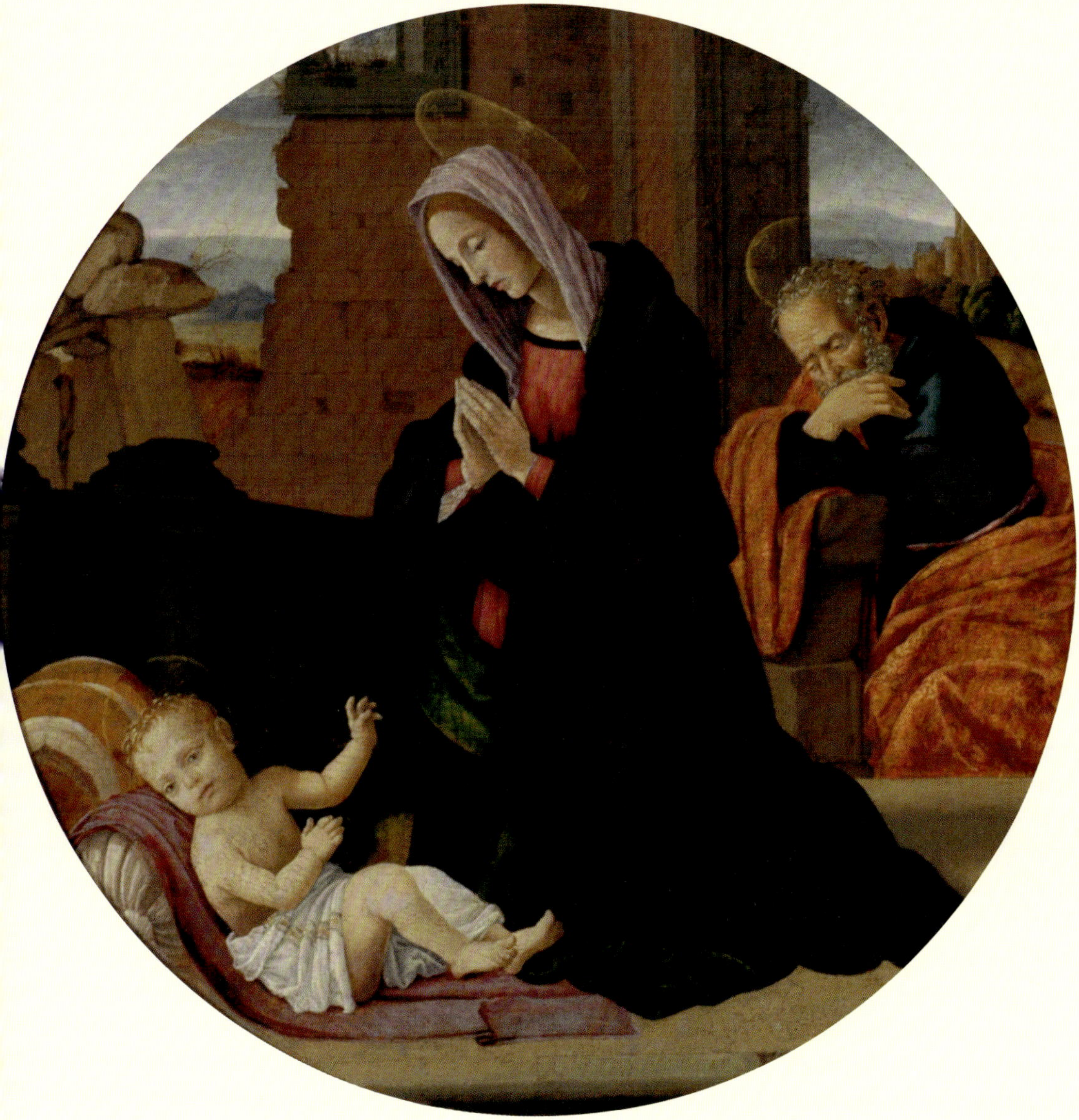

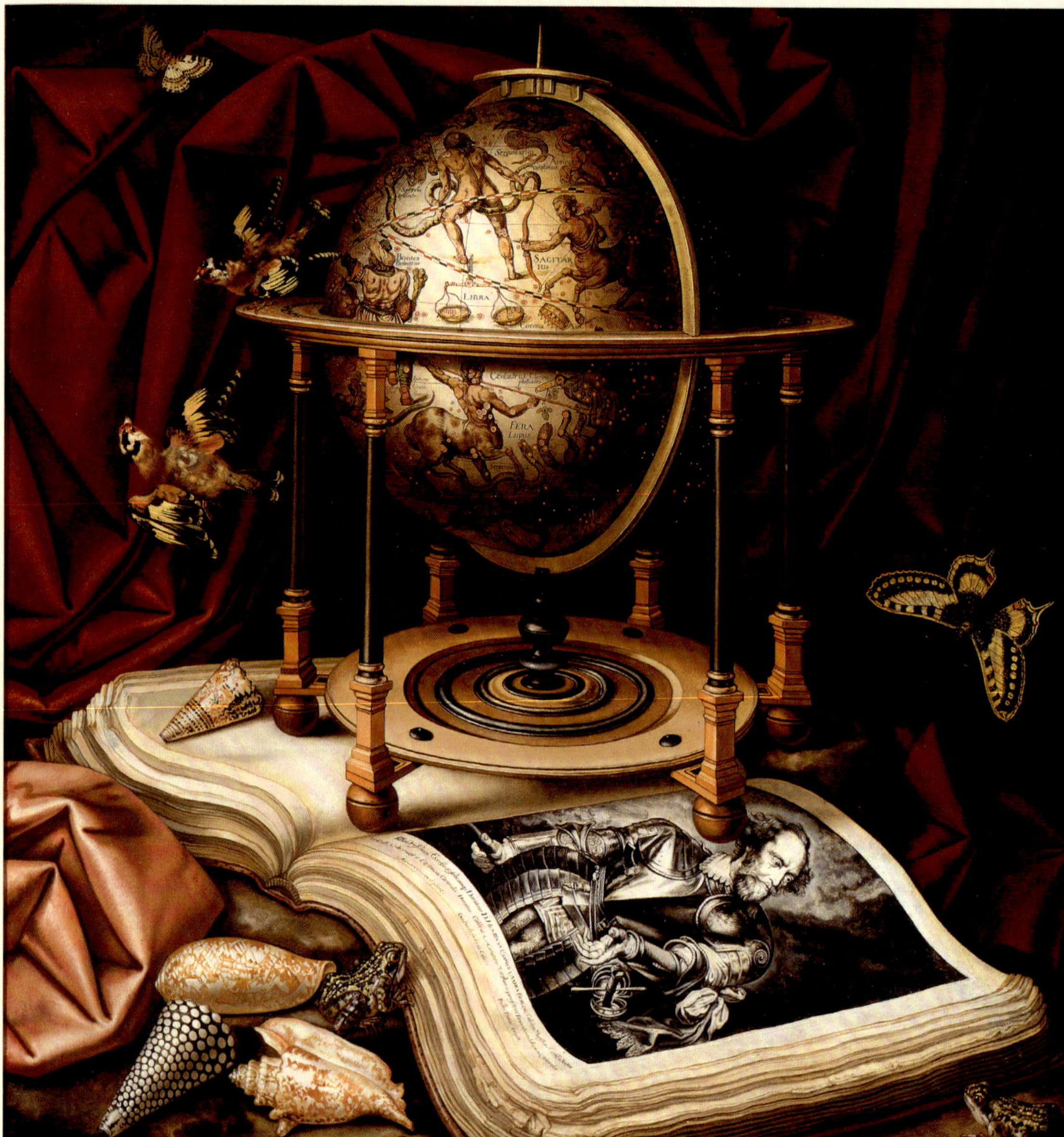
LIBRA
FERA

2

Vanitas Still Life with Celestial Globe and a Book
CARSTIAN LUYCX (1623-after 1657), attributed
Canvas, 90 x 95 cm, Rijksdienst voor het Cultureel Erfgoed, NK3067

In 1925, Dirk A. Hoogendijk (1895-1975) established an art gallery in Amsterdam. He quickly became one of the leading art dealers in paintings in the Netherlands, selling many works by famous masters. A highlight of his career appeared to be the sale of the painting *The Supper at Emmaus* by Johannes Vermeer to the Boijmans Museum in 1937. When after the war the seemingly extraordinary piece turned out to be a falsification, the discovery also backfired on Hoogendijk. He continued his art trade, however, albeit on a more modest scale than before the forgery scandal. The still life attributed to the Antwerp painter Carstian Luycx was acquired by Hoogendijk before the start of the German occupation. He sold it in September 1940 to Walter Andreas Hofer, who especially became well-known as an art agent for Hermann Göring. The painting eventually ended up in the collection of the Führermuseum in Linz in 1944.

3

The Doctor's Visit, c. 1665-1668
JACOB OCHTERVELT (1634-1682)
Canvas, 48 x 42 cm,
Rijksdienst voor het Cultureel
Erfgoed, NK1984

The Doctor's Visit by Jacob Ochtervelt was purchased by the art gallery Kunsthandel P. de Boer in Amsterdam in 1937. De Boer sold the piece in 1943 to the Wallraf-Richartz Museum in Cologne. During the interbellum, De Boer was one of the most respected art dealers in old master paintings in the Netherlands, after the Goudstikker gallery and together with Hoogendijk. The gallery was established in 1922 by Pieter de Boer (1894-1974), who ran it together with his younger brother Rudolf. It quickly became one of the most important Dutch dealerships in old art. Before 1933, Kunsthandel P. de Boer had a few supporting branches in Germany as well. The gallery also published catalogues but these were not as luxurious as those issued by Goudstikker.

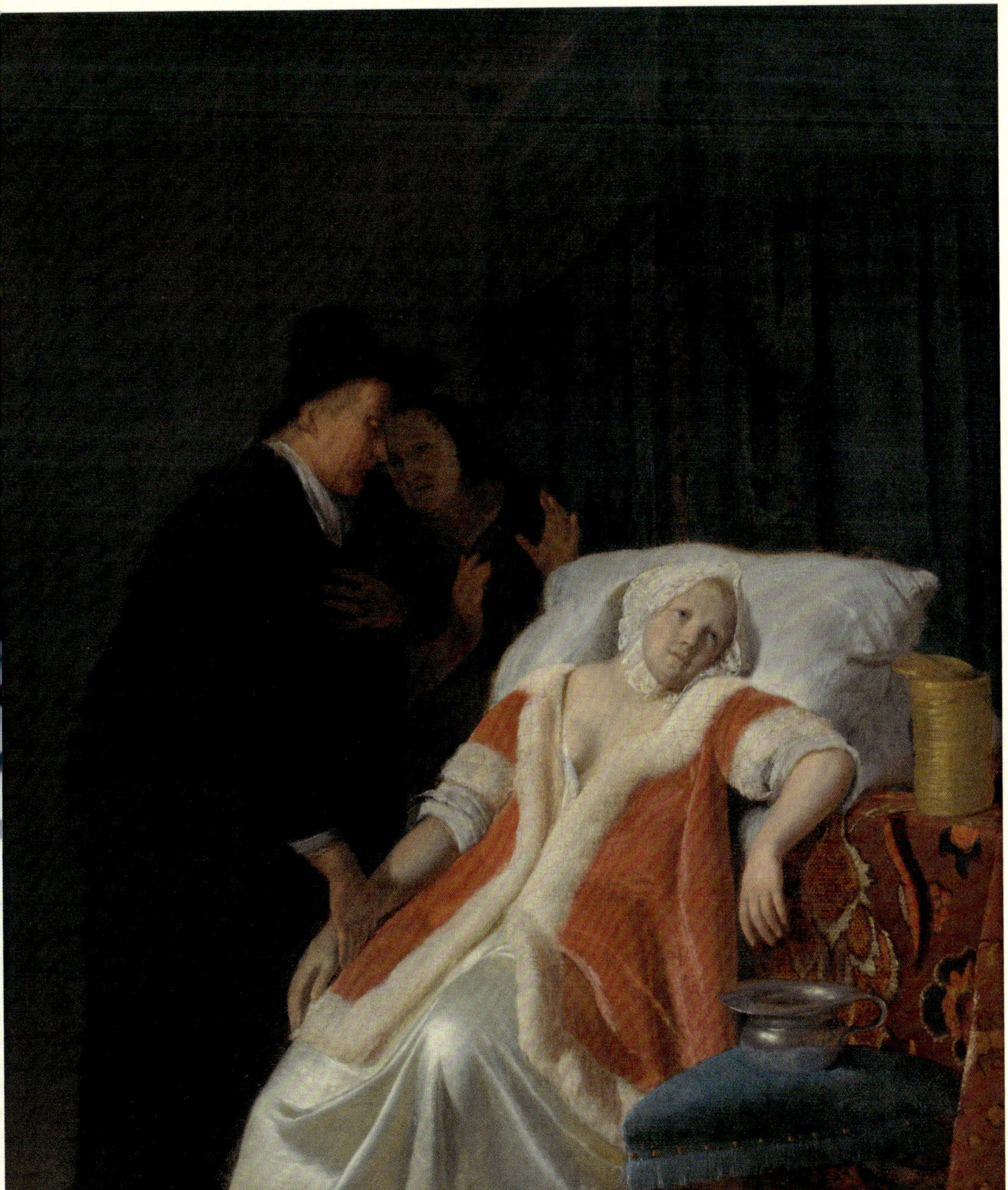

4

Wigbold Slicher and Elisabeth Spiegel as Paris and Venus with Amor, 1656
FERDINAND BOL (1616-1680)
Canvas, 118 x 157 cm, Dordrechts Museum, Dordrecht, on loan from RCE, NK1701

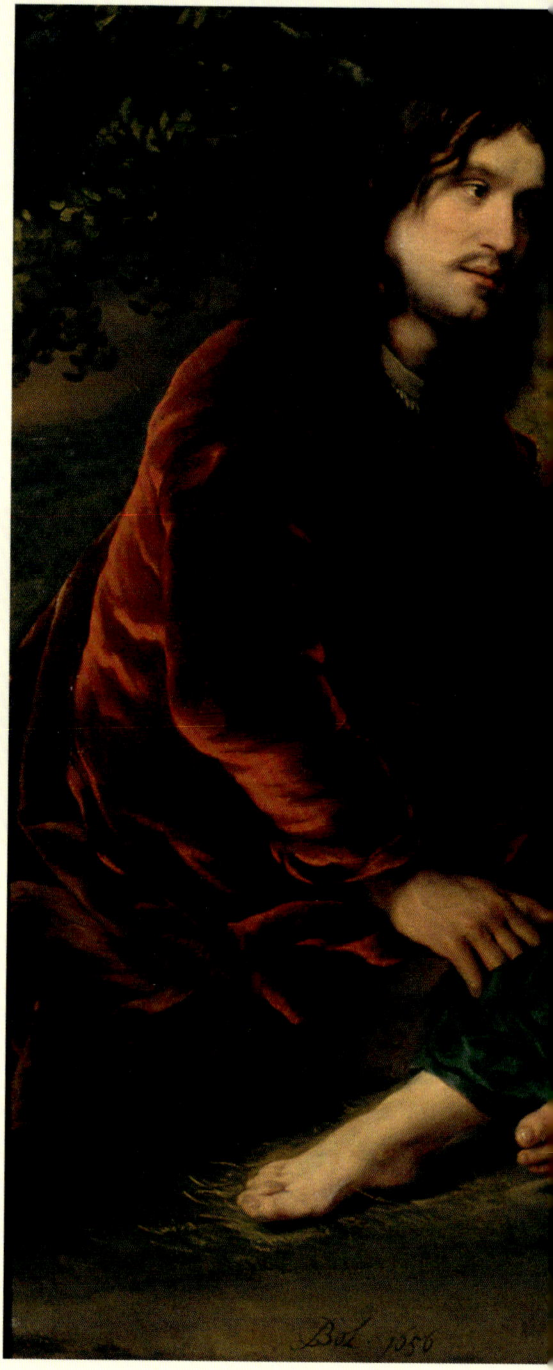

The art dealing firm Katz was established in Dieren in 1883 by David Katz. It began as a furniture store but his two sons Benjamin Katz (1891-1962) and Nathan Katz (1893-1949) transformed the business into one of the largest art dealers of old master paintings in the Netherlands in the 1930s. Branches of the firm were opened in Switzerland and in The Hague on the first of May in 1940. During that year's summer, the Katz brothers sold a portion of their large stock to Alois Miedl, who had taken over Kunsthandel Goudstikker. Business continued to flourish in the early period of the German occupation. However, the Katz gallery was placed under non-Jewish management in 1941, in accordance to the command of the German authorities. Nathan Katz fled to Switzerland with his family in February 1942. Benjamin also managed to flee soon after. When the war ended, the management of the art firm was restored to the Katz family. Benjamin recontinued the gallery in the Netherlands until his death, while Nathan and his son remained in Switzerland.
The depicted painting by Ferdinand Bol was sold by the Katz gallery in 1940 to the museum director Hans Posse, whose responsibilities included procuring the art collection for the intended Führermuseum in Linz.

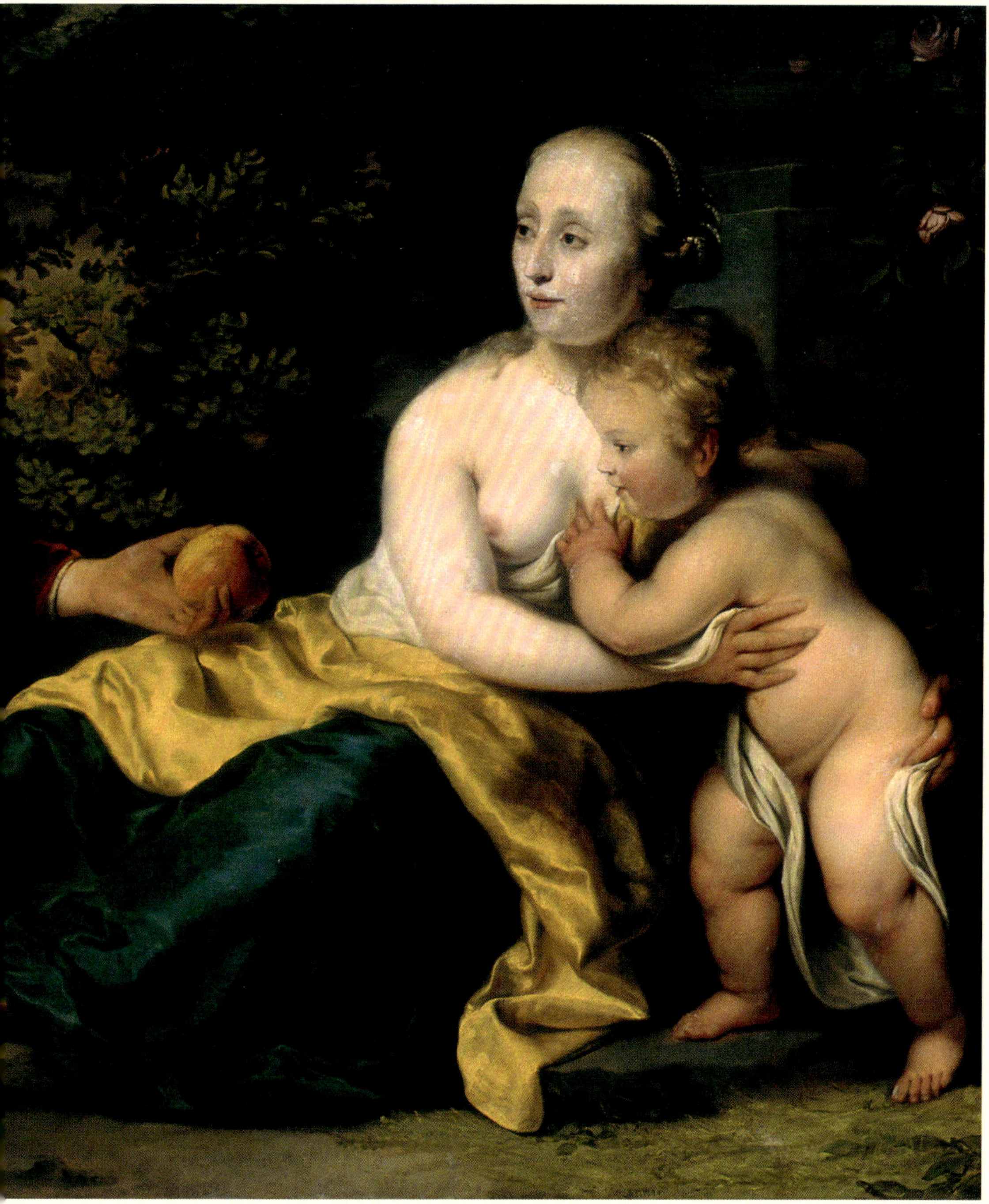

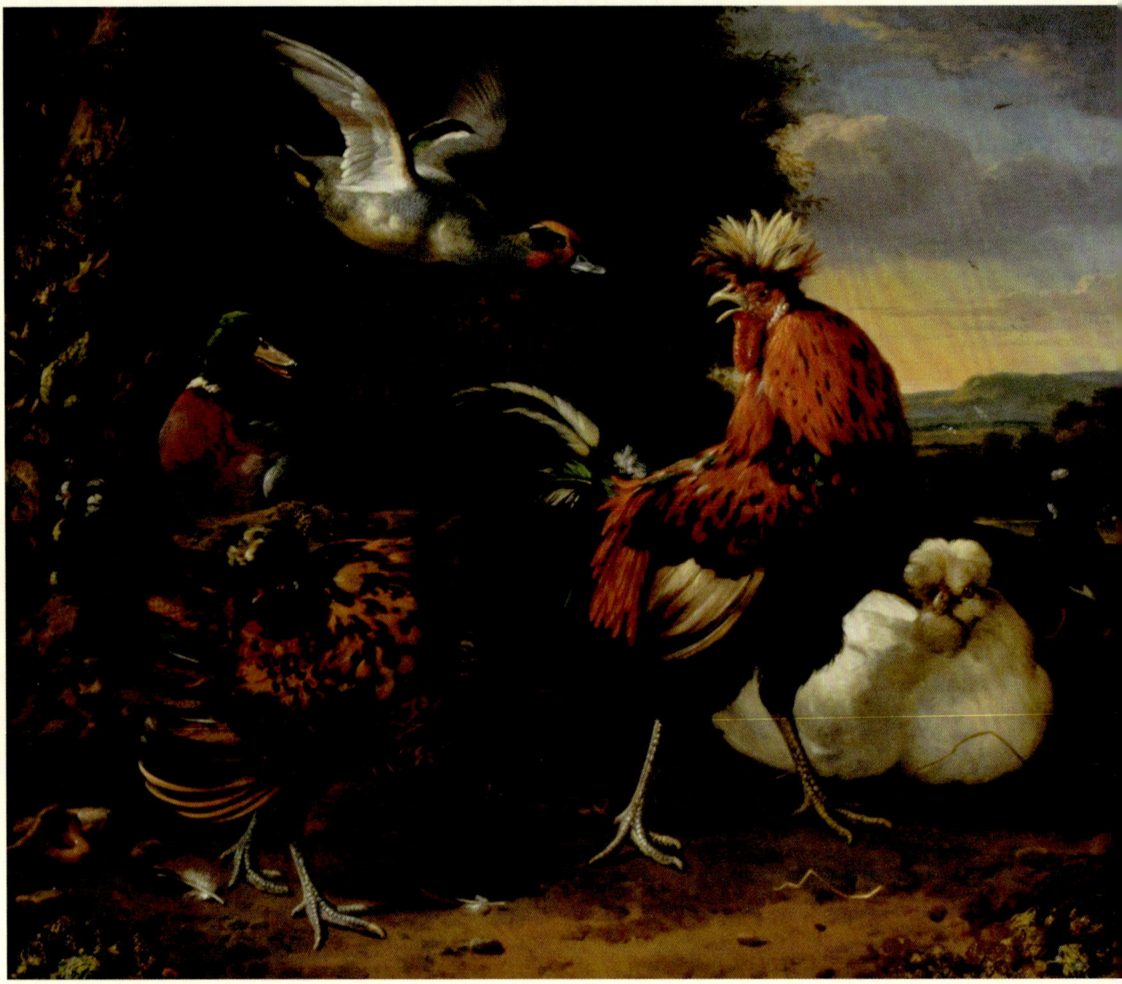

5

Poultry in a Landscape
MELCHIOR D'HONDECOETER
(1636-1695)
Canvas, 100 x 118 cm,
Private Collection

The owner of this painting was an economist and art collector of German-Jewish descent, who had fled to the Netherlands with his wife in 1938. The couple was active in the resistance movement in Enschede during the war. After a period in hiding, the private collector was arrested and detained in 1944. He survived the war, as did his wife and child. The collector had sold the d'Hondecoeter painting in 1942 to the art gallery Paul Cassirer & Co., which sold it on to the Wallraf-Richartz Museum in Cologne. The poultry scene was recovered from Germany after the war. The collector's multiple attempts to redeem possession of the painting did not lead to a final settlement of his claim. Following the advice of the Restitutions Committee, the work was finally returned to the collector's daughter in 2006. The committee had considered it plausible that the owner, a stateless resident of Jewish descent, was unable to practise his profession during the occupation and was forced to sell the d'Hondecoeter for subsistence. The fact that he and his wife participated in the resistance also played a role in the committee's concluding advice.

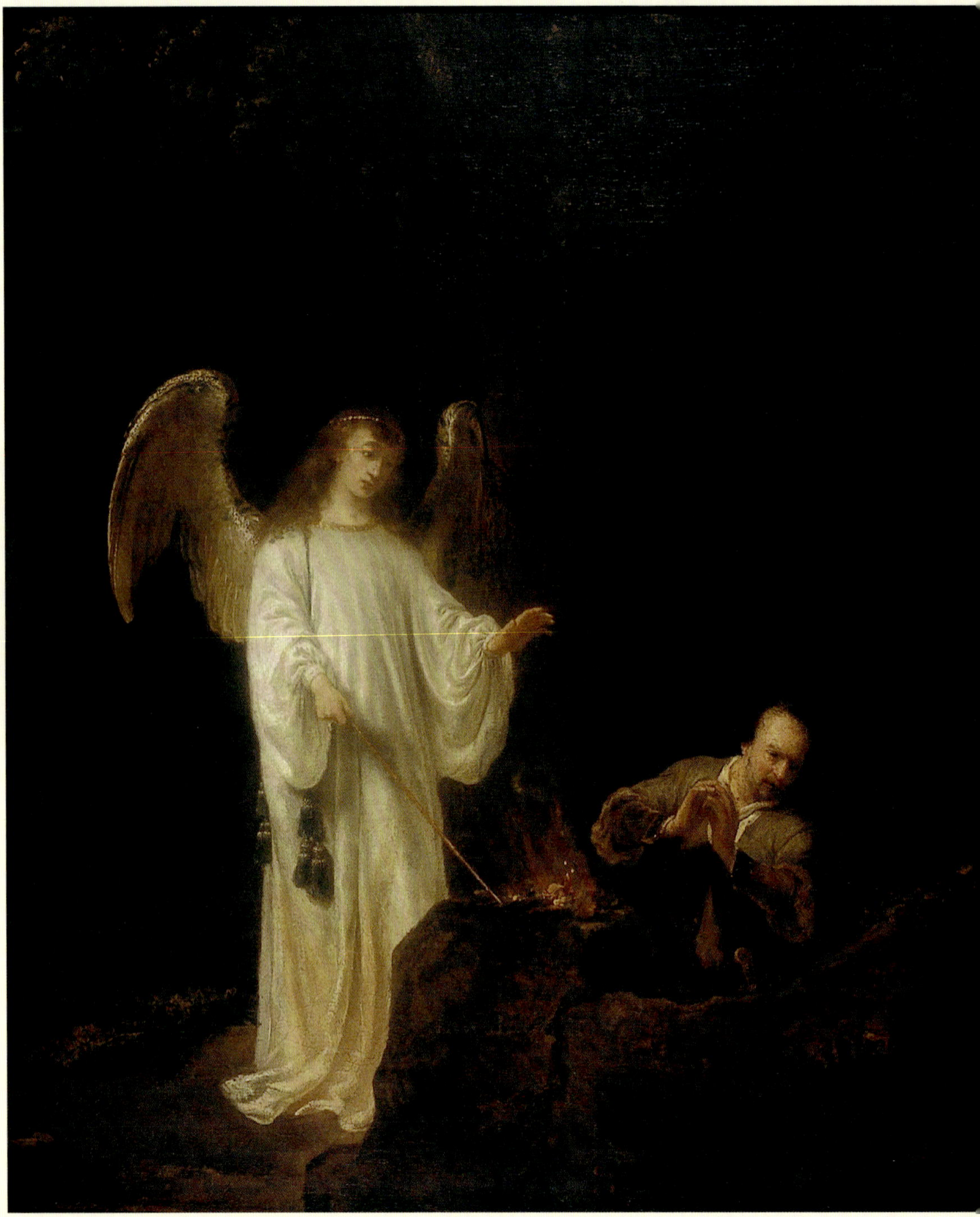

6
Gideon and the Angel, c. 1641
FERDINAND BOL (1616-1680)
Canvas, 83 x 71 cm,
Museum het Catharijneconvent, Utrecht,
on loan from RCE, NK2484

The Austrian art dealer Kurt Walter Bachstitz (1882-1949) began an art gallery after World War I, which soon included branches in New York and The Hague in addition to divisions in Vienna and Berlin. The Hague branch was opened in 1920 and became the gallery's headquarters in 1937, the year that Bachstitz left Vienna with his family and settled in the Netherlands. The Bachstitz gallery was internationally orientated, not only dealing in paintings but also in exquisite applied art and art from classical antiquity. In 1941, Bachstitz formally withdrew from the art firm. He was arrested in 1943, after being classified as a 'full Jew', but he was released on Göring's orders after the intervention of his brother-in-law Walter Andreas Hofer and temporarily exempted from deportation. In 1944, he was given permission to travel to Switzerland after the circumstances had forced him to dissolve his marriage and to surrender a painting by Jan Steen and two antique necklaces to the occupying authorities. Bachstitz had acquired the painting by Ferdinand Bol in the 1930s from the renowned Von Auspitz collection. Hans Posse purchased it in August 1940 for the Führermuseum to be built in Linz.

7

Double Portrait of a Couple, c. 1632-1640
CORNELIS DE VOS (1584/85-1651)
Canvas, 145.5 x 127 cm,
Bonnefantenmuseum, Maastricht,
on loan from RCE, NK1791

The auctioneer Anton Mensing, owner of the Frederik Muller auction house, was also a fervent collector of book bindings, shipping instruments, maps and atlases, paintings, prints, drawings and so forth. His 112-piece collection of paintings with works by artists such as Rembrandt, Bartholomeus van der Helst, Jacob van Ruysdael, Pieter Saenredam and Jan Steen was auctioned off in 1938, at the Frederik Muller firm of course. This double portrait by the Antwerp painter Cornelis de Vos was also part of Mensing's collection. At the 1938 sale, the canvas remained unsold. It was not until four years later that Mensing's heirs were able to sell the painting to Erhard Göpel for the benefit of the Führermuseum.

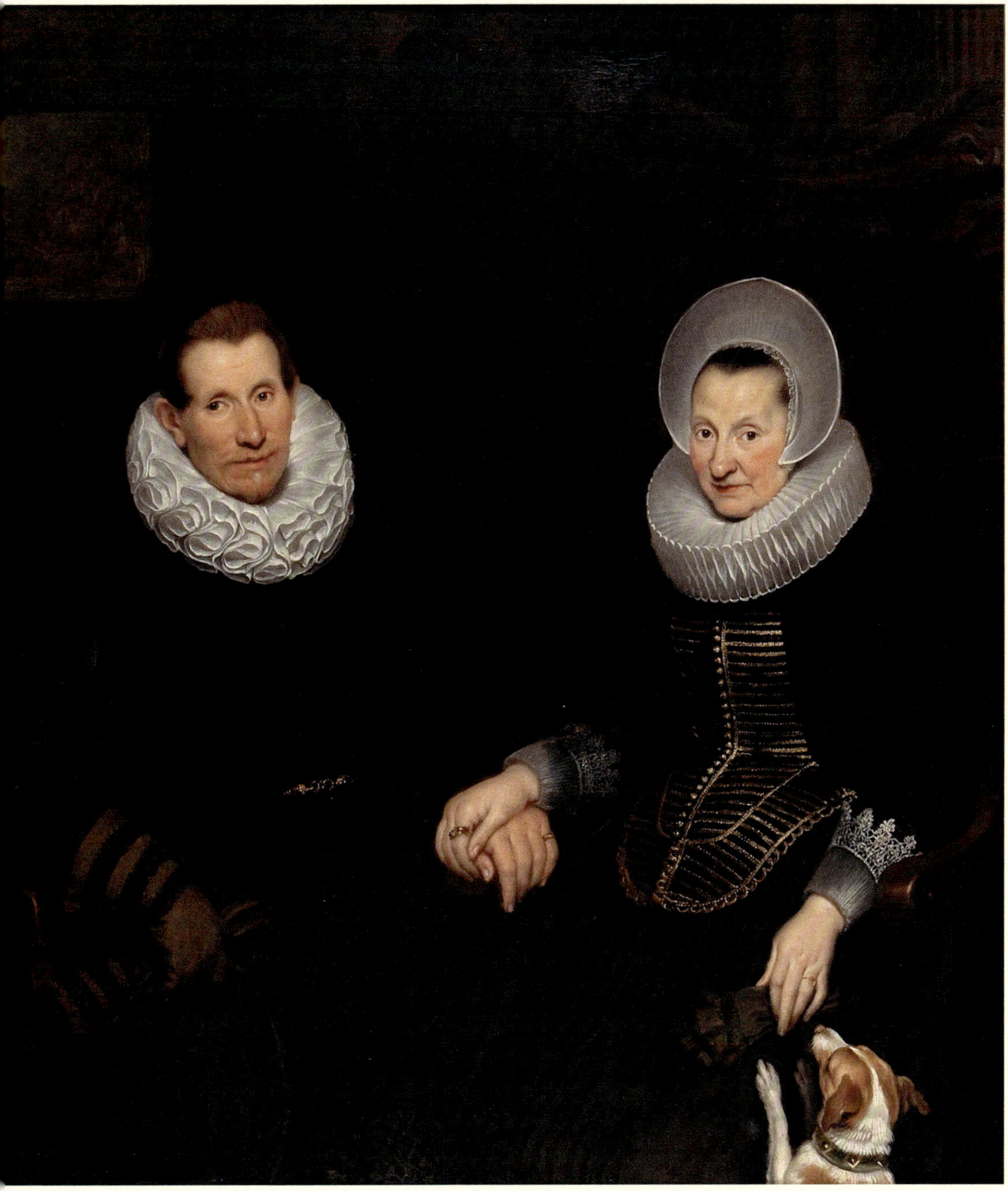

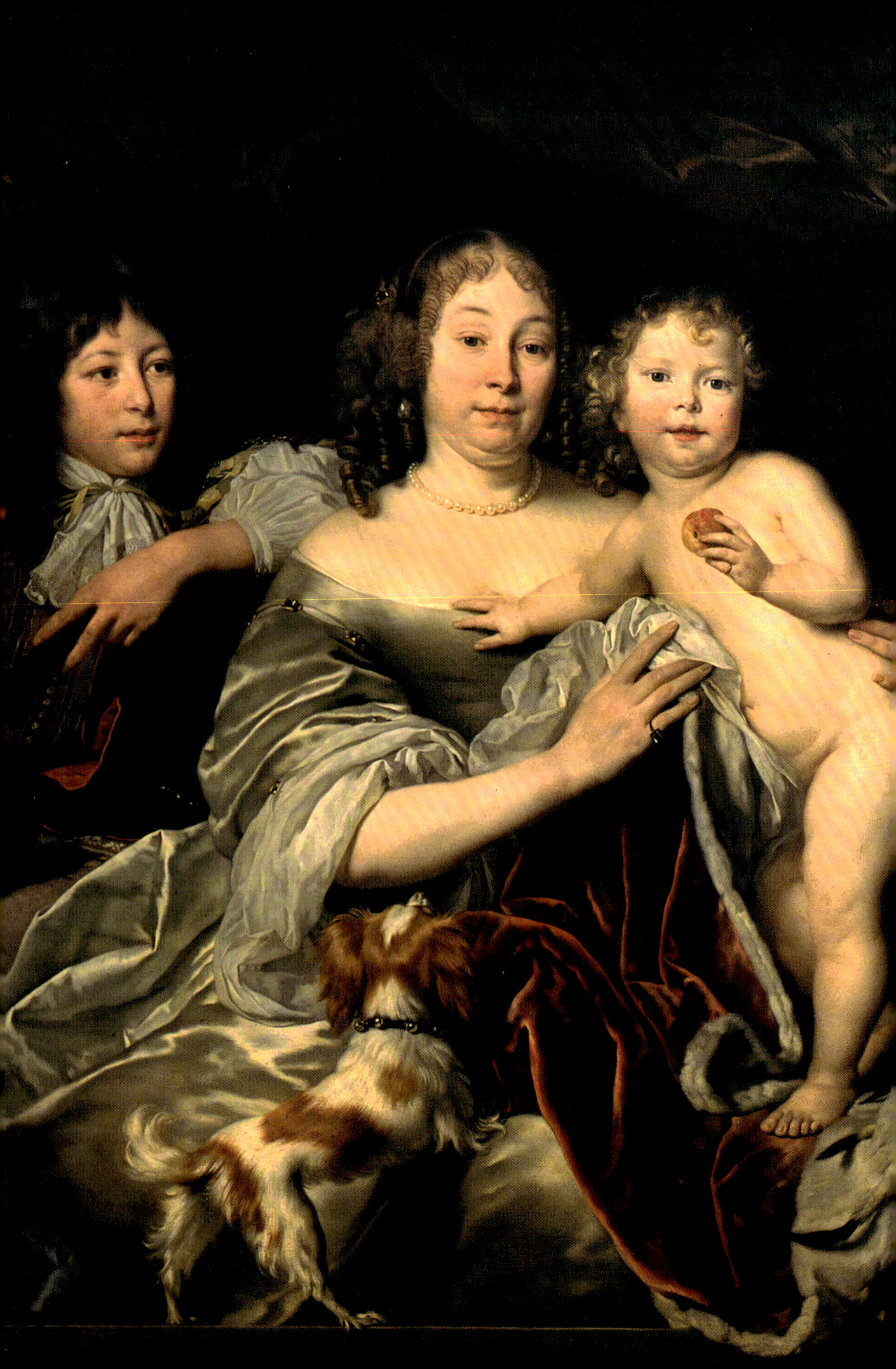

II THE DEVELOPMENT OF ART PRICING DURING THE OCCUPATION

The monetary value of artworks was generally low since the 1929 crash. In the Netherlands, this changed significantly upon the German invasion in May 1940. Immediately after the Dutch surrender on May 14, the Germans, led by Adolf Hitler and his Führermuseum and Hermann Göring with his private collection, grabbed their opportunity to expand their collections via the abundant Dutch market. They did so partly through regular purchases from dealers and sometimes acquired works from private owners. Their fiery interest in art, which was shared by other German collectors and museums, caused a rapid rise in prices (fig. 8). Many art dealers who had accumulated a large stock of artworks under the poor economic circumstances were now able to successfully sell some of those stocks at a rapid pace. This in turn made it necessary for the dealers to acquire new objects. The increased prices motivated private owners to sell art from their own collections, resulting in a time of booming business. The majority of transactions was entirely voluntary, even by our current standards. Vital exceptions were the properties of Jewish owners whose future was so bleak that they fled immediately after the German invasion, leaving their belongings behind or even committing suicide. Furthermore, some sold their works of art early on during the war in order to finance their flight to unoccupied areas.

The most spectacular transactions in the first months of the occupation concerned the sale in the early summer of 1940 of almost the entire trading stock of Kunsthandel Goudstikker to Hermann Göring and that of the firm itself to Alois Miedl. Because Miedl had acquired a virtually empty shell, he worked to refill the stock in the summer and autumn of 1940, purchasing paintings from other dealers (fig. 9). It is obvious that many art dealers at the time and in the following years greatly benefited from the German collecting frenzy. The buying rage of the Germans not only meant a notable increase in the prices of art objects and antiques, but was also a catalyst for the market for types of artworks for which collectors' interest had been quite limited before the war, and which were therefore still reasonably inexpensive. For example, this applied to many nineteenth-century paintings, such as those by the Romantic school, which were coveted by German collectors and therefore skyrocketed in price (fig. 10). This development also contributed to the big boom in the art trade. It was precisely in the field of nineteenth-century art that a tremendous number of new dealers emerged, many of whom were amateurs in this field and not members of any professional organisation. Moreover, they were seldomly registered with the Chamber of Commerce. There was also a rise in the auction business: the activities of several auction houses were of modest size before the outbreak of the war grew enormously, while all sorts of new sale rooms were also opened.

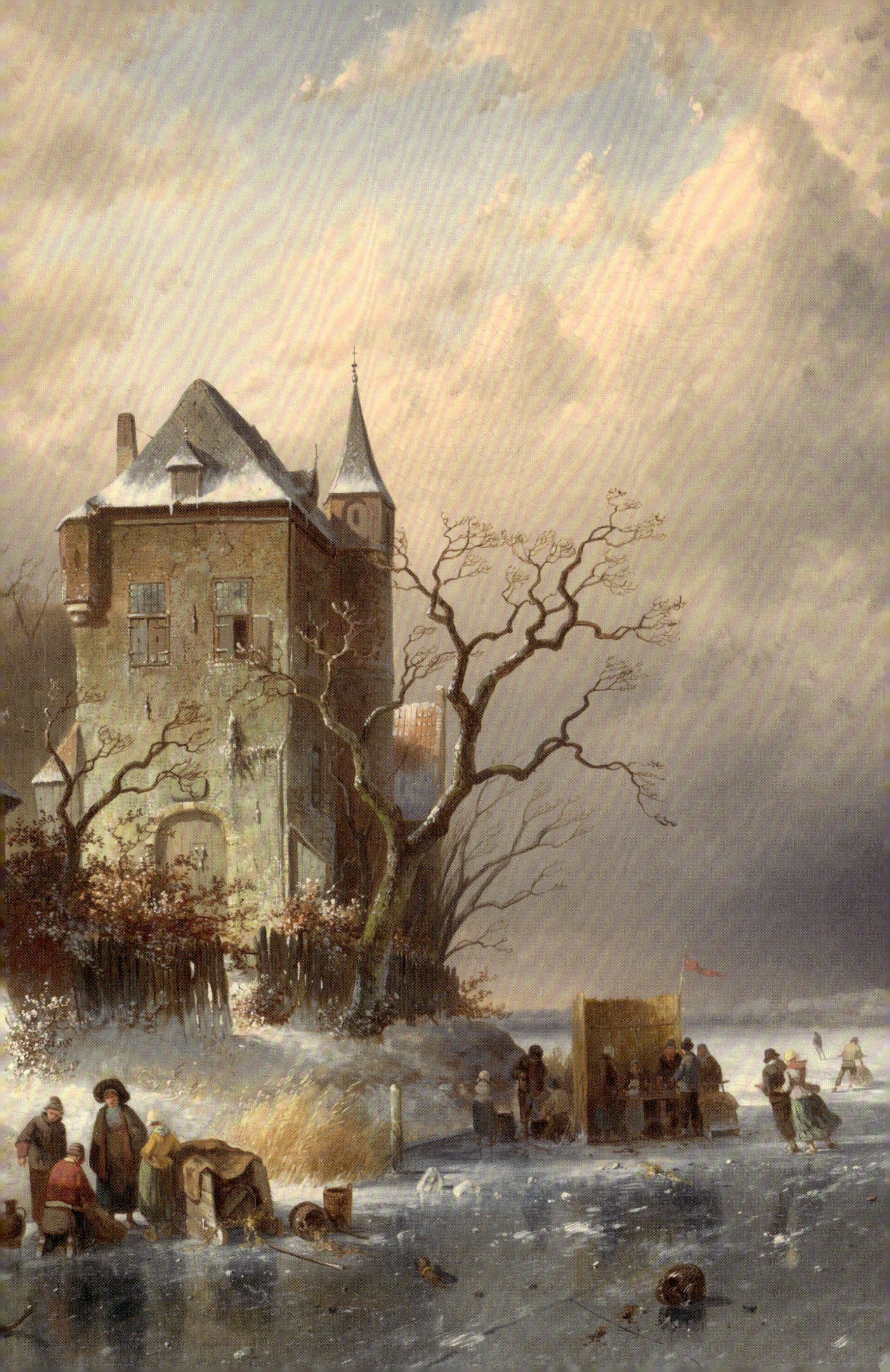

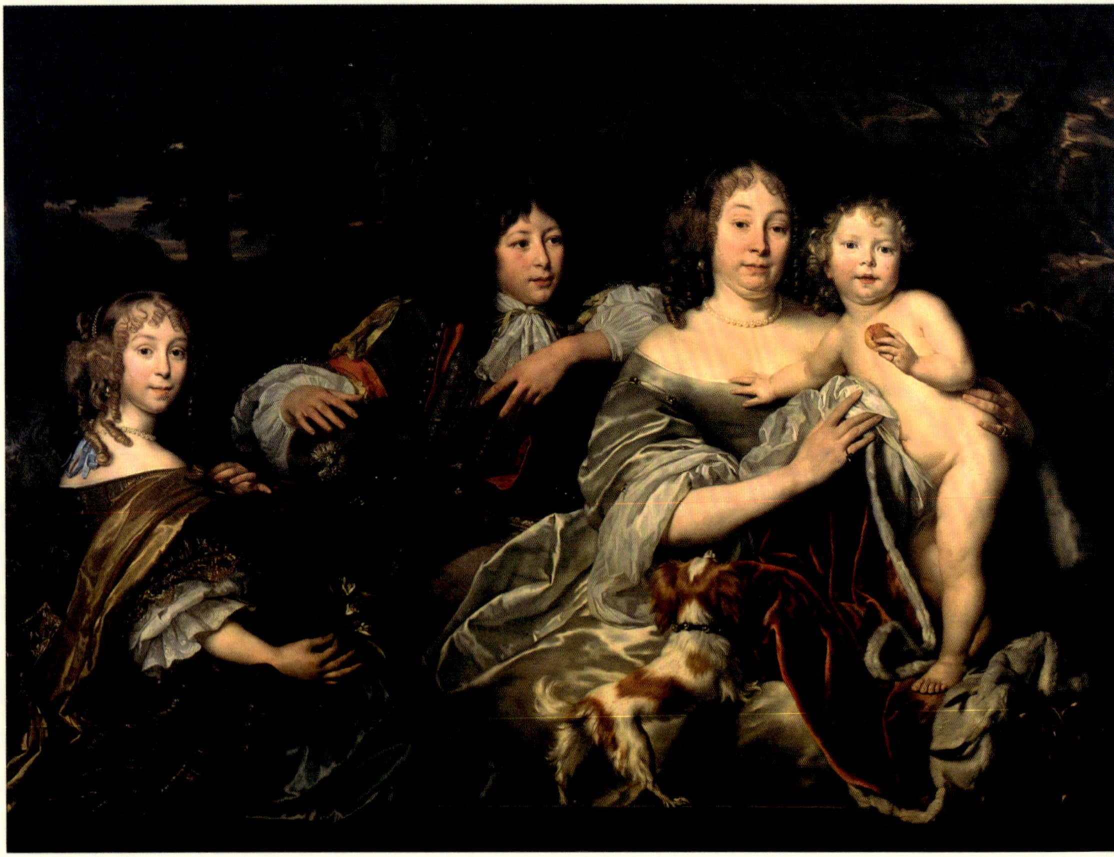

8
Albertina Agnes, Princess of Orange, with her three children, 1668
ABRAHAM VAN DEN TEMPEL (1622/23-1672)
Canvas, 141 x 191 cm, Fries Museum, Leeuwarden, on loan from RCE, NK2609

Although some art dealers were still able to prosper during the crisis years, there were also galleries that were threatened by the situation of the art market. They struggled with the increasing stock inventory and low sales. Nicolaas Beets (1878-1963), a lawyer who ran an art gallery in Amsterdam from 1920 onwards, was forced to auction off part of his stock in early 1940. The auction, held at Frederik Muller in early April 1940, was a fiasco, as bids stayed exceptionally low and many works of art were even left unsold. For example, an important piece such as the group portrait of the widow and children of the Frisian stadholder Willem Frederik, painted by Abraham van den Tempel, did not reach the limit of 4,000 guilders and remained Beets' property. However, in July 1940, he sold it without effort for 5,000 guilders to his colleague Hoogendijk, who sold it again a month later for 30,000 guilders to one of the Führermuseum's agents.

The group portrait by Van den Tempel is not the only unsold work from Beets' auction that experienced a sharp rise in value within months. For example, in April there was not even a bid in the room for twenty guilders for a drawing by 16th-century artist Pieter Coecke van Aalst but in October, Beets easily sold it to Alois Miedl for 250 guilders.

9

Portrait of a sixty-year old Woman, 1597
PIETER PIETERSZ. (c. 1540-1603)
Panel, round, 42 cm (diam),
Koninklijk Kabinet van Schilderijen,
Mauritshuis The Hague

This portrait of a woman was sold by the Katz gallery in Dieren to the art dealer Goudstikker-Miedl in Amsterdam in August 1940. The work then went to Bankhaus Witzig & Co. in Munich. After the war, the painting was recovered from Germany. Because there was not a museum with interest in the work, it was sold in 1952 by the Frederik Muller & Co. auction house in Amsterdam, on behalf of the Dutch State. The lack of interest is all the more astonishing given that in 1953, the at the time still unrecognised companion piece to this painting, a portrait of a sixty-year-old man, was acquired for the Mauritshuis by A.B. de Vries from the Katz gallery. When the woman's portrait reappeared at auction again in November 1995, it finally was recognised as the companion piece of the previously acquired man's portrait. It was purchased by a private individual who donated it to the Mauritshuis. The pair of portraits, which had been separated since at least 1879, were reunited again.

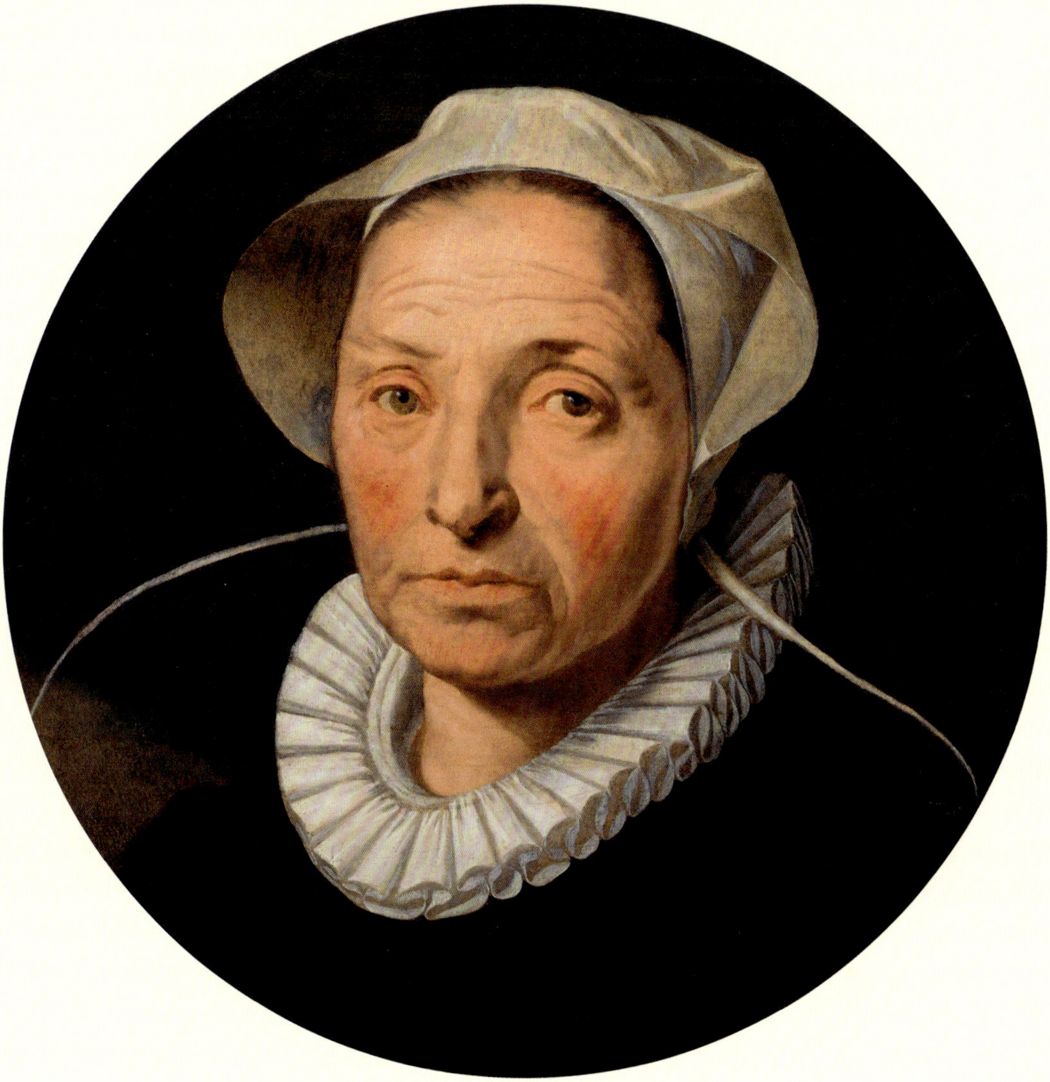

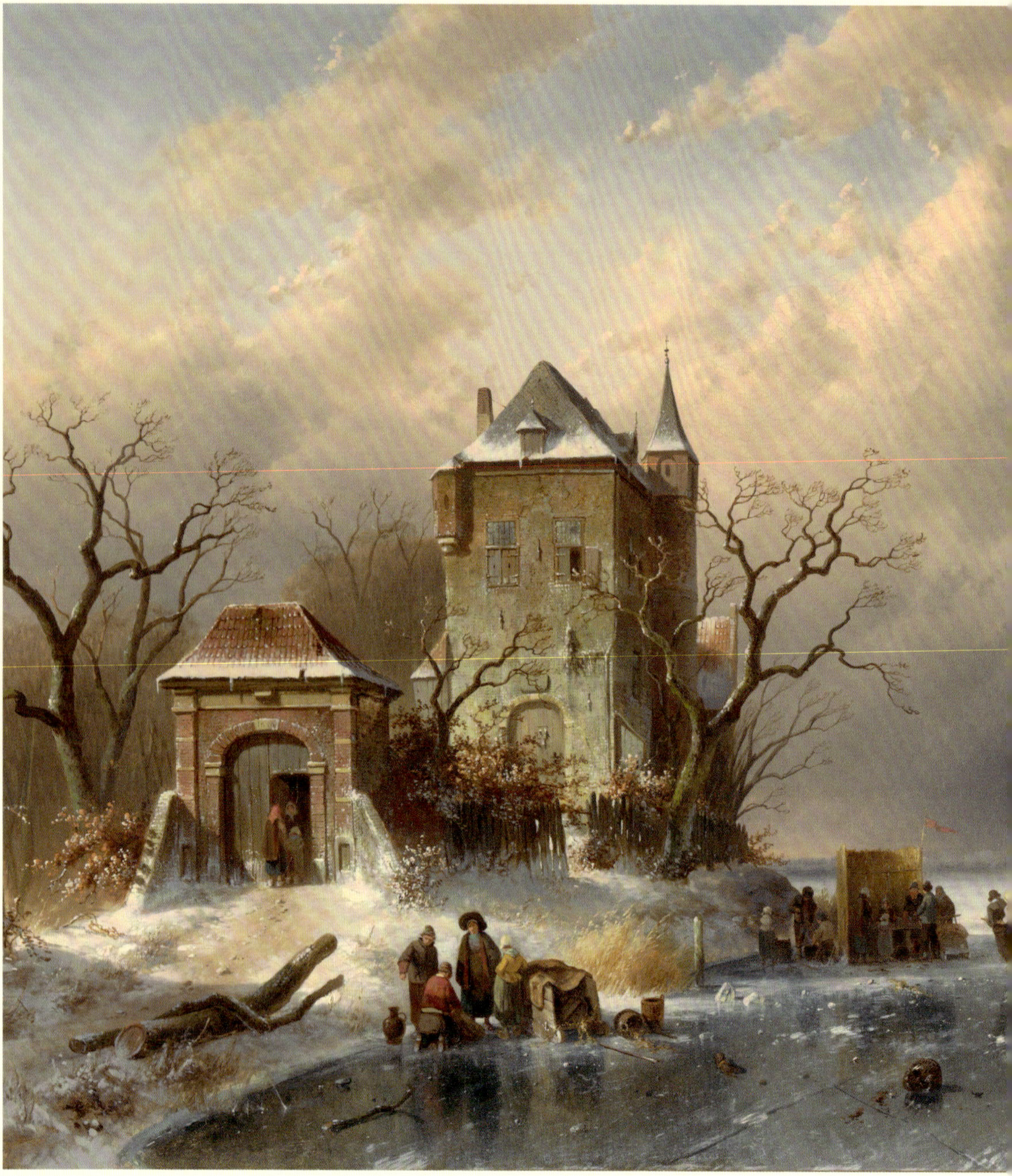

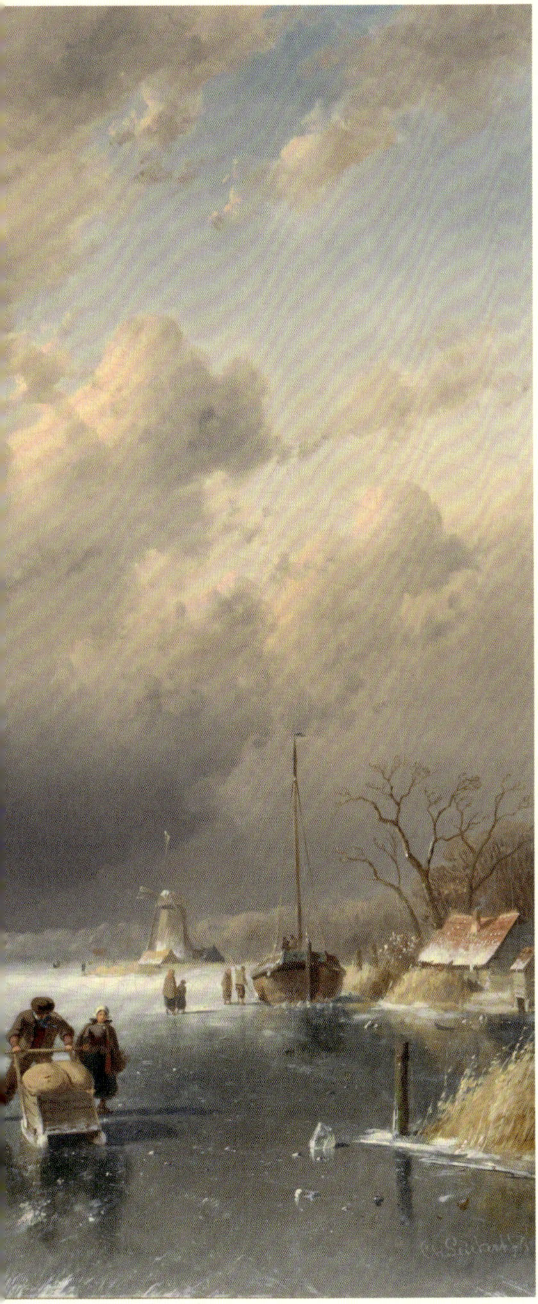

10
Winter Landscape with Skaters, 1866
CHARLES LEICKERT (1818-1907)
Canvas, 82.5 x 122 cm, Rijksdienst voor het Cultureel Erfgoed, NK2060

Between 1940 and 1945, the prices for paintings on the Dutch art market skyrocketed. According to a post-war report by the art dealer Evert Douwes, prices for old paintings were six times higher in 1943 than in 1940, and those for works from the Romantic era were as much as eight times higher. One of the main German buyers for nineteenth-century paintings was the art dealer G. Paffrath in Düsseldorf. Almost ninety works from the current NK Collection passed through his hands and the majority of them are works from the Romantic era.

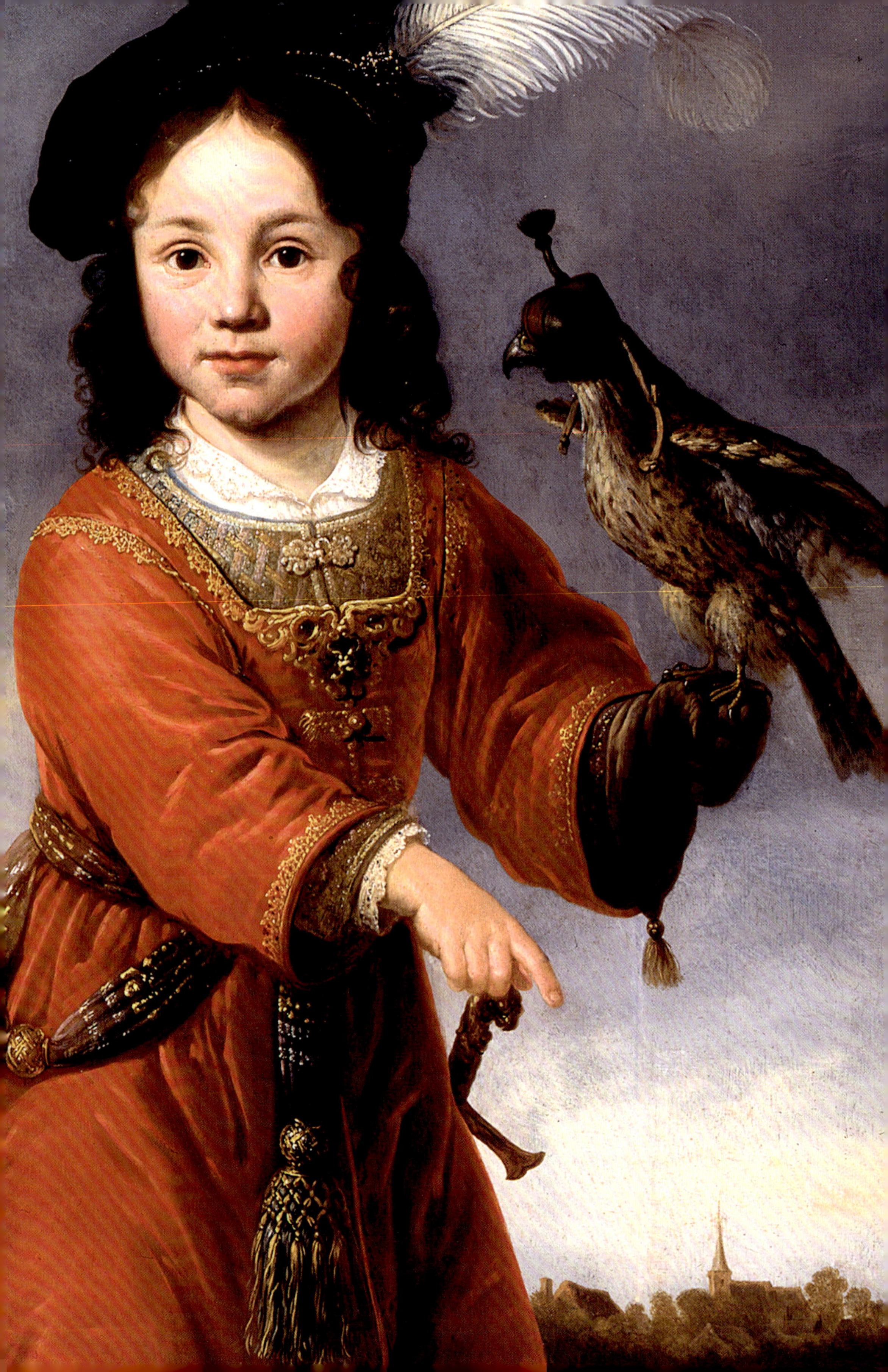

III THE JEWISH ART TRADE DURING THE OCCUPATION

On 10 May 1940, the German invasion of the Netherlands began, followed by the Dutch capitulation five days later. The fear of living under Nazi rule drove many Jews to suicide or attempts to flee the country in these days. Fierce anti-Semitism and anti-Jewish legislation in Germany and Austria were a warning that these extreme measures were also to be expected in the Netherlands. The best-known example of a Jewish art dealer who chose not to wait for such events to happen was Jacques Goudstikker. He managed to board the last Dutch freighter to leave the port of IJmuiden with his family on 14 May 1940. The ship was due to set sail for South America after a stopover in England. Goudstikker's attempt to flee ended in tragedy on the night of 15-16 May with a fatal fall into the ship's hold (fig. 11).

After the panic of the first weeks of the occupation, a moderate calm returned to the Netherlands. The Germans established a civilian occupation regime in the Netherlands, led by Austrian lawyer Arthur Seyss-Inquart. The new regime initially showed a friendly face. The German authorities aimed for a 'self-nazification' of society and intended to gently guide the Germanic fraternal people towards (re)integration into the German Reich. Immediate harsh anti-Jewish actions or measures would create unrest and were therefore deemed counterproductive. The German occupier pretended that a 'Jewish issue' did not exist in the Netherlands. Meanwhile, diligent preparations were quietly being made to isolate and eliminate the Jewish citizens of the Dutch population.

The occupying forces had tightened their grip on society and an administrative separation of Jews and non-Jews was implemented before the end of 1940. The pressure on the Jewish population gradually increased. Step by step, Jews were banned from public life, robbed of their possessions, denied their rights, and finally murdered in extermination camps. Their systematic dispossession, deportation and murder greatly contributed to the devastating effect of the persecution. Of the approximately 140,000 Jews in the Netherlands, 73% did not survive the war, a percentage far exceeding that in Belgium, Luxembourg and France.

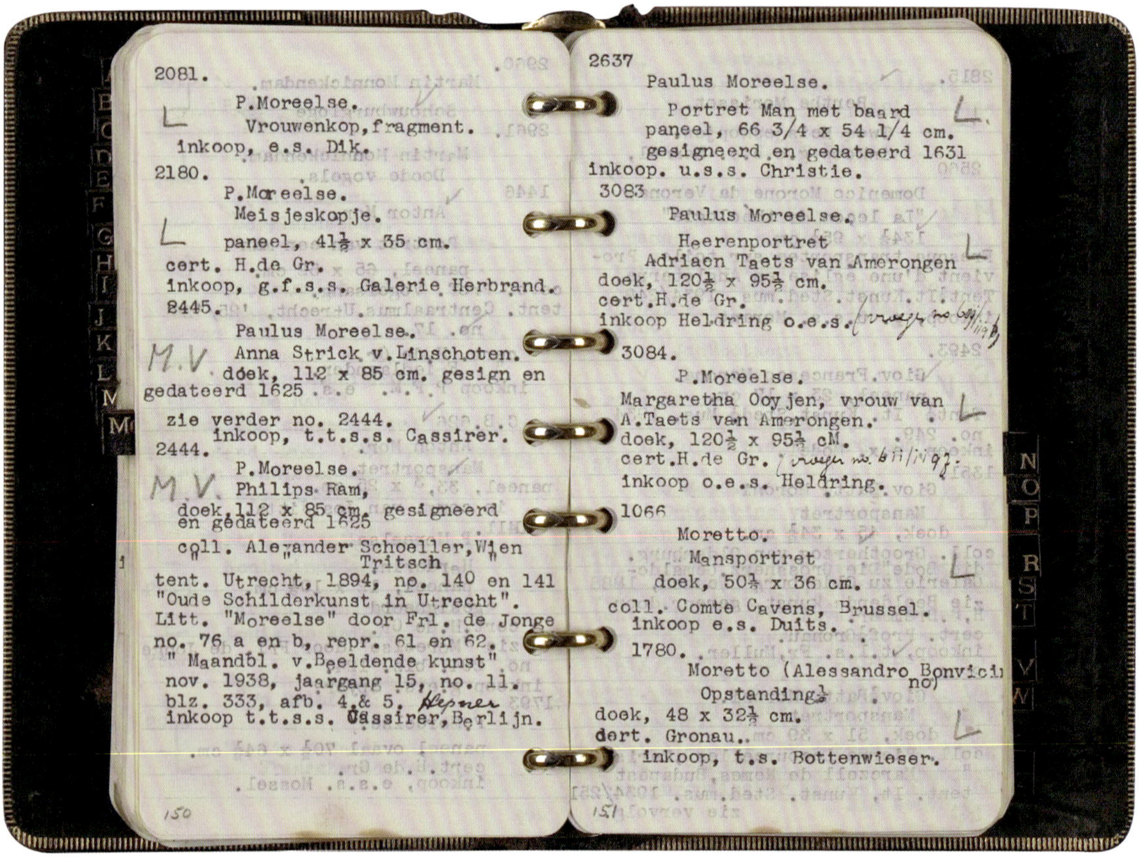
2081.
P.Moreelse.
Vrouwenkop, fragment.
inkoop, e.s. Dik.
2180.
P.Moreelse.
Meisjeskopje.
paneel, 41½ x 35 cm.
cert. H.de Gr.
inkoop, g.f.s.s. Galerie Herbrand.
2445.
Paulus Moreelse.
Anna Strick v.Linschoten.
doek, 112 x 85 cm. gesign en gedateerd 1625
zie verder no. 2444.
inkoop, t.t.s.s. Cassirer.
2444.
P.Moreelse.
Philips Ram,
doek, 112 x 85 cm. gesigneerd en gedateerd 1625
coll. Alexander Schoeller, Wien
" " Tritsch "
tent. Utrecht, 1894, no. 140 en 141
"Oude Schilderkunst in Utrecht".
Litt. "Moreelse" door Frl. de Jonge
no. 76 a en b, repr. 61 en 62.
" Maandbl. v.Beeldende kunst"
nov. 1938, jaargang 15, no. 11.
blz. 333, afb. 4 & 5.
inkoop t.t.s.s. Cassirer, Berlijn.

2637
Paulus Moreelse.
Portret Man met baard
paneel, 66 3/4 x 54 1/4 cm.
gesigneerd en gedateerd 1631
inkoop. u.s.s. Christie.
3083
Paulus Moreelse.
Heerenportret
Adriaen Taets van Amerongen
doek, 120½ x 95½ cm.
cert. H.de Gr.
inkoop Heldring o.e.s.
3084.
P.Moreelse.
Margaretha Ooyjen, vrouw van A.Taets van Amerongen.
doek, 120½ x 95½ cM.
cert. H.de Gr.
inkoop o.e.s. Heldring.
1066
Moretto.
Mansportret
doek, 50½ x 36 cm.
coll. Comte Cavens, Brussel.
inkoop e.s. Duits.
1780.
Moretto (Alessandro Bonvicino)
Opstanding
doek, 48 x 32½ cm.
cert. Gronau.
inkoop, t.s. Bottenwieser.

Jacques Goudstikker's Black Book, 1940

When Jacques Goudstikker fled the Netherlands on 14 May 1940, he took with him his little black book, which listed the inventory of his entire collection of paintings, drawings and sculptures. It was later the property of his widow, Dési von Halban (1912-1996), and was transferred to the Stadsarchief Amsterdam after her death. The information in the book has always been the main reference basis for the Goudstikker heirs in their search for the art dealer's dispersed possessions.

The looting of Jewish property was also systematic. The German authorities provided a legal basis for their activities by issuing regulations with the force of law. Several administrative bodies were officially set up in order to carry out the confiscations, forming an intricate looting bureaucracy. The revenues of the confiscations were used, among other things, to fund the deportation of Jews.

THE ART MARKET

Most major art dealers sold their ware directly to German clientele during the occupation. Initially, Jewish dealers also had the opportunity to make a profit. This population group was not yet prohibited from doing business at the start of the war. Yet many of them, especially those who had experienced or followed the political developments in Germany, must have feared that this commercial freedom would not last long.

During the occupation, countless transactions in the art market took place without direct pressure or intimidation. Numerous German buyers were able to fall back on a supplying network that had already been established long before the war. The Amsterdam art dealer Evert Douwes wrote in a 1948 report: 'The Museum Directors came to see if there were any acquisitions for their museum, among them were some with whom we had been in contact for years and with whom, because of our like-minded interest, we had become more or less familiar or friends over the years'. However, a German client at the door could be a distressing experience. Freedom of doing business was a relative concept at this time, especially for a Jewish entrepreneur. Such was the case for, among others, the art dealer Gustav Cramer from The Hague, who had emigrated from Germany in the 1930s because of his Jewish origins. In July 1940, the German art historian and museum director Hans Posse called on him. Posse was one of Hitler's representatives and was responsible for the large-scale acquisitions of art for a Führermuseum to be set up in Linz as well as other collections. Reportedly, Posse demanded from Cramer to sell two well-known paintings by Italian masters, thereby setting the price himself. Cramer was, 'as a Jew having escaped from Germany, obviously in no position to oppose to the forced sale of these paintings'.

Hermann Göring on the steps of the art gallery Kunsthandel Goudstikker, Herengracht 458, Amsterdam, 1941

Göring regularly selected the pieces for his collection himself and was therefore not entirely dependent on the sleuthing or advice of his agents and buyers.

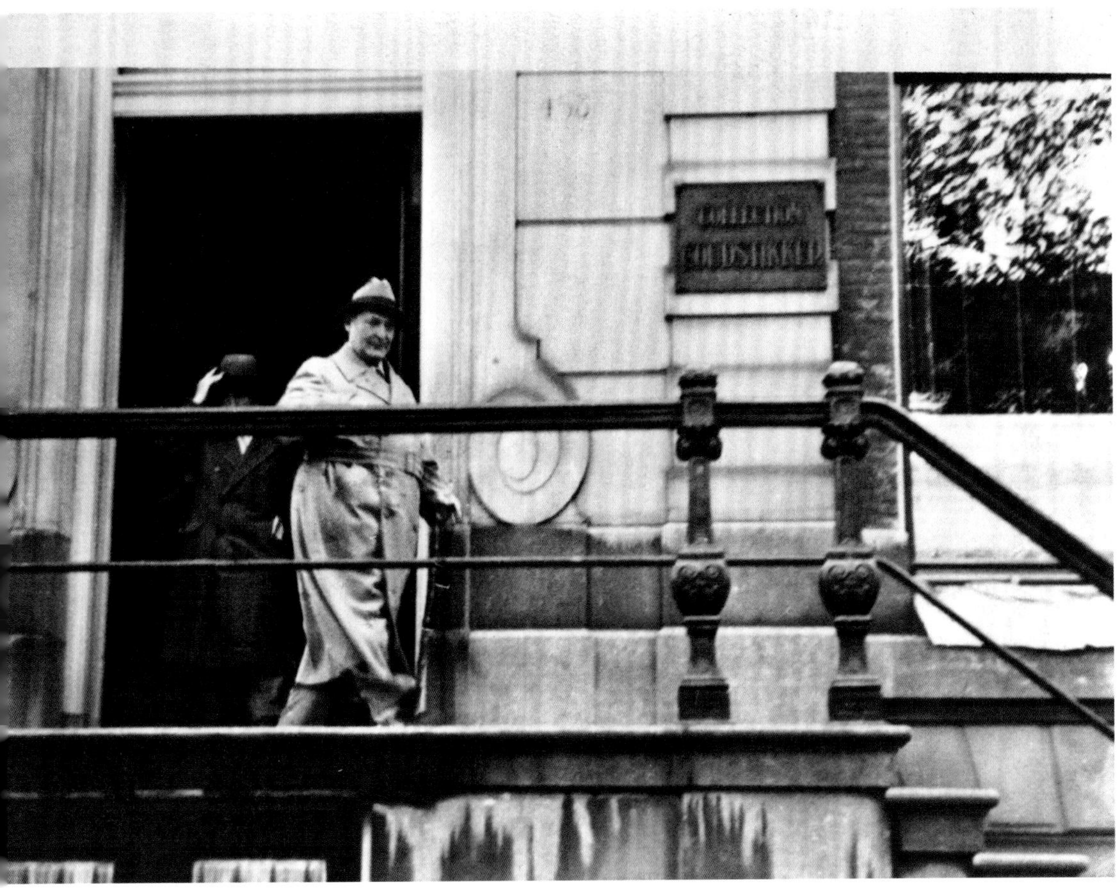

ARYANIZATION OF THE JEWISH ART TRADE

Besides through purchases on the art market, the occupying forces also acquired cultural goods in other ways. The persecution of Jews brought a multitude of art treasures within reach, including those from the Jewish art trade. A significant step in increasing isolation of the Jewish population was the 'Entjüdung' (dejudification) of the Dutch economy, which amounted to keeping Jews out of business. In September 1940, it was rumoured that the German authorities would begin to expropriate Jewish companies. Shortly afterwards, it would turn out that this was not idle gossip. In October 1940, a regulation was issued stipulating that all commercial firms in which Jews had any influence were required to register with the German authorities. Forebodingly this regulation defined precisely what was to be understood by 'a Jew'. The purpose of this mandatory registration became evident when the ordinance for the removal of Jews from business followed (VO 48/41) in March 1941. It enabled the German authorities to appoint administrators ('Treuhänder') to companies to completely take over the rights of their owners or directors. This allowed the occupying forces to dispose of businesses as they pleased. The aim was to liquidate as many smaller Jewish companies as possible and to take over economically important enterprises or put them up for sale. So-called 'Liquidationstreuhänder' were appointed to the former and 'Verwaltungstreuhänder' ('Verwalter' for short) to the latter. All costs were to be paid by the companies themselves. About 22,000 companies applied. Of these, 9,000 to 13,000 were dissolved and circa 2,000 were 'Aryanised', i.e. put under management or sold to an 'Aryan' buyer. In addition, about 2,000 companies were granted 'Selbstarisierung', in which the Jewish director or manager was replaced by a non-Jewish one with the consent of the responsible authorities. These were generally businesses with limited Jewish influence. What happened to the remaining companies is unknown.

The art trade itself was also affected by these measures as this niche was most strongly represented in Amsterdam, which traditionally had a thriving Jewish community. A relatively large proportion of Amsterdam's art dealers and antique dealers were of Jewish origin. These included several German and Austrian entrepreneurs who had fled their country after Hitler's rise to power. Albert Heppner was such an art dealer, having emigrated from Berlin with his wife in 1933, establishing a dealership in old paintings in Amsterdam. The internationally operating Austrian art dealer Kurt Walter Bachstitz chose The Hague as his home base in 1937. In this city, he had already established the Bachstitz Gallery as early as 1920. After the German invasion of the Netherlands in May 1940, Jewish refugees were once more confronted with grave difficulties. In 1941, Jewish citizens were increasingly separated from the rest of society. Among other regulations, they had to surrender all of their assets, were banned from public places, were expelled from associations and were no longer free to travel without permission. The progressive disenfranchisement made Jews' professions and lives increasingly difficult, including those of art dealers. The VO 48/41 regulation laid the foundation for the 'Entjüdung' of the Jewish art trade.

Various measures and restrictions followed. In the autumn of 1941, for instance, a series of art dealers and antique shops were unexpectedly closed and sealed off. Around the same time, the art dealer P. de Boer, the acting chairman of the Association of Dealers in Old Art in the Netherlands ('Vereniging van Handelaren in Oude Kunst in Nederland', VHOK), was summoned to the office of the *Beauftragte* for the city of Amsterdam. There, he was ordered to inform the Jewish members of the association that they had to cancel their membership. Furthermore, dozens of Jewish companies had to deal with the Dienststelle Mühlmann, an organisation erected solely for the acquisitions of art objects for Nazi Germany. The Dienststelle was headed by the Austrian art historian Kajetan Mühlmann, a personal friend of Seyss-Inquart, who had previously looted art treasures in Poland for the benefit of the Third Reich. Mühlmann and his associates scavenged for objects of interest in Jewish art shops. Large quantities of artworks were 'taken over'. These artworks were passed on to prominent Nazis and other buyers, or sold at auction in Germany and Austria.

The German authorities made a meticulous inventory of Jewish art dealers in the Netherlands. The financial situation and other circumstances of each business were charted. A decision regarding their future followed. Most businesses and enterprises were liquidated. Several other, often more profitable businesses were appointed a German or Dutch Verwalter. A few of these businesses were sold over time, sometimes to the Verwalter himself, or were liquidated. A limited number of Jewish art galleries were allowed 'Selbstarisierung' (fig. 12 and 13). The appointed Verwalters were by no means all skilled. The shortage of experienced candidates meant that one person was occasionally employed to multiple companies. There were also quite a few changes in the management of a business after the take-over. According to the guidelines, the Verwalter had to apply and guarantee

Bernard Houthakker (1884-1963, far right) with his brothers Eduard Abigedor and Josephus Houthakker, 1920

The art gallery Kunsthandel Houthakker was founded in 1909 by Bernard Houthakker and was located at 98 Rokin in Amsterdam since 1926. Houthakker was one of the driving forces behind numerous initiatives in the Dutch art trade, including the major national exhibition of old master works of 1929 at the Rijksmuseum. He was secretary of the Association of Dealers in Old Art in the Netherlands ('Vereniging van Handelaren in Oude Kunst in Nederland') from its foundation in 1911 until 1941, becoming its chairman after the liberation in 1945 until 1954. To evade the anti-Jewish measures by occupying forces, Houthakker arranged that his business was taken over by 'Aryan' acquaintances in 1941. Nevertheless, a former pub owner from Berlin acted as manager over the gallery for a time and caused the business extensive damage. Bernard Houthakker was one of the individuals who belonged to the so-called Barneveld Group. The group consisted of some 700 Jewish prominents who were initially exempted by the Nazis from the Arbeitseinsatz and deportation and were accommodated in Barneveld and Doetinchem. It was from Barneveld that Houthakker was deported to Theresienstadt via Westerbork and eventually allowed to enter Switzerland with other members of the Barneveld Group as part of an 'exchange' in February 1945. Bernard Houthakker reopened his art gallery a year later.

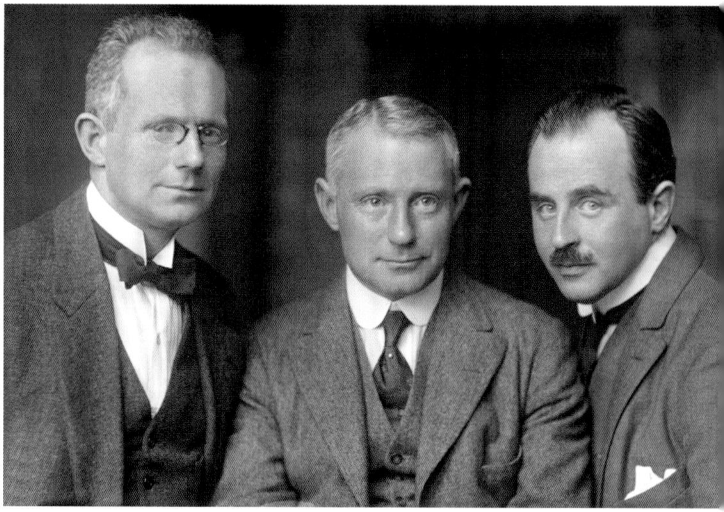

exemplary National Socialist management. This included removing all Jews from the company. If this made a proper continuation of the business impossible, an exception could sometimes be made. In that case, however, it had to be ensured that these Jews had no influence whatsoever on the management and that they would be removed as soon as possible. In practice, the Verwalter had widely varying views of their duties. Some hardly interfered in the business, while others kept a tight rein on all things. Some managers were primarily focused on self-enrichment and plundered the business, while showing little or no concern for the fate of the Jewish owners and their families. Others, on the other hand, tried to keep the business owners at work as long as possible, intervening several times to prevent them from being deported and managed to delay the dissolution of the business. These two extremes, and the whole spectrum in between, are clearly revealed in post-war testimonies of Jewish survivors.

Various art dealers applied different tactics to evade the control of the German authorities in their business. Sometimes they managed to save their business by transferring it to non-Jewish friends or acquaintances. One example is Bernard Houthakker's shop on the Rokin in Amsterdam (fig. 14). This business was preserved because in 1941 it was taken over by an 'Aryan' company, the art dealership Rembrandt van Rijn N.V. This rescue operation was jeopardised when a German manager was unexpectedly appointed over the business after all. This was a former pub owner from Berlin, who believed he was entitled to freely dispose of all the firm's property and lined his own pockets at the company's expense. However, the responsible German authorities caught up to him eventually and he lost his lucrative position. Another example is the antiques shop S. van Leeuwen on Noordeinde in The Hague (fig. 15). The owner of this one-man business, Salomon van Leeuwen, was no longer allowed into his store by a Verwalter appointed in 1942 and forcedly went into hiding. However, he had a confidant in the business. In 1944, this man managed to have the firm donated to the adult daughter and young son of Salomon van Leeuwen, both of whom had a non-Jewish mother. This amounted to a loss of 8,000 guilders, as the Verwalter demanded a ransom for his departure.

In 1942, the situation for the Jewish population in the Netherlands became severe and life-threatening. Jews were deported in great numbers and transported to camps. Those who still had the opportunity to show up in their shops took great risks. Among non-Jewish art dealers were those who unashamedly profited from the distress of their fellow professionals. However, there were attempts to help. Many displayed a combination of reactions, in which a combination of both self-interest and compassion can be found, without the line between the two. The post-war witness accounts from the archives show the complexity of these issues and the extent to which views of another's behaviour during the occupation could differ.

AFTER THE LIBERATION

At an eventful meeting of the VHOK in Amsterdam on 28 May 1945, those present shared what they knew about the fate of their brothers in trade and a moment of silence was observed. Some Jewish traders and their families survived the war, for example by going into hiding or by qualifying for exemptions. Many others were deported and murdered in extermination camps. Those who returned after the liberation not infrequently found, upon returning home, a looted business that had to be rebuilt from scratch. The survivors or their relatives also faced an often lengthy and difficult bureaucratic process of legal rehabilitation.

It is difficult to get a complete picture of the financial scale of the liquidations and sales of Jewish businesses in the Netherlands. Many of the archives that could have shed light on this issue were destroyed, disappeared or are no longer complete. Estimates from both during and after the war vary from around 150 million to around 600 million guilders.

11

Portraits of Philips Ram and Anna Strick, 1625
PAULUS MOREELSE (1571-1638)
Canvases, 113 x 85 cm, Centraal Museum, Utrecht, on loan from RCE, formerly NK2719 and NK2718

The pair of portraits of the couple Philips Ram and Anna Strick were purchased by the art dealer Jacques Goudstikker from his Berlin colleague Cassirer in 1930 but were still unsold in May 1940. They were among the works purchased by Hermann Göring in 1940. After the war, both paintings were recuperated to the Netherlands. In 2006, the Dutch State returned them to the Goudstikker heirs, along with a large number of other works from the gallery's old trading stock. Subsequently, the Dutch State bought back these two portraits by Moreelse from the heirs, along with several other paintings.

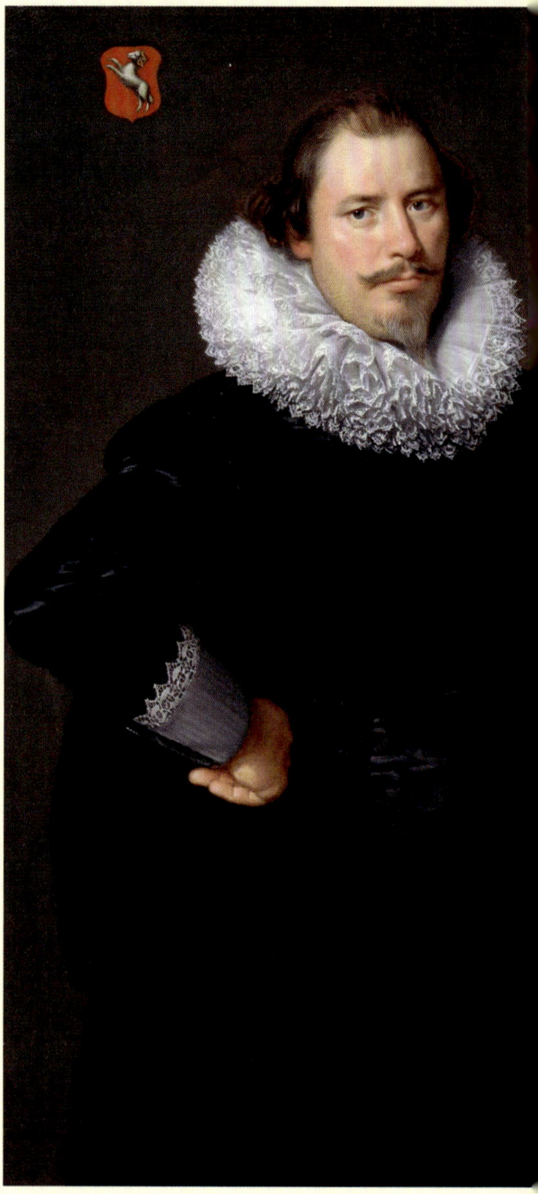

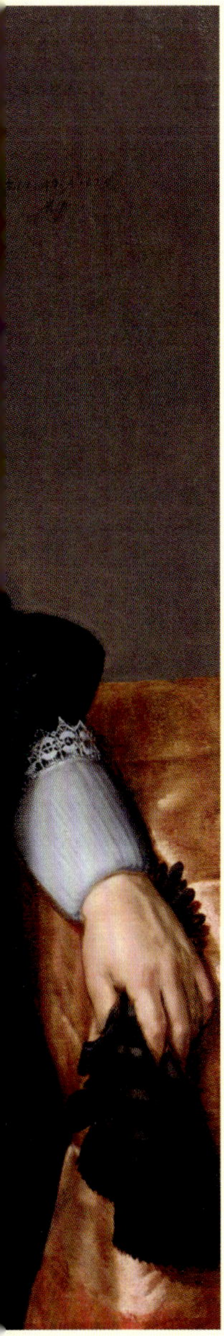

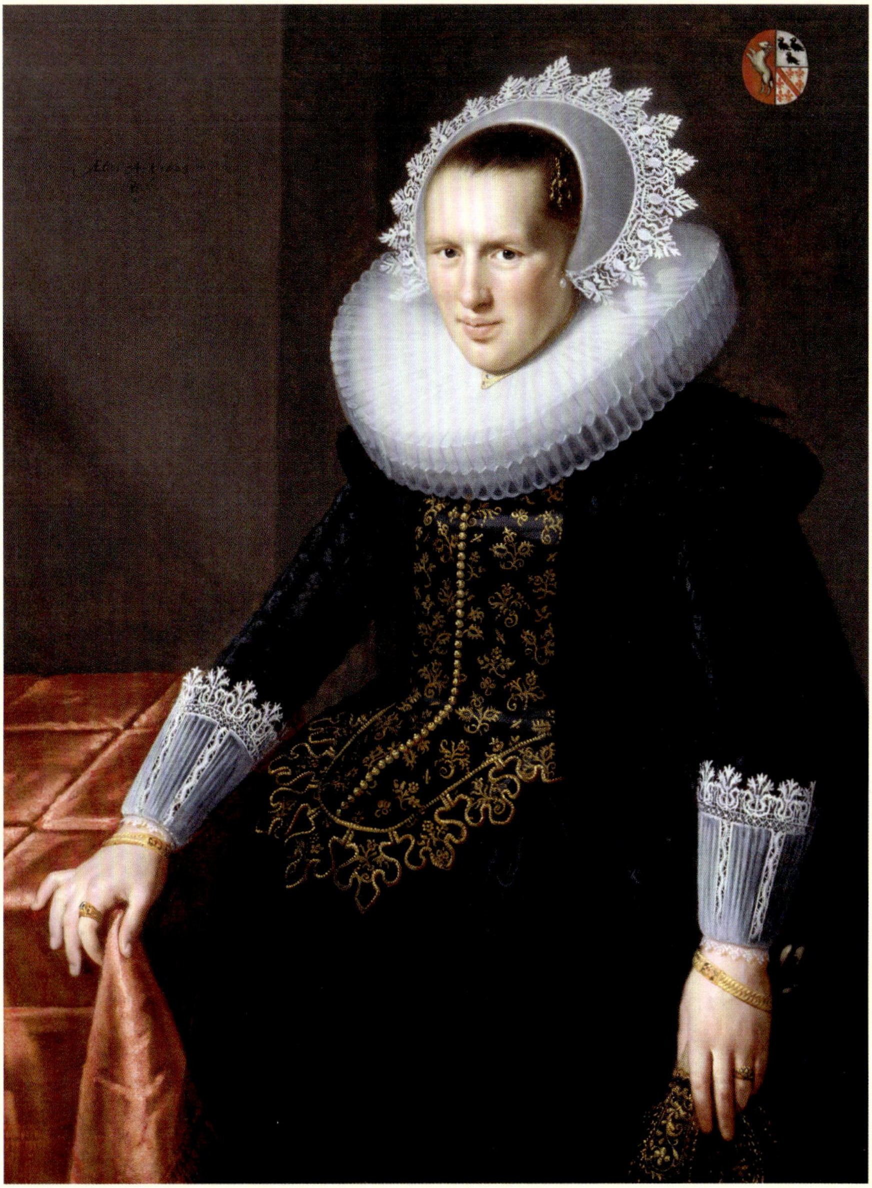

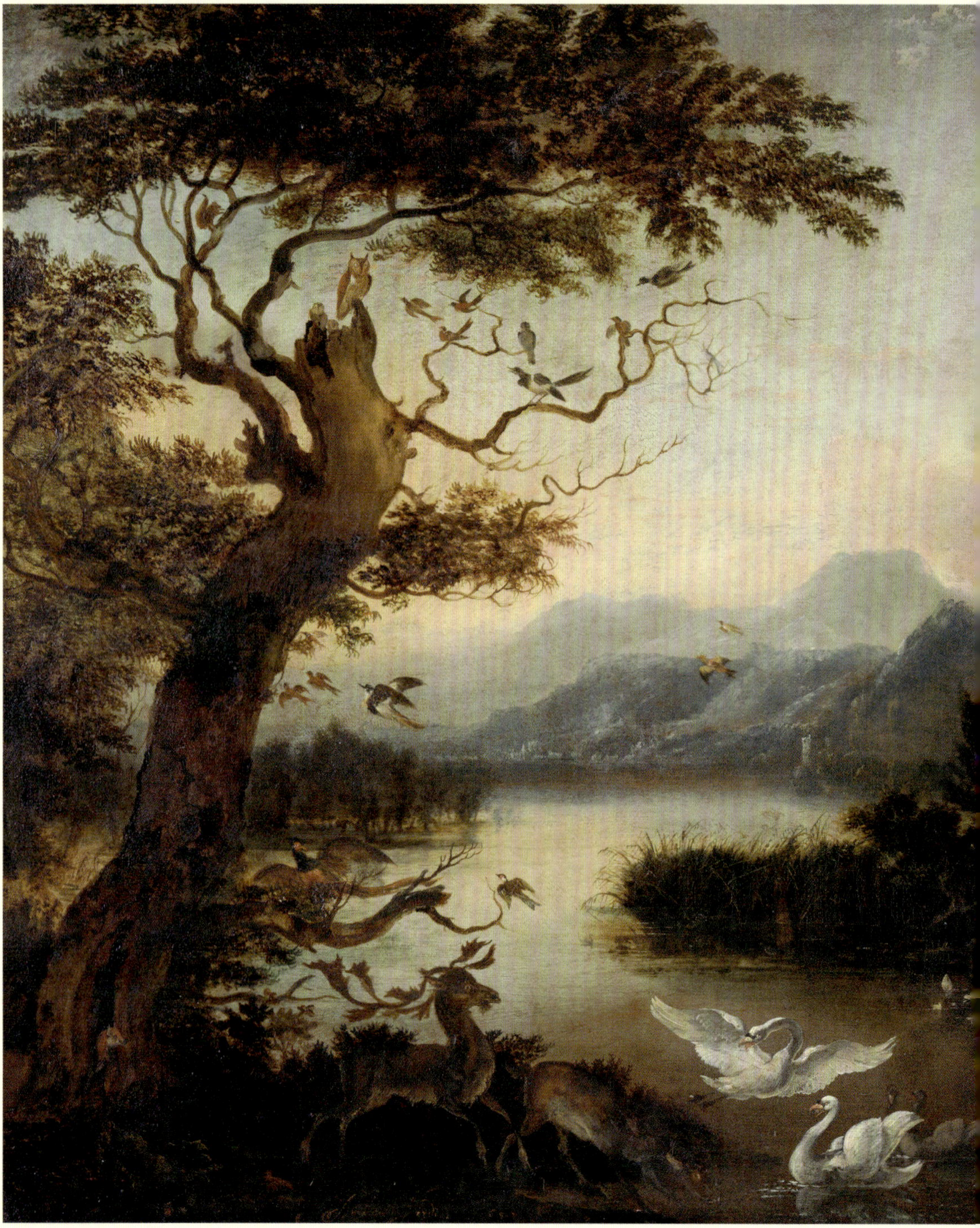

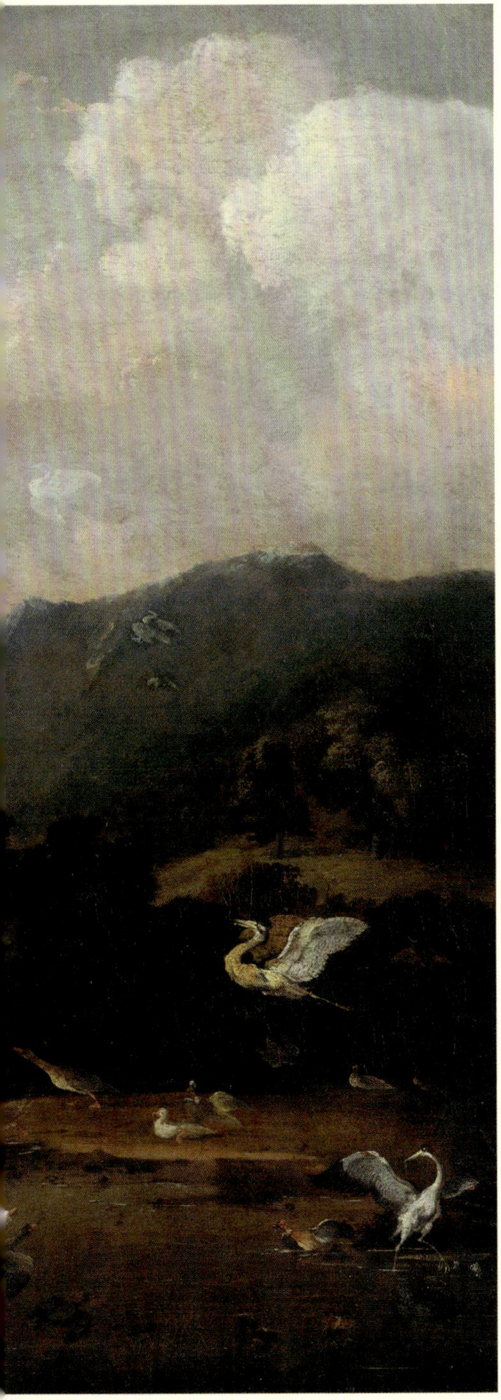

12
A Mountain landscape with a Lake with Deer and Fowl
ABRAHAM HONDIUS (1625-1695)
Canvas, 81 x 104 cm, Rijksdienst voor het Cultureel Erfgoed, NK1759

This painting was on the English art market in the 1930s and was sold in 1944 by the art gallery Kunsthandel A. Nijstad in Lochem through an art agent to the Sonderauftrag Linz. Kunsthandel Nijstad was headed by Abraham (Bram) Nijstad (1895-1960) from 1925. The gallery was one of the Jewish art dealers who survived the occupation period unscathed by the German 'Selbstarisierung'. In 1941, the management of the gallery was transferred to a non-Jewish art dealer, J.H. Borghouts in Utrecht. A staff member of the company looked after the branch in Lochem for the duration of the war. Nijstad himself was initially given protection by one of Hitler's agents but he and his sons Harts and Saam were eventually detained. All three survived the war and rebuilt the gallery after the liberation.

13

Portrait of Michiel Pompe van Slingelandt, 1649
JACOB GERRITSZ. CUYP (1594-1652)
Panel, 106.5 x 78 cm, Dordrechts Museum, Dordrecht, on loan from RCE, NK1695

This painting was part of a Dutch private collection in the 1930s and was the property of the art dealers Katz in Dieren in 1940. During the occupation of the Netherlands, the Katz brothers not only did business with the Goudstikker-Miedl gallery but also frequently sold works directly to Germany. This portrait by Jacob Cuyp was acquired by Walter Andreas Hofer for Hermann Göring as early as 1940.

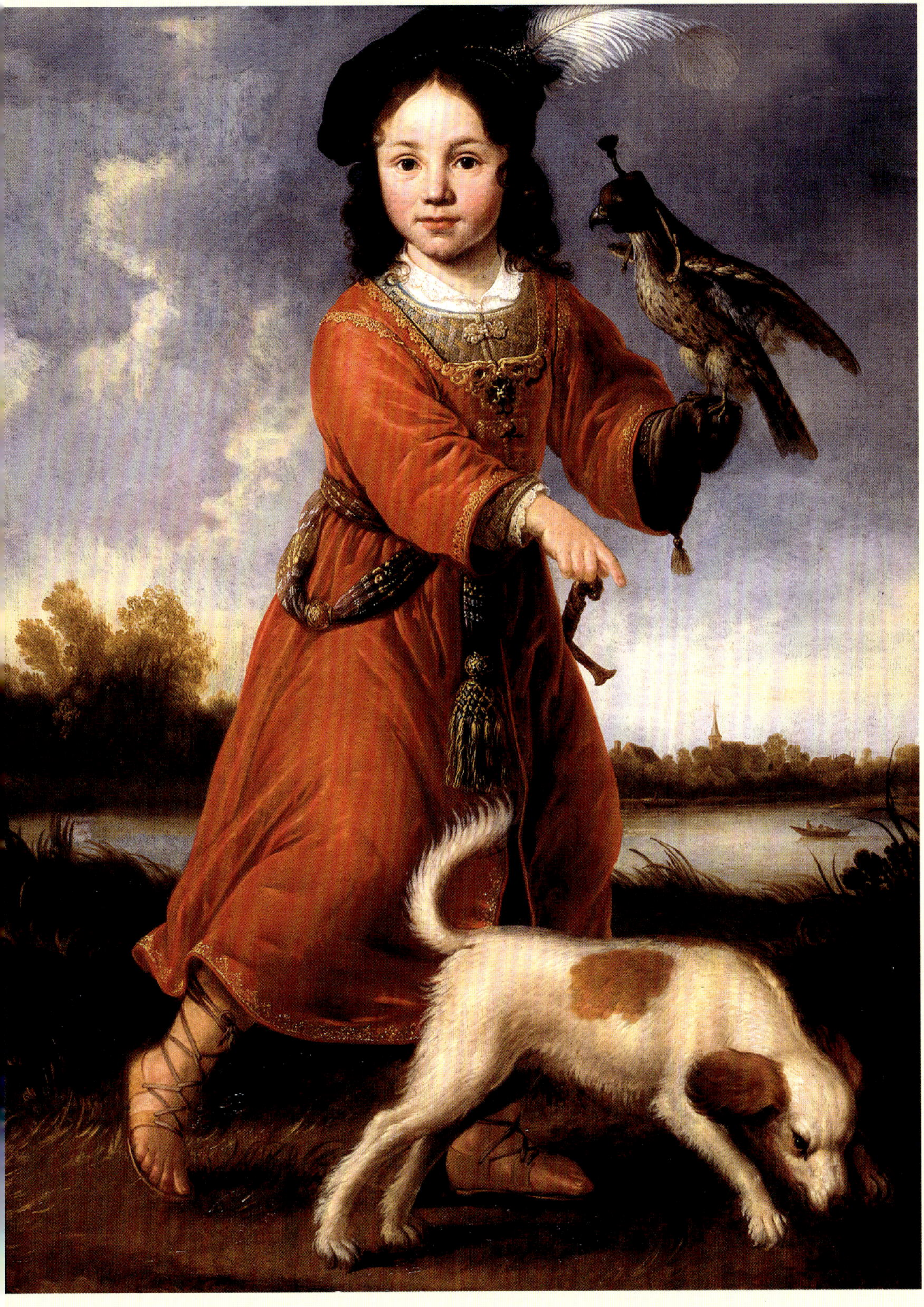

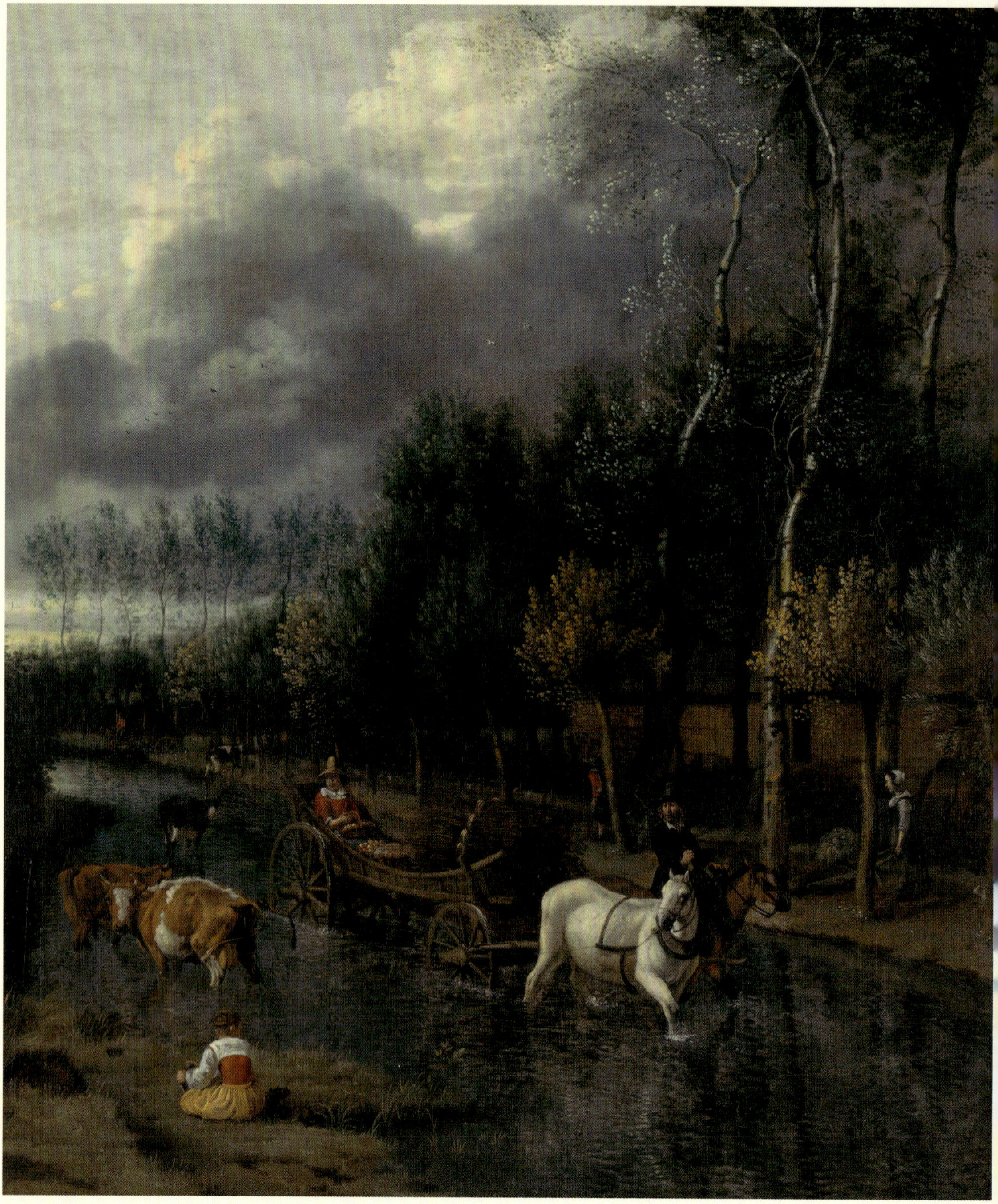

4
.andscape with a Farmer's Wagon in a Ford
AN SIBERECHTS (1627-c. 1700)
Canvas, 117 x 105 cm, Rijksdienst voor
1et Cultureel Erfgoed, NK1687

The Amsterdam art dealer Houthakker purchased this painting on the English art market in the 1930s and sold it in late 1940 to the Dienststelle Mühlmann, a German organisation tasked with the acquisition of works of art for Germany. The landscape was added to the collection for the Führermuseum in Linz. After the war, Houthakker officially declared it a forced sale, but declined the opportunity to buy it back.

15

A Seventeenth-Century Beech Wood Chest with Inlaid Panels
61 x 162.5 x 52 cm, Private Collection

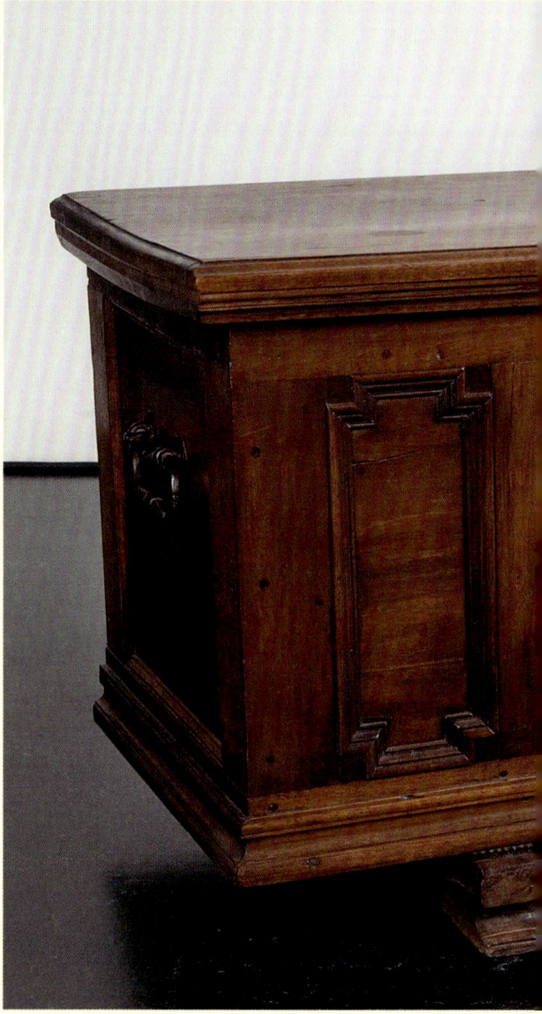

This chest was acquired in 1944 by a German from Salomon van Leeuwen's antiques store in The Hague. The German authorities had appointed a *Verwalter* to take over the management of the antiques gallery in 1942. As a result, Van Leeuwen no longer had access to his business and lost his means of income. The Verwalter had to be 'bought out' for a large sum of money in order to recontinue the gallery two years later by transferring the ownership to two of Van Leeuwen's children, who, unlike their father, were not subject to the anti-Jewish restrictions according to the German regulations. In late 2007, Salomon van Leeuwen's children filed a claim for this chest, which had been recovered from Germany after the war. Although the chest was sold after the gallery was formally handed over to van Leeuwen's children in 1944, the Restitutions Committee ruled that this was a case of sale under duress. Salomon van Leeuwen and his family had been forced into hiding and had serious financial problems, partly because Van Leeuwen did not receive any income from his antiques business during the *Verwaltung*. Therefore, in line with the Restitutions Committee's advice, the chest was returned to Van Leeuwen's son, who had inherited the gallery from his father.

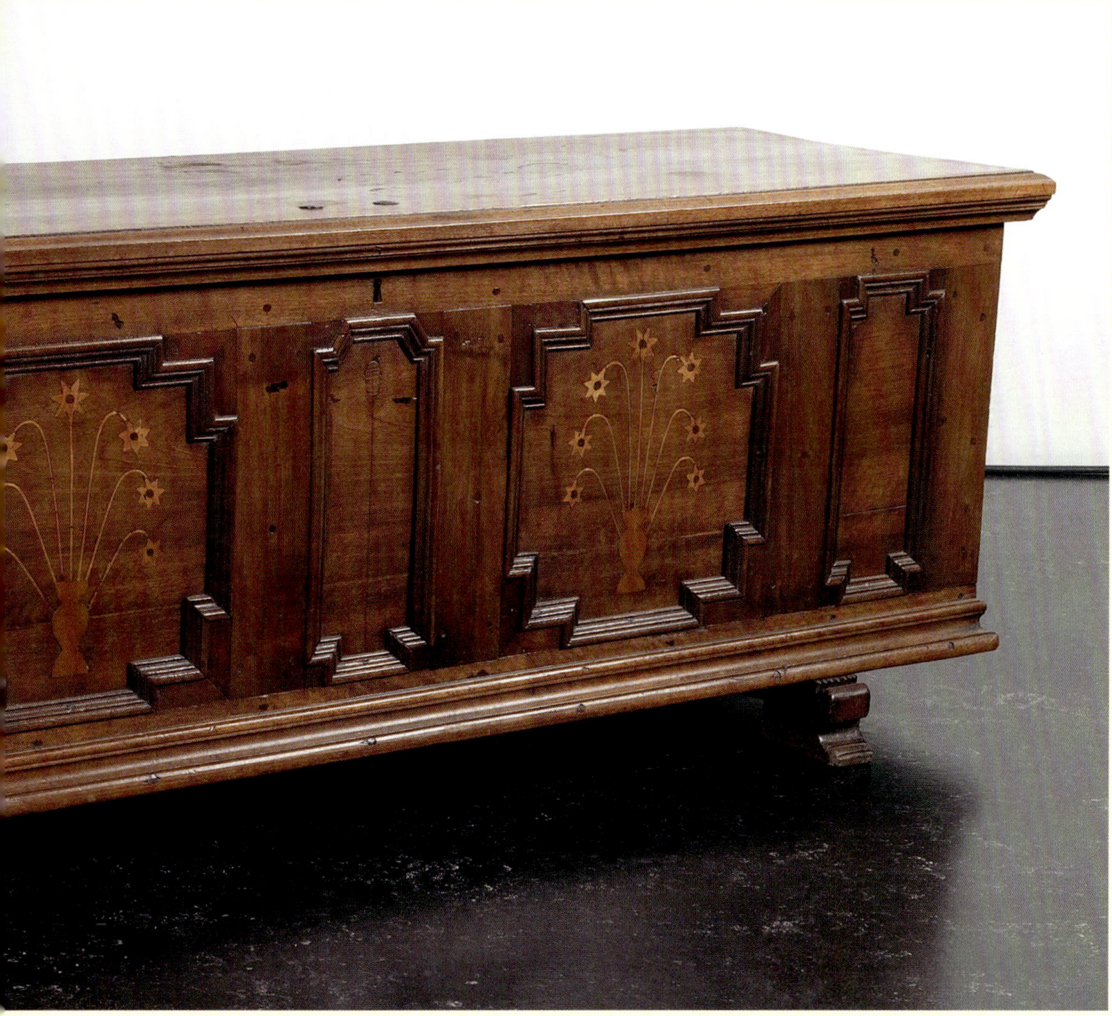

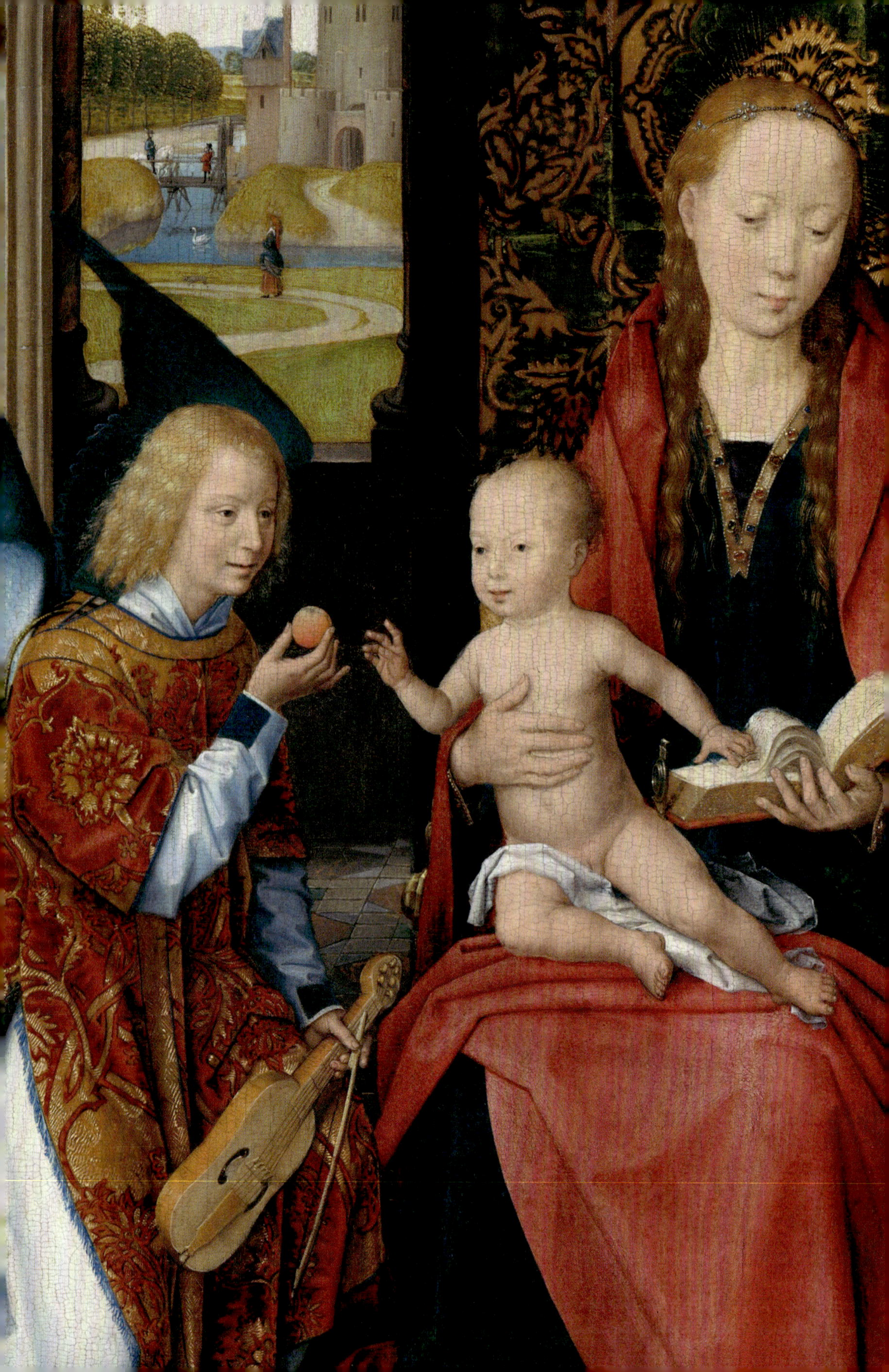

IV JEWISH OWNERS DURING THE OCCUPATION

In all of the occupied countries, the Nazi regime aimed for the maximum possible expropriation of the Jews. The methods used to achieve this objective varied extensively from country to country. For example, the murder of Jews and the looting of their property in Eastern Europe often took place simultaneously and in the same location. In the occupied countries of Western Europe, on the other hand, the Nazis created a physical distance between the confiscation of their victims' property and the places where they were murdered. Furthermore, there were major differences in the rapidity of looting and in the processes involved. More time was given to such measures in the Netherlands. For example, the anti-Jewish measures that already existed in Nazi Germany were put into effect immediately in Austria after the *Anschluss* of 1938. As mentioned in the previous chapter, the persecution of Jews in the Netherlands was implemented as a step-by-step, carefully directed process based on legal and official regulations. The looting of Jewish cultural property took place in the same manner. Both the expropriation of Jewish art dealers and the looting of Jewish collectors' property proceeded as a bureaucratic process.

'ENEMY ASSETS'

After the capitulation of the Dutch army on 15 May 1940, the Nazis occupied the Netherlands. During the occupation, the existing Dutch administrative structure was largely maintained. The country was placed under a civilian administration, headed by Arthur Seyss-Inquart. Initially, he gave priority to restoring public order and winning over the Dutch population to accept National Socialism. Large-scale looting did not take place during this first phase of the occupation, but specific categories of goods were confiscated. These were mainly objects from so-called Feindvermögen, which were the property of enemies of Germany, such as the British, or Dutchmen in enemy territory. These properties had to be put under German administration based on regulation VO 26/40 of June 1940. Some of these enemy assets belonged to Jewish refugees, whether from Germany or of other origins. After Hitler's rise to power in 1933, the

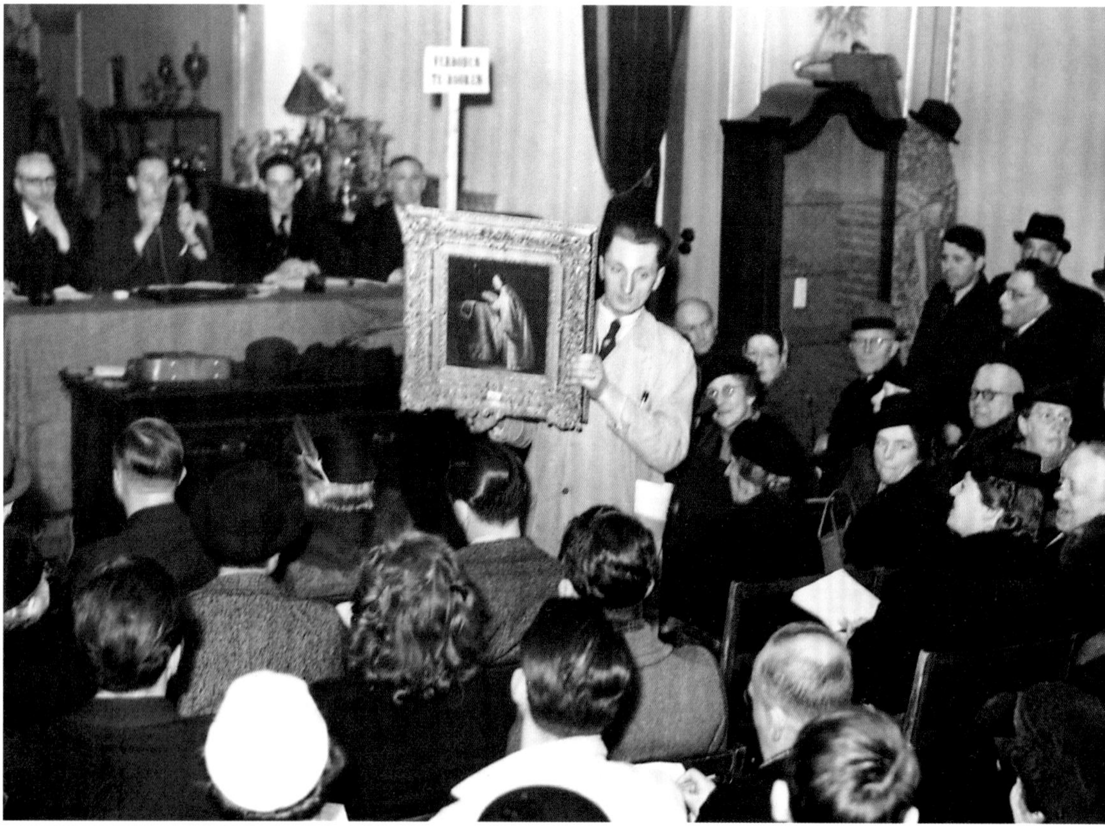

An auction at Van Marle & Bignell, The Hague, 1941

The Hague auction house Van Marle & Bignell flourished during the occupation of the Netherlands thanks to the countless sales it managed on behalf of the Germans. It was particularly for the *Sammelverwaltung feindlicher Hausgeräte* that thousands of objects were sold at auction.

Netherlands became a refuge and transit country for tens of thousands of Jews who had fled from National Socialism. Most of them travelled on to other countries, but had occasionally left behind property in the Netherlands. After the German invasion, these possessions, such as stored household effects at transport companies, were confiscated as soon as possible. To manage these confiscated household goods, the department Sammelverwaltung feindlicher Hausgeräte (SFH) was established. This organisation, based at Scheveningen, offered important German buyers the opportunity to acquire the best works of art and antiquities from the confiscated properties. O the remaining goods, some were leased to German officials in the Netherlands or transferred to German cities affected by air raids. However, by far the majority of objects of Jewish origin were sold at auction in the Netherlands.

One example is formed by the precious household effects owned by Milly Antonia von Friedländer-Fuld, the widow of a German coal magnate. She left the Netherlands in 1939, leaving some of her possessions with the De Gruyter & Co transport company in Amsterdam. There, the goods were seized in 1941 and most were sold at auction in The Hague later. Suicide could also bring art property within reach of the occupying forces as early as the first phase of the war. Fear of a future under Nazi rule drove many Jews in the May days of 1940 to take their fate in their own hands. Among others, banker and art collector Paul May and his wife Rosine Fuld ended their own lives on 15 May 1940. Their daughter Ellen had fled the Netherlands with her family. In 1941, part of the May-Fuld couple's valuable estate was auctioned off as enemy property in Amsterdam.

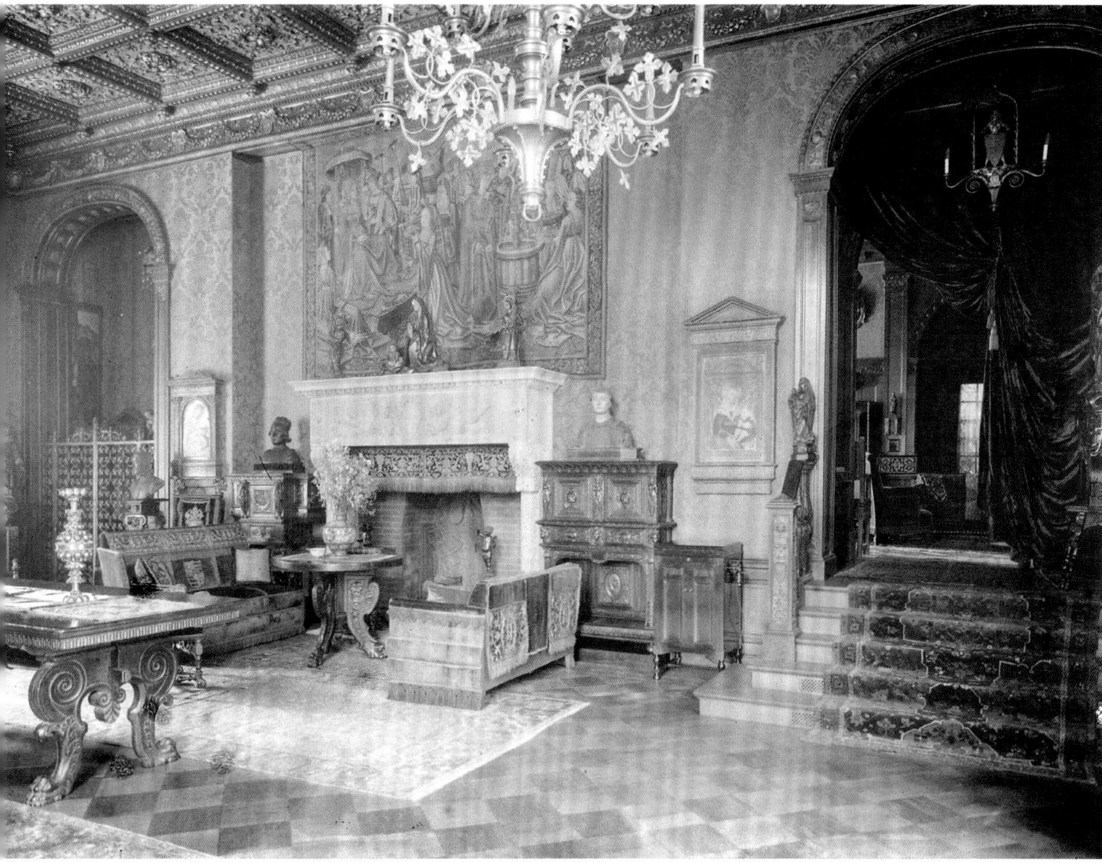

The interior of De Hartekamp in Heemstede, the residence of Catalina von Pannwitz-Roth (1876-1959), Argentinian of Jewish descent

Catalina von Pannwitz-Roth was the widow of the wealthy German lawyer Walter von Pannwitz, who had assembled a fine collection of paintings by masters from the 15th to 17th centuries. After Walter von Pannwitz's death in 1920, his widow settled with their daughter Ursula at De Hartekamp country house in Heemstede and used it as a gathering place for German upper circles. She was close friends with the former German emperor Wilhelm II and also received members of the Von Lippe-Biesterfeld princely family at her estate. There were also friendly ties with the family of the banker Fritz Gutmann, who resided in the nearby Huize Bosbeek. During the war, Catalina von Pannwitz managed to escape from the Netherlands thanks to her art collection. She sold six paintings to Hermann Göring in October 1940, in exchange for an exit visa to Switzerland (fig. 16).

One German organisation that was active in locating and amassing art from the outset was the Dienststelle Mühlmann. This agency, which will be discussed in Chapter V, had the task of tracking down valuable objects and allocating them to German buyers, including prominent Nazis. Among other things, the bureau investigated whether Dutch art dealers had interesting objects from enemy assets in their stock. After the war, art dealer Houthakker stated that a delegation from the Dienststelle had come to his gallery to 'very carefully sniff everything out'. For example, a painting by Jan Swart of Groningen was partly owned by a firm in London and was taken over through a transaction. Houthakker explained: 'As a Jew, I was of course unable to prevent this and the sale came about against my will – under duress'.

LIRO REGULATIONS

Most art confiscations took place from 1941 to 1943. In January 1941, all Jews were required to register. From March 1941, Jewish businesses were placed under German control. Managers were appointed who could liquidate or sell the company. Then, in August of that year, under the First Liro Regulation (VO 148/41), Jews were forced to deposit their monetary assets, including securities, with the bank Lippmann, Rosenthal & Co., Sarphatistraat (Liro) in Amsterdam. This was a looting agency set up by the Germans as a branch of the Jewish banking firm of the same name on Nieuwe Spiegelstraat in Amsterdam. In fact, the looting agency had nothing to do with the renowned Jewish firm and had merely adopted the name to avoid unrest over the obligation

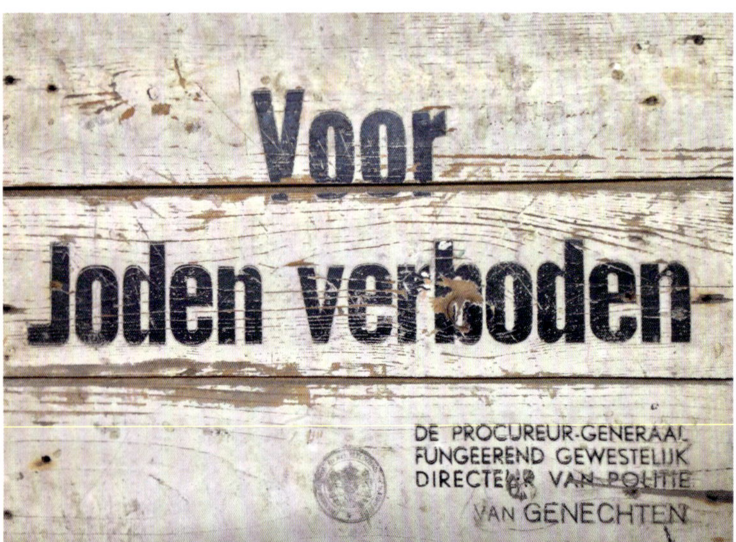

Wooden street sign *Voor Joden verboden* ('Prohibited for Jews'), 1941-1945

During the occupation, the Nazi regime implemented more and more measures that affected the rights and freedom of Jews. A September 1941 regulation had a major impact on their position in publi[c] life. Jews were no longer permitted to enter parks, zoos, restaurants, museums, libraries and sports venues. They were also no longer allowed to attend public markets or auctions.
This wooden street sign *Voor Joden verboden* was donated to the Anne Frank House by the granddaughter of [a] woman who removed it from a street i[n] protest during the war.

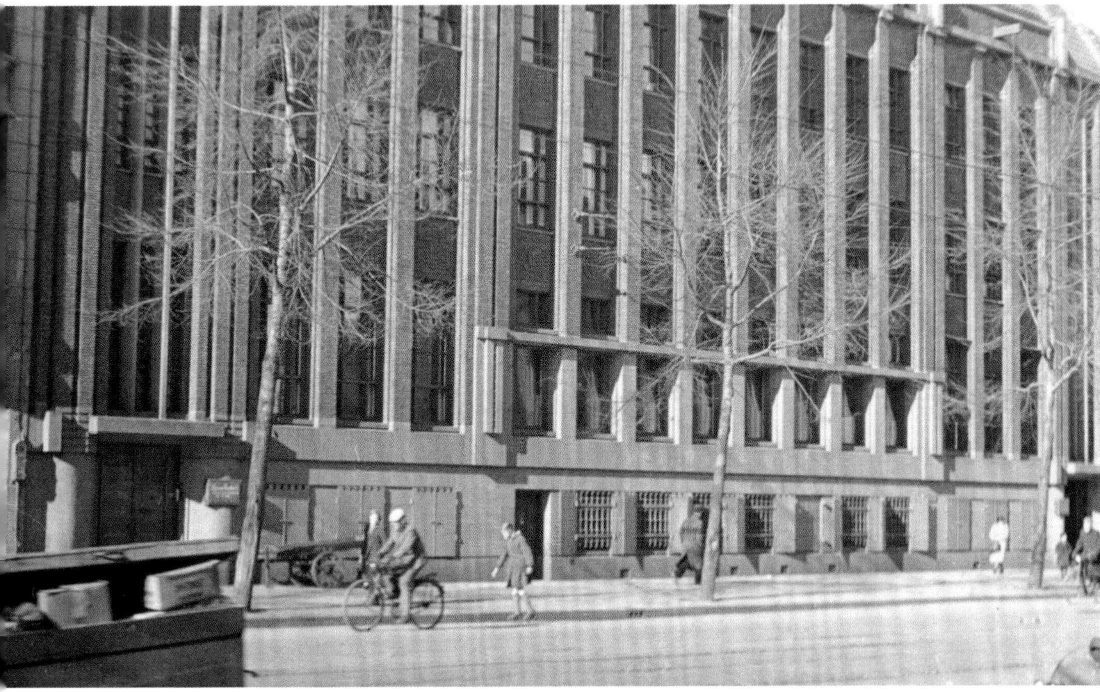

he building at Sarphatistraat 47-55 in Amsterdam, where the occupiers established the bank Lippmann, Rosenthal & Co. (Liro) in 1941, March 1944

When the Liro Bank was established, the impression was intentionally given that it was a regular bank, an affiliate branch of the Jewish bank of the same name at the Nieuwe Spiegelstraat, which had already been founded in the mid-nineteenth century. In reality, the new 'branch' was erected for Jews to deposit their capital and valuables. The many works of art handed over here were sold off at auction or otherwise.

to surrender their belongings. The occupying forces pretended that Liro would manage the Jewish assets. However, the real aim was total expropriation. In May 1942, the obligation to surrender possessions was further extended. According to the Second Liro Regulation (VO 58/42), from then on Jews also had to surrender other assets to Liro, including 'collections of all kinds of art objects, objects of gold, platinum or silver, as well as processed and uncut precious and semi-precious gems and pearls'. From then on, enormous numbers of objects poured into the looting institution. At Liro, the items handed over were handled by a special department. The highest quality works of art and antiquities were kept for important German buyers, with preferential rights for the Dienststelle Mühlmann, among others. The large mass of Liro goods ended up on the German and Dutch art market, especially in Amsterdam and The Hague. Numerous Dutch individuals and companies profited from the sale of these looted goods. Auction houses that were already known during the war to bring large quantities of Jewish property under the hammer were Van Marle & Bignell in The Hague and Mak van Waay in Amsterdam. The first-mentioned auction house was mainly used to sell 'Jewish enemy property' and the latter was employed to sell the Liro goods.

THE DUTCH MUSEUMS

German authorities left the collections of Dutch museums largely untouched, with a few important exceptions, such as the removal of three sixteenth-century German Renaissance masterpieces from the Rijksmuseum Kröller-Müller and the confiscation of the collection of the Jewish Historical Museum in Amsterdam (fig. 21). However, the Nazi authorities did confiscate artworks belonging to Jewish collectors that had been housed in Dutch museums for protection. However, they did not manage to track everything down. Several museums succeeded in protecting Jewish art property. They withheld data, hid or destroyed documentation and accepted objects as 'donations' to keep them out

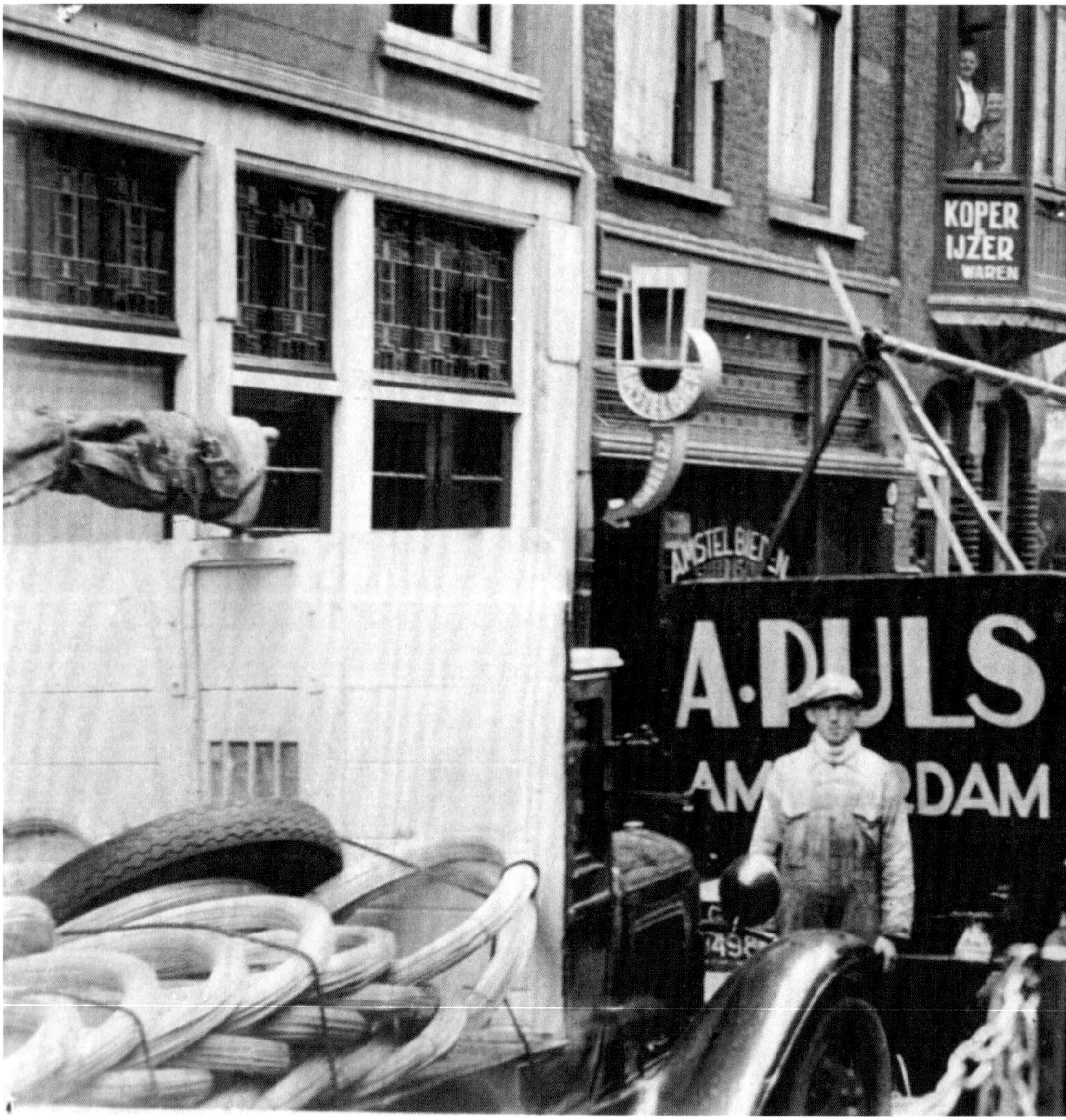

of the Germans' grasp. In addition, the Department of Education, Science and Cultural Protection (DOWK) strained to ensure that Jewish art property was permitted to remain in museums, which was successful in a number of cases. This allowed several Jewish owners to have their artworks returned after the war, although the restoration of rights was difficult at times. In addition to these attempts by museums to save Jewish art property from German confiscation, it occurred that institutions acquired Jewish looted art themselves during the war, including purchases on the art market. Many such cases went unnoticed for decades and only came to light in the last two decades, partly as a result of recent museum investigations (see Chapter VII).

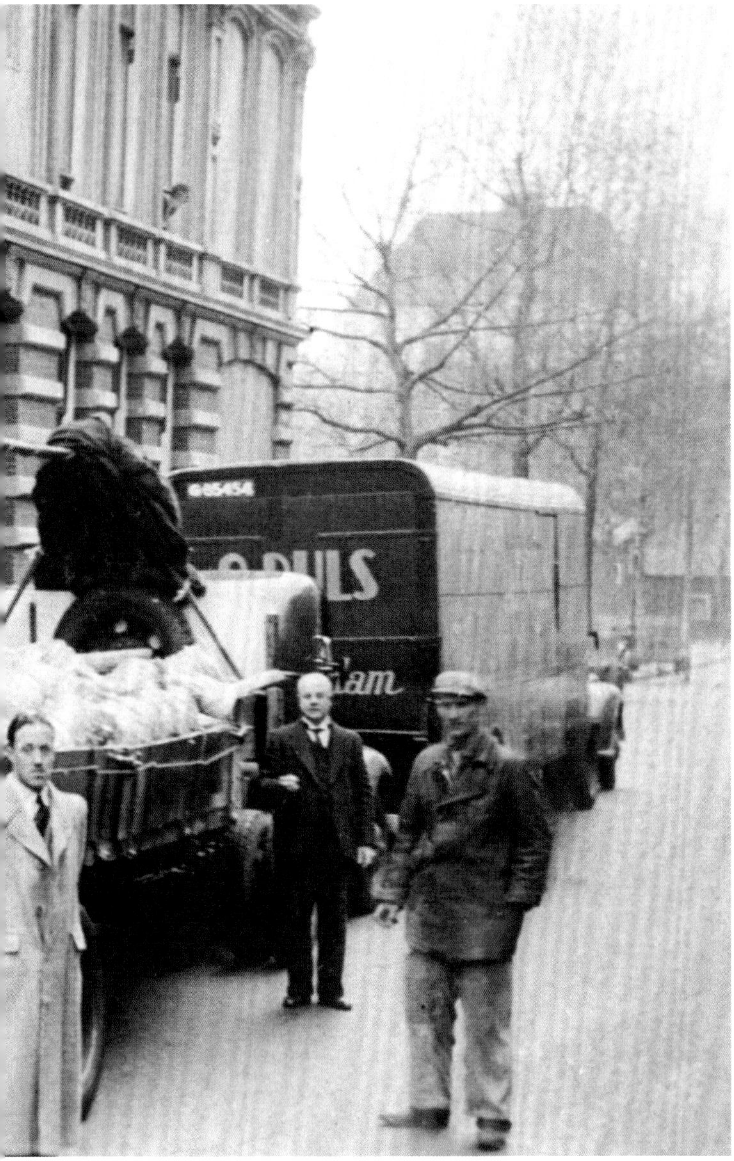

Transport by Puls

The Amsterdam based transport company A. Puls was methodically involved in the eviction of Jewish homes ordered by the Germans. As a result, the term 'to puls' became a synonym in the Dutch language for the emptying of deportees' houses.

DEPORTATIONS

Large-scale deportations of Jews began in the summer of 1942. Initially, Jewish citizens were ordered to report for work in Germany but soon they were arrested straightaway, on the streets or during house raids. They were then transferred to the transit camp Westerbork. From there, every few days the dreaded train departed to the east, usually with Auschwitz and Sobibor extermination camps as final destinations. In September 1943, the last major razzia was held in Amsterdam. The Germans then deemed the capital 'Judenrein'. A total of around 102,000 Jews deported from the Netherlands were murdered during the occupation.

After the deportation of Jews, their homes were emptied. For this task, the Einsatzstab Reichsleiter Rosenberg (ERR) was responsible. This looting organisation was headed by Nazi ideologue Alfred Rosenberg and was active in several occupied countries, partly for the confiscation of cultural goods. At the head of the Dutch branch of the ERR was Albert Schmidt-Stähler, who kept office at Keizersgracht 264 in Amsterdam. The household effects of deported Jews were first inventoried by the Hausraterfassungsstelle, an official department of the German administration. The ERR then had the houses emptied by Dutch and German transport companies. This happened at least 29,000 times during the occupation. Because of the frequent involvement of the Amsterdam moving company A. Puls in the evictions, a new verb emerged in the vernacular: 'to pulse'. Goods the ERR had no interest in were handed over to Liro. Most of the 'pulsed' household goods were auctioned off after removal, transported to Germany or stolen. In this way, large-scale works of art and antiques also disappeared out of view. Not everything was lost. Several people were able to house valuable goods in time with neighbours and other acquaintances, popularly referred to as 'bewariërs' (Aryan keepers). Some of these items were returned to Jewish survivors after the war, but other objects remained where they were.

INVOLUNTARY SALE AND EXCHANGE OF GOODS

A significant proportion of the art that came into German hands was purchased rather than confiscated. The wartime art market flourished considerably. Many Dutch dealers and private individuals seized the opportunity to profit with both hands. However, this does not mean that every sales transaction was voluntary. Sales by Jewish owners were often directly related to their vulnerable position in a country under Nazi rule. Some owners sold artworks as early as the beginning of the war for fear of future confiscations. For example, the merchant E.L. Branau, who came from Germany, stated after the war that his father-in-law had sold several works of art in 1940 and 1941, reasoning that on the basis of the events in Germany it was sufficiently clear that these objects from Jewish property would sooner or later be expropriated in one way or another (*'man auf Grund der Erfahrungen aus Deutschland genuegend bekannt war mit der Tatsache, dass diese Dinge aus juedischem Besitz doch frueher oder spaeter auf irgend eine Weise enteignet werden wuerden'*). Selling art was also a means to fund an escape plan for safety. After the war, Amsterdam art dealer Otto Busch stated that he had hidden a painting by Floris van Schooten from the Nazis for some time. Eventually, he sold the work through a Dutch intermediary to flee from the Netherlands: 'Since in 1942, as a Jew, I practically could no longer dispose of money [...]. I was forced [...] to sell to Germany a still life by Floris van Schooten, which I had sent into hiding. I thought I would need the proceeds to escape to England, an operation which did not succeed.' Hugo Kaufmann, an Amsterdam-based banker of German-Jewish descent, also hoped to escape the Netherlands. He sold several paintings by old masters in 1941 in preparation for his planned departure. For a time, it seemed that Kaufmann would be able to secure an exit visa if he met certain financial conditions set by the German authorities. Kaufmann initially met all the requirements, but the Nazis changed their minds and decided not to let him go. He was arrested in July 1942 and was murdered with his wife and three children in Auschwitz a few months later.

As the war progressed, it became increasingly difficult for Jews to earn a living. They lost their sources of income, had to surrender their assets to Liro and were increasingly cornered. In August 1941, there was still an exemption from the surrender of assets up to 1,000 guilders, but in May 1942 this was reduced to 250 guilders. From 1943, individual Liro bank accounts were dissolved and all assets were deposited in a collective account ('Sammelkonto'). In this situation, art could offer a last resort. Selling hidden paintings or other artworks could sometimes help make ends meet. In a post-war letter to the Dutch authorities for restoration of rights, the Hague lawyer and prosecutor H.A. Tels described how difficult it had been to support his family of five. The 250 guilders per month guaranteed by the Liro for living expenses was insufficient, as well as being paid irregularly and sometimes not at all. The sale of works of art, including old family possessions, provided a solution: 'I had sent a few of my paintings into hiding with a friend. I was forced to gradually have some of these paintings sold [...] in order to keep my head above water'. The proceeds

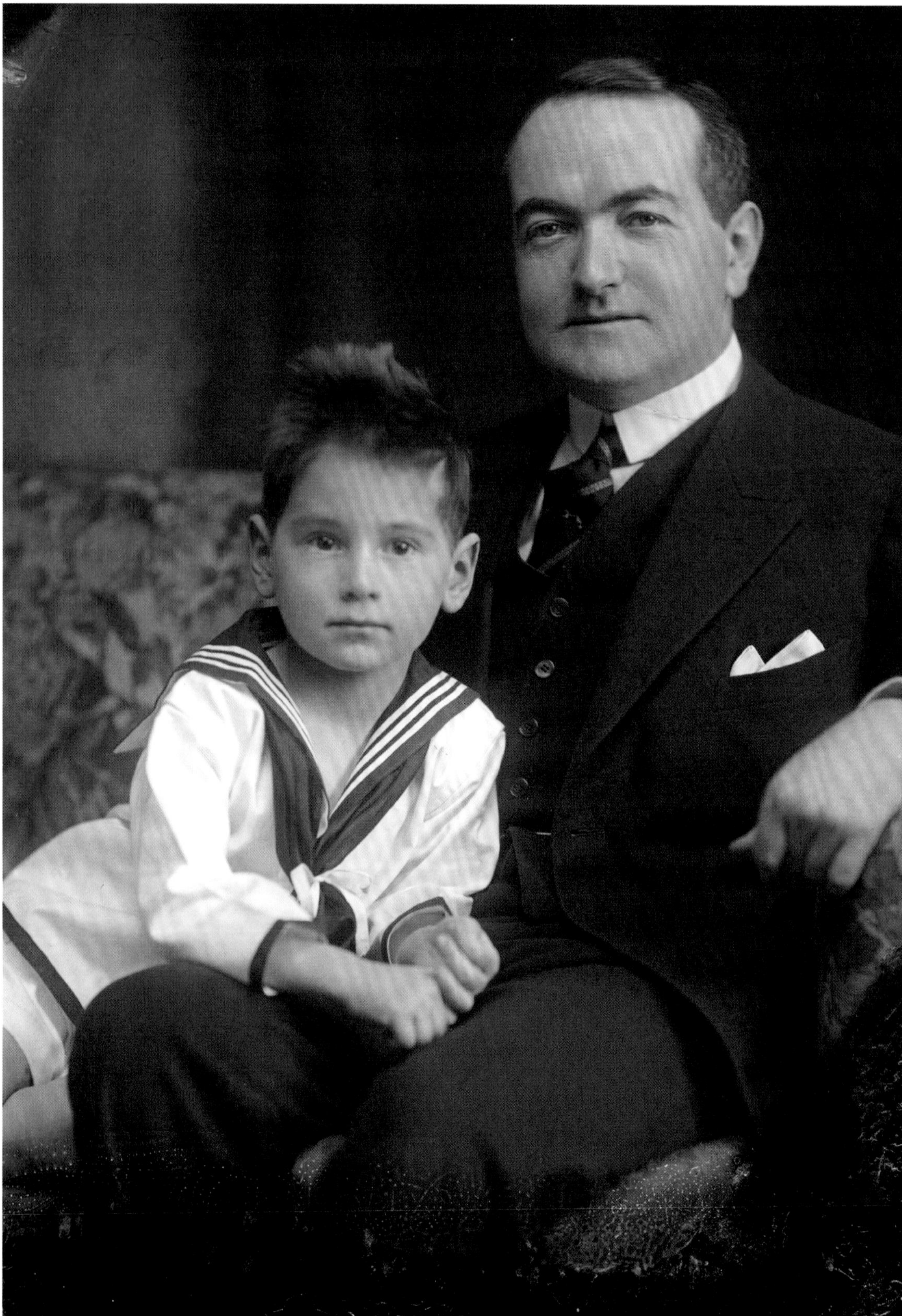

had also been used 'after we were all interned, to have food parcels sent to the various camps regularly for about two years'.

Many Jews handed over or sold valuables in the hope of obtaining an exit permit or a 'Sperre', an entry on a list that gave a reprieve from deportation. Sometimes this enabled them to save their own lives. However, guarantees were often false or protection was only temporary and people were deported after some time anyway. Works of art were also used as a means to buy freedom. The Nazi elite's urge to collect was so great that several families were able to escape death by handing over coveted paintings by old masters. This applied not only to private collectors, but also to art dealers. For example, during the occupation, the Amsterdam art dealer P. de Boer transferred a painting by Salomon van Ruysdael to a buyer for the Führermuseum in Linz. His representative explained after the war that he had done this to help his Jewish parents-in-law emigrate to Switzerland with the Germans' permission. This operation was successful. The couple had arrived in Switzerland under the escort of a German police officer, after which the painting had been collected from De Boer's house. It is one of the examples of how human lives could be saved by sacrificing one or more works of art in times of war.

Portrait of Fritz Gutmann (1886-1944) with his son Bernhard

The German art collector Fritz Gutmann, who resided in Heemstede, was forced to sell a large quantity of objects, both paintings and applied art, from his collection to several German dealers in 1942. A few works were returned to his heirs as early as 1952 but most were not restituted until 2002 onwards (fig. 22-24).

16
Man with Beard and Turban
REMBRANDT (1606-1669), follower of
Panel, 73 x 59.5 cm, Rijksdienst voor het Cultureel Erfgoed, NK1602

This painting belonged to the collection of Catalina von Pannwitz (see p. 63). The study of an old man's face, at the time attributed to Rembrandt, was among of the six artworks sold by Von Pannwitz to Hermann Göring in October 1940, in exchange for an exit visa to Switzerland. Paintings by Rembrandt were highly appreciated by the prominent Nazis. In their mutual rivalry to acquire paintings by the artist, the *Man with Beard and Turban* must have been a coveted possession for Göring. The attribution to Rembrandt was rejected after the war. As is the case with so many pieces originally ascribed to the artist, the painting was eventually downgraded to the work of a follower or imitator.
After the liberation, Catalina von Pannwitz declined the opportunity to buy back the paintings acquired by Göring from her collection.

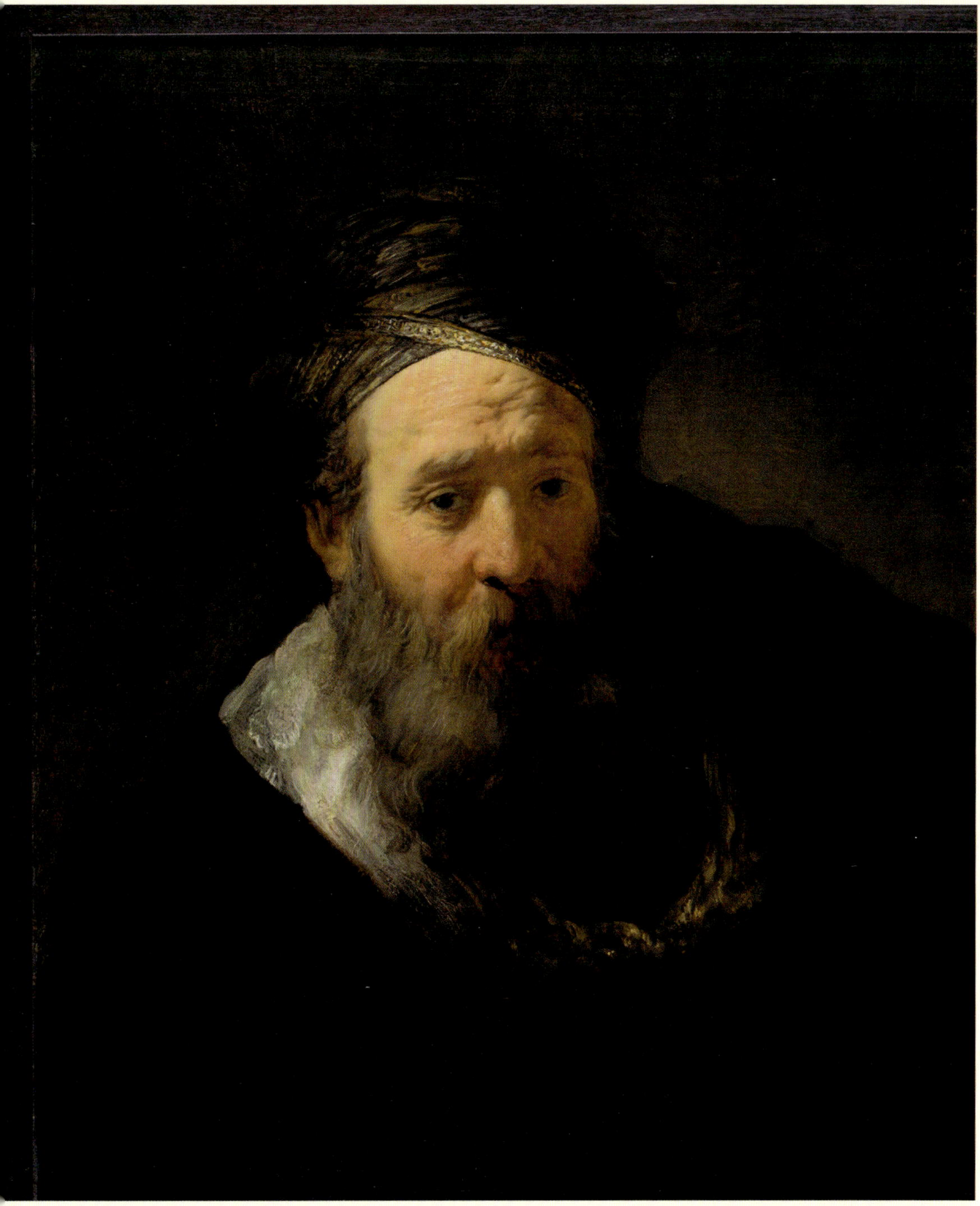

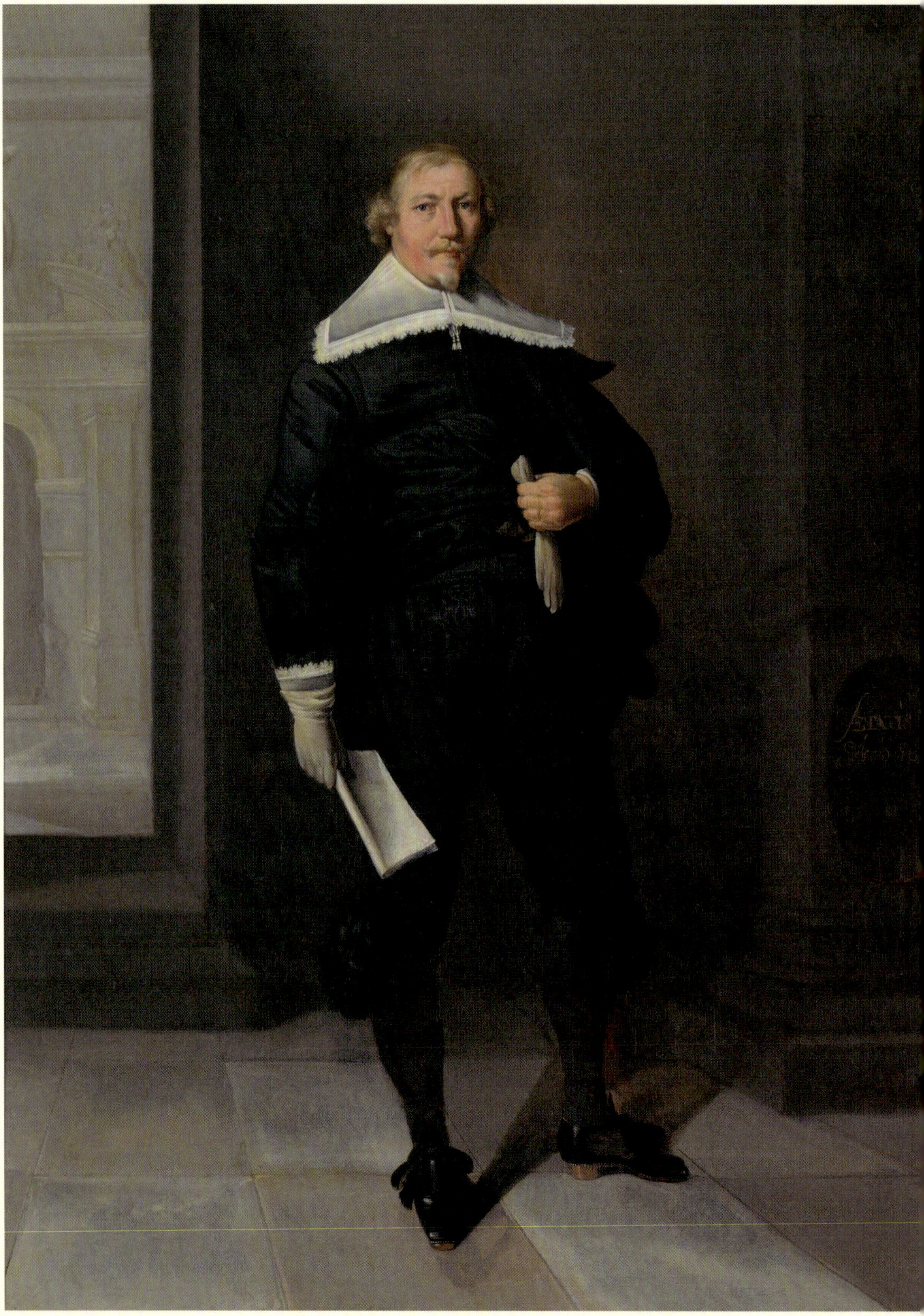

17

Portrait of a Man, 1643
HARMEN WILLEMSZ. WIERINGA (c. 1590-1650)
Panel, 71 x 54 cm, Rijksdienst voor het Cultureel Erfgoed, NK2558

Robert May (1873-1962) was partner of the renowned bank Lippmann, Rosenthal & Co. on the Nieuwe Spiegelstraat in Amsterdam, which was placed under the management of the German Verwalter A. Flesche by the German authorities in July 1940. After the war, May stated that Flesche had behaved correctly as a Verwalter. From May 1942, in accordance with regulation VO 58/42, Jews were forced to hand over their art objects and other valuables to the looting bank Liro on the Sarphatistraat. May, on the other hand, was ordered to bring his painting by Wieringa to the Rijksmuseum for safekeeping. There it was confiscated by the Dienststelle Mühlmann in 1943, after which the work ended up in Hermann Göring's collection. May survived the war but decided not to reclaim the painting when it was recovered from Germany after the war.

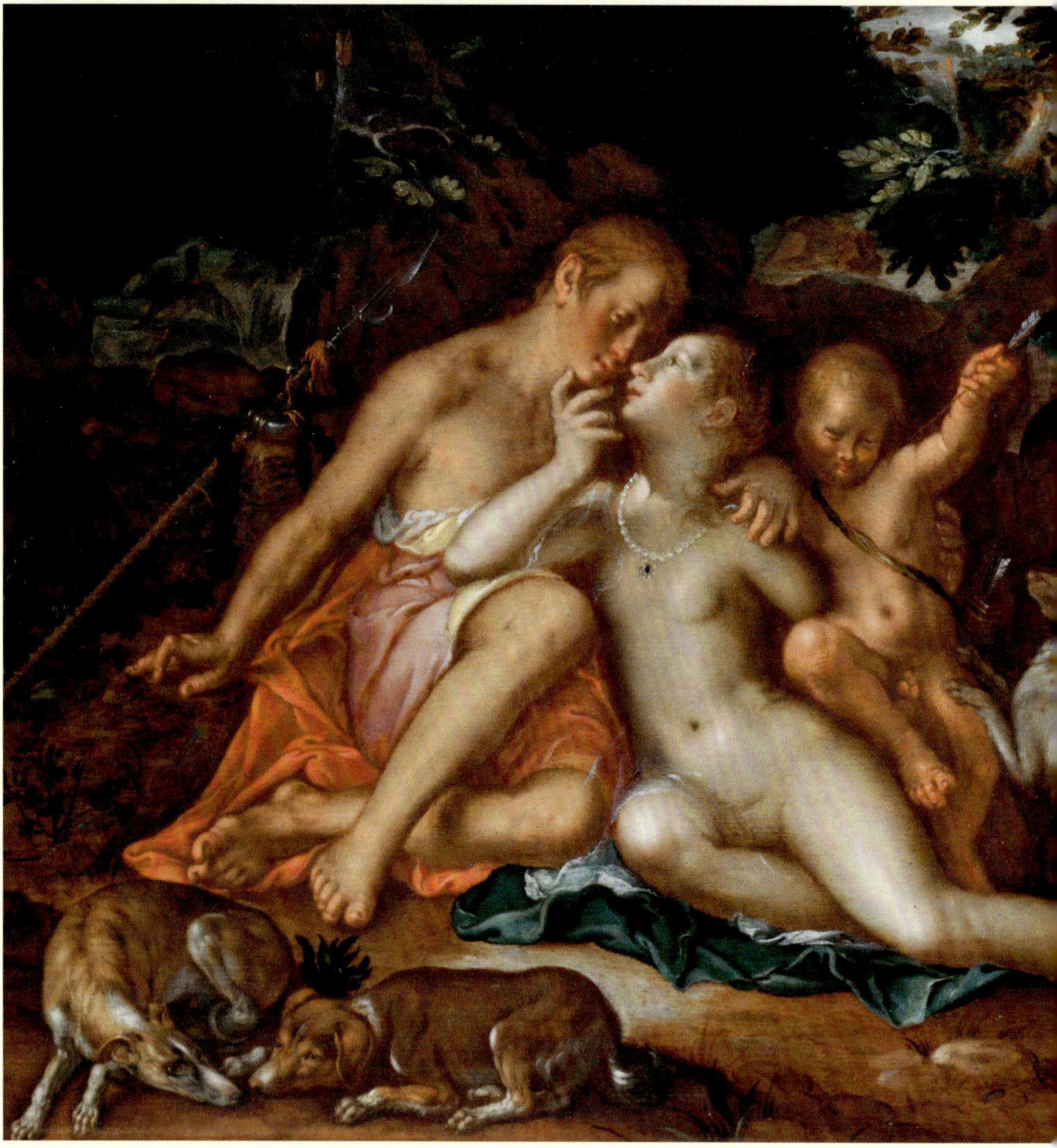

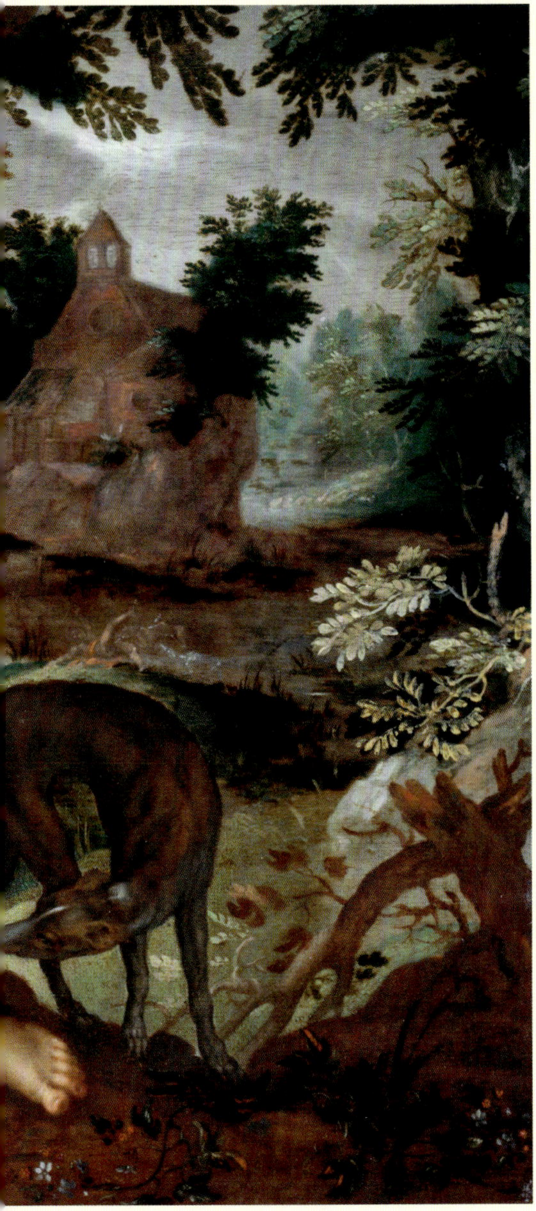

18

Venus and Adonis, c. 1607-1610
JOACHIM WTEWAEL (1566-1638), attributed
Panel, 39 x 60 cm, Private Collection, on loan to the Centraal Museum, Utrecht

This painting, at the time still considered to be a work by the German artist Hans Rottenhammer, was owned by Isaac Goudeket, who was murdered in Sobibor in 1943. The work came to the Liro through confiscation. It was probably never transported to Germany during the war because after the liberation, it was found in a Foreign Ministry building used by the Germans. In 2005, in accordance with the advice of the Restitutions Committee, the *Venus and Adonis* was returned to the heirs of its rightful owner.

19
Landscape with a Fortress
ABRAHAM BEGEYN (1637-1697)
Canvas, 73.5 x 131.5 cm, Rijksdienst voor het Cultureel Erfgoed, NK3097

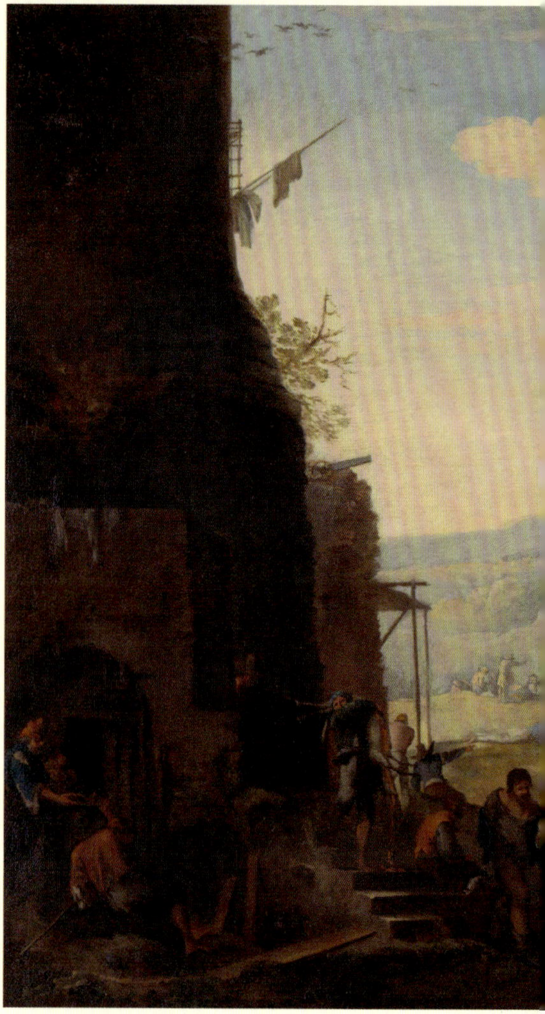

The provenance of many paintings in the NK Collection still remains unclear. According to the available information, this landscape by the painter Abraham Begeyn changed owners several times during the war and eventually ended up at the Liro. However, it is not known which private collector or dealer handed over the painting to the looting bank. Countless works of art from Jewish property surrendered to Liro were never recovered after the war. As for the successfully traced Liro works, it frequently proved impossible to determine who the original owners were. The Liro's registry records were often inaccurate and incomplete and parts of the archive had been lost over the years.

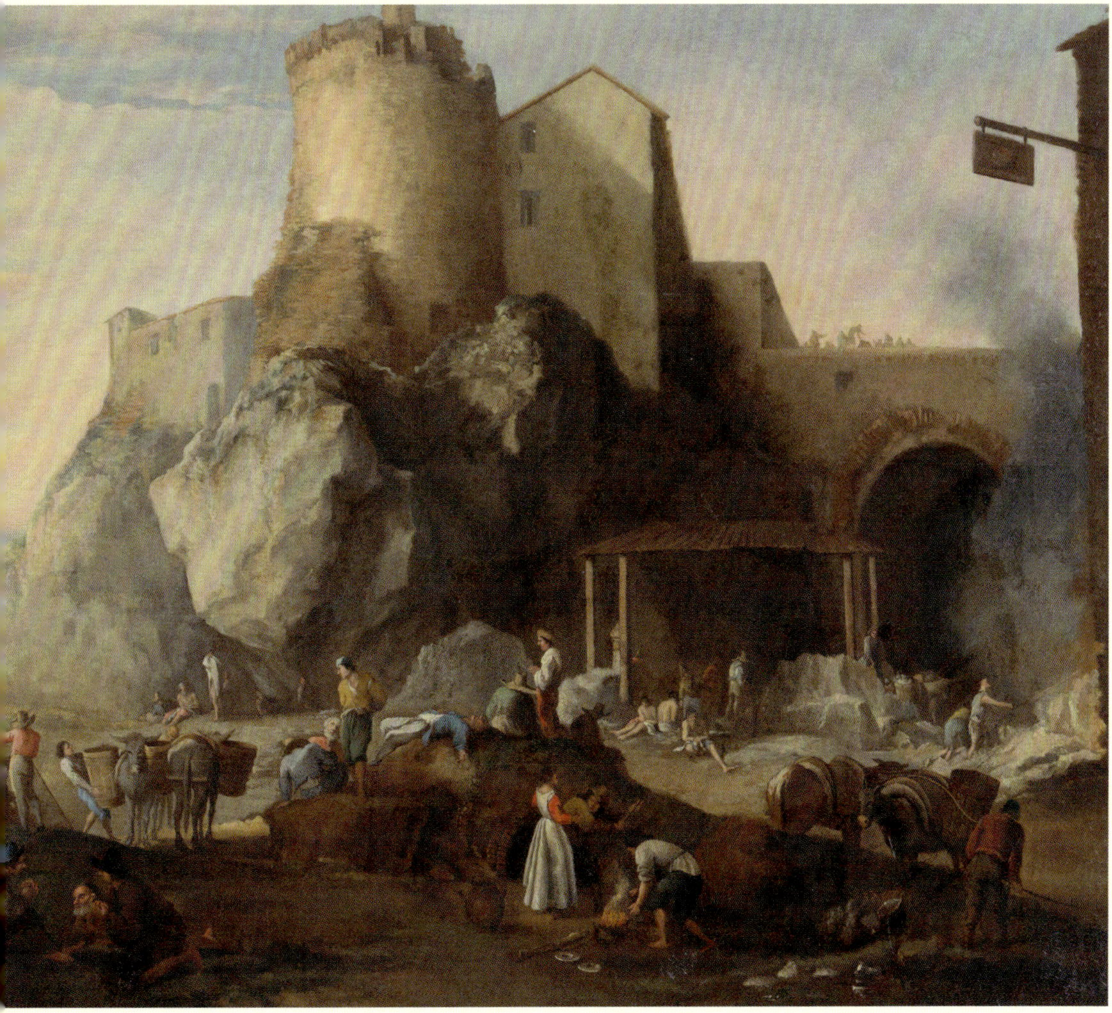

20
Elegant Company Making Music on a Terrace
DIRK HALS (1591-1656)
Panel, 53 x 84 cm, Frans Halsmuseum, Haarlem

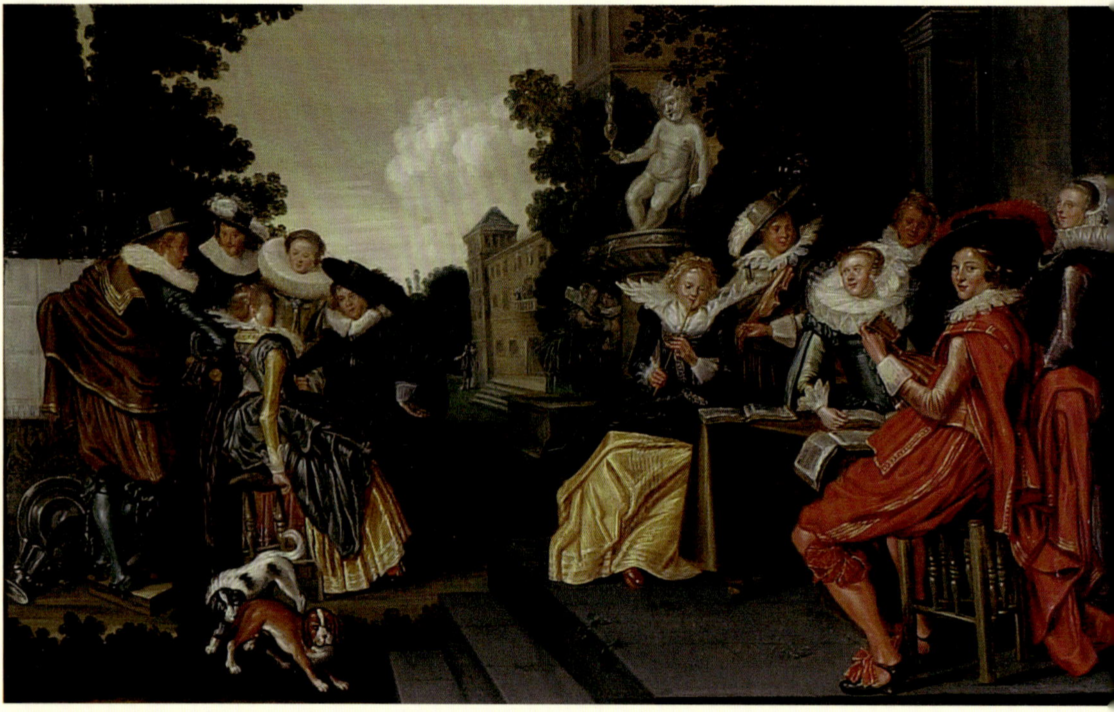

This painting was the property of the Jewish entrepreneur Maurits de Kadt from Aerdenhout. De Kadt attempted to flee the Netherlands in May 1940 but the ship that was to carry him to safety struck a mine. Wounded, De Kadt returned home. In August or September 1940, he sold the Dirk Hals painting through an art agent to the German organisation Dienststelle Mühlmann. At the time, De Kadt was in preparation for another attempt to escape from the Netherlands. He managed to obtain an exit visa and left the Netherlands in October 1940 with the United States as his destination. After the painting was recovered from Germany after the war, De Kadt requested the return of the work in 1948. The SNK, however, was not convinced that the work had been sold involuntarily and rejected the appeal. In 2003, De Kadt's son submitted another claim for the painting in the NK Collection. The Restitutions Committee concluded that De Kadt had sold the work under the art agent's duress and in circumstances that forced him to obtain an exit visa to flee the country. The request was granted and the ministry of Education, Culture and Science returned the work to De Kadt's heirs in accordance with the advice of the committee. In 2012, the Frans Halsmuseum in Haarlem was able to purchase the painting for its collection; the Dirk Hals had been on loan to the museum before the restitution. This was made possible by the financial support of the Association of Friends of the Frans Halsmuseum.

21
Amulet with Hebrew Inscription,
Silver, 8.5 x 0.8 x 9.1 cm,
oods Museum, Amsterdam

On 24 February 1932, the Jewish Historical Museum was officially opened in a tower room of the Waag building in Amsterdam. The museum was closed down after the German invasion in May 1940. Most of he collection had by now been stored for afekeeping in a bunker in the dunes of Castricum. In 1943, the occupying forces confiscated the museum's collection. By order of the German looting organisation Einsatzstab Reichsleiter Rosenberg (ERR), over 600 objects were transported Frankfurt am Main. They were brought to the Nazi ideologist Alfred Rosenberg's Institut zur Erforschung der Judenfrage in Frankfurt am Main. Frantic attempts by the Netherlands to prevent this confiscation came to nothing. Of the more than 600 seized objects, only 200 were found after the war. This amulet is one of those recovered objects.

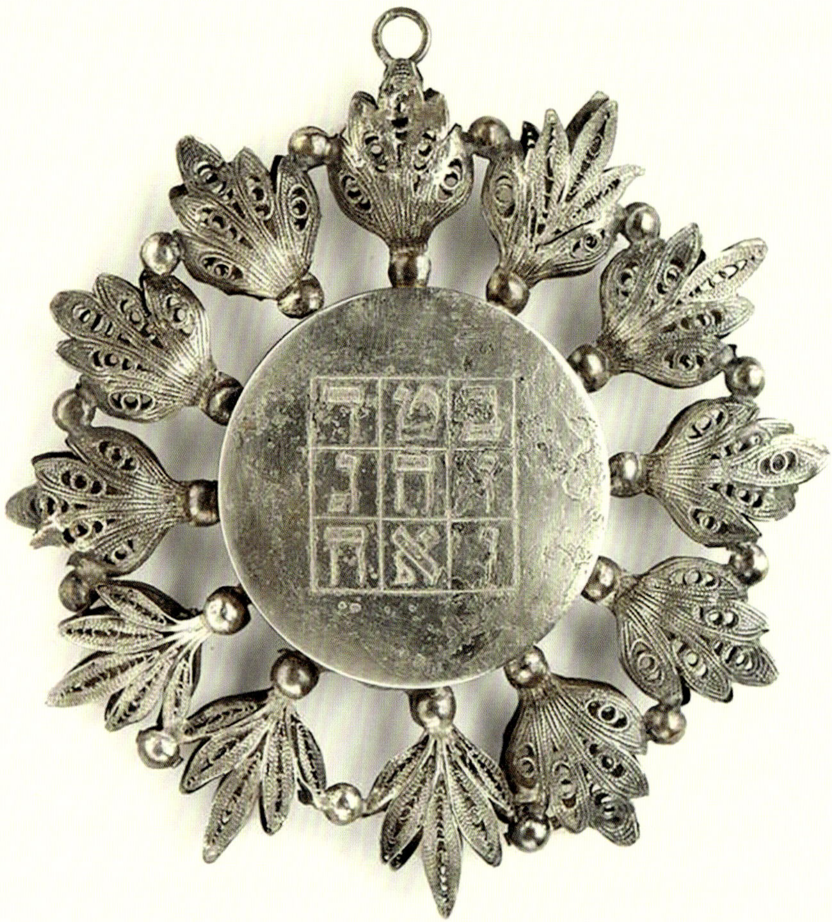

22

Deer Hunt in a Forest
JAN HACKAERT (1628-in or after 1685)
Canvas, 69 x 54 cm, Koninklijk Kabinet van Schilderijen, Mauritshuis, Den Haag

This painting belonged to the banker and art collector Fritz Gutmann (1886-1944). It hung in the dining room of his villa on the country estate Bosbeek in Heemstede. In 1942, Gutmann was forced to sell the landscape and many other pieces from his collection to the German art dealers Julius Böhler and Karl Haberstock. Gutmann and his wife fell victim to the persecution of Jews in 1944. Hackaert's painting was recovered from Germany after the war but it took the intervention of a judge to have the painting returned to Mr. and Mrs. Gutmann's two adult children. In a ruling dated 1 July 1952, the judge ruled that the works of art sold to Böhler and Haberstock were to be returned to the Gutmann heirs, on the condition that the sale amount received at the time was transferred to the State. The family then selected and reclaimed a few of the recovered works, including this painting. They later sold it and the Hackaert landscape eventually came into the possession of the Mauritshuis through purchase in 1971. However, many other objects from the Gutmann collection remained in the NK Collection after the ruling of 1952. Following new restitution claims, these works of art were returned to the heirs on the advice of the Restitutions Committee from 2002 onwards.

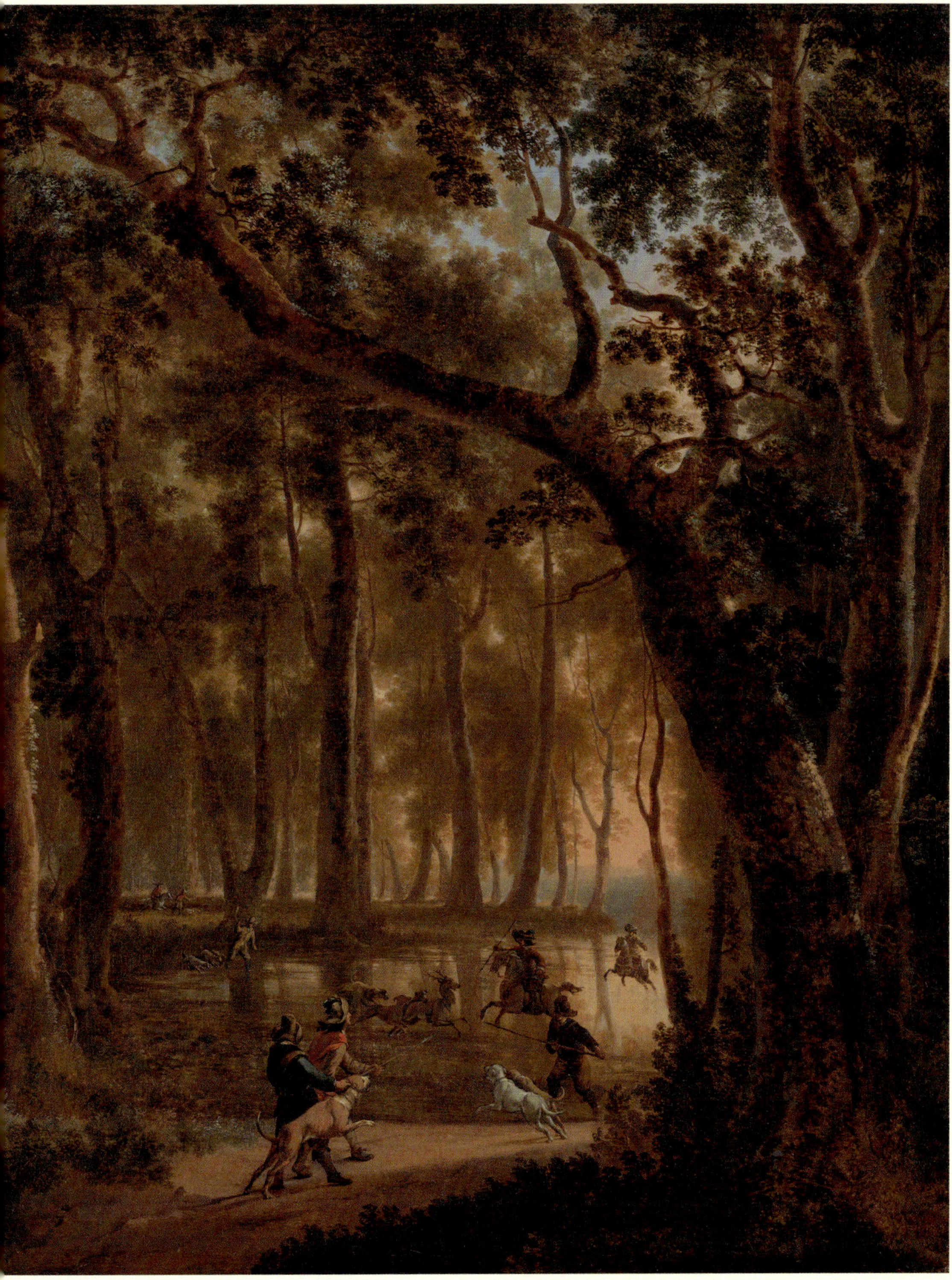

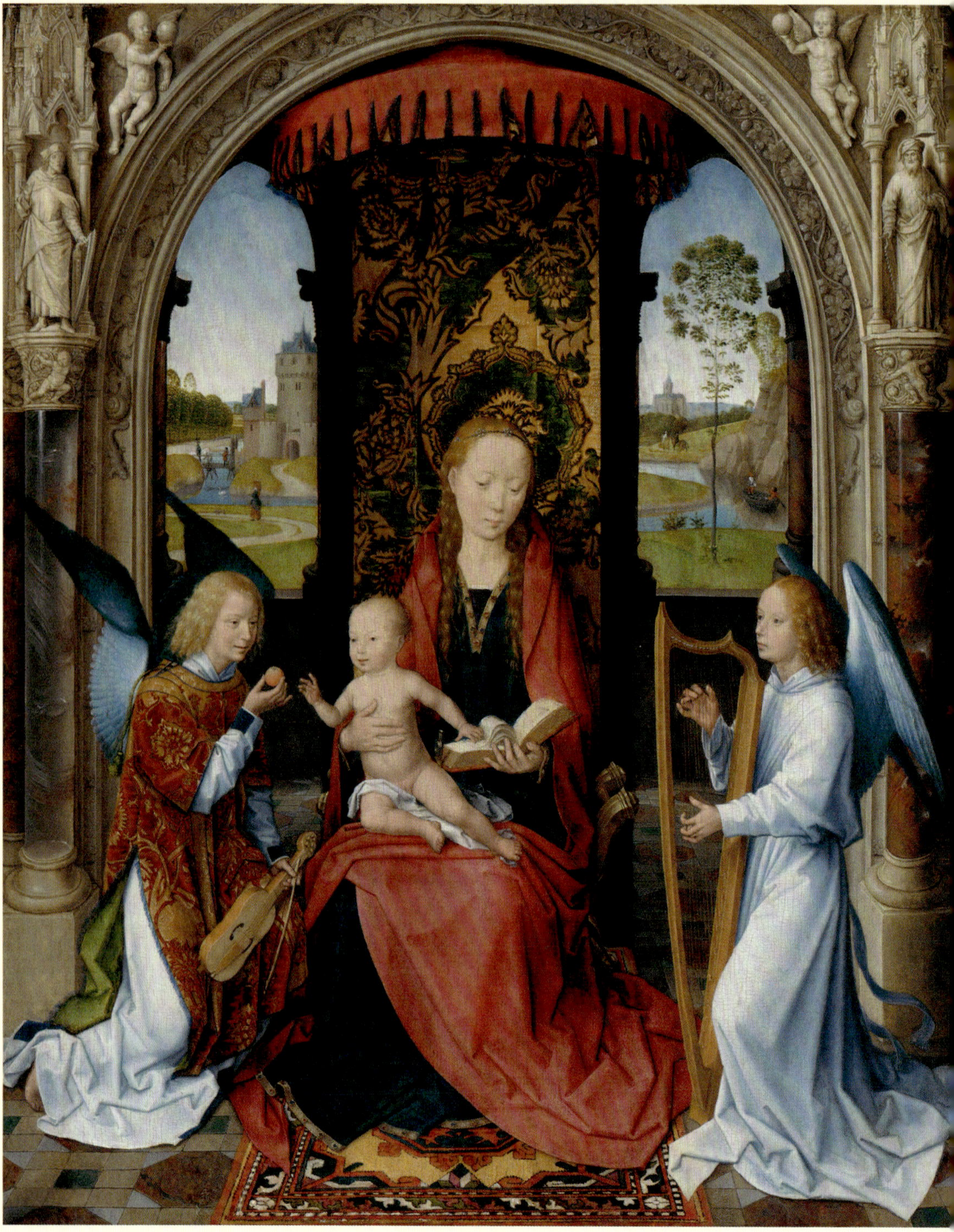

23

Madonna and Child with Angels Making Music
HANS MEMLING (c. 1433-1494), copy after
Panel, 65.5 x 47.5 cm,
Stichting P. en N. de Boer, Amsterdam

This painting was owned by the banker and art collector of Jewish-German descent Fritz Gutmann (1886-1944). He lived with his wife Louise von Landau on the country estate Bosbeek in Heemstede. Under the threat of the war, the Gutmann couple decided to sell or send off as many works of art from their collection as possible for safekeeping. They prepared an escape plan but were detained in 1943 by the SS. The Gutmanns were murdered in concentration camps in 1944. Their children, Bernhard and Lili, strived for justice for many years after the war. The restitution of several works of art recovered to the Netherlands was burdened because the SNK doubted whether there had been involuntary loss of possession. It was not until a judgment by the responsible court of justice in 1952 that Gutmann's heirs were finally able to claim these works, including this painting after Memling. After being returned to the Gutmann heirs, the work was purchased by the Amsterdam art dealer Pieter de Boer to add it to his private collection, which later became a foundation.

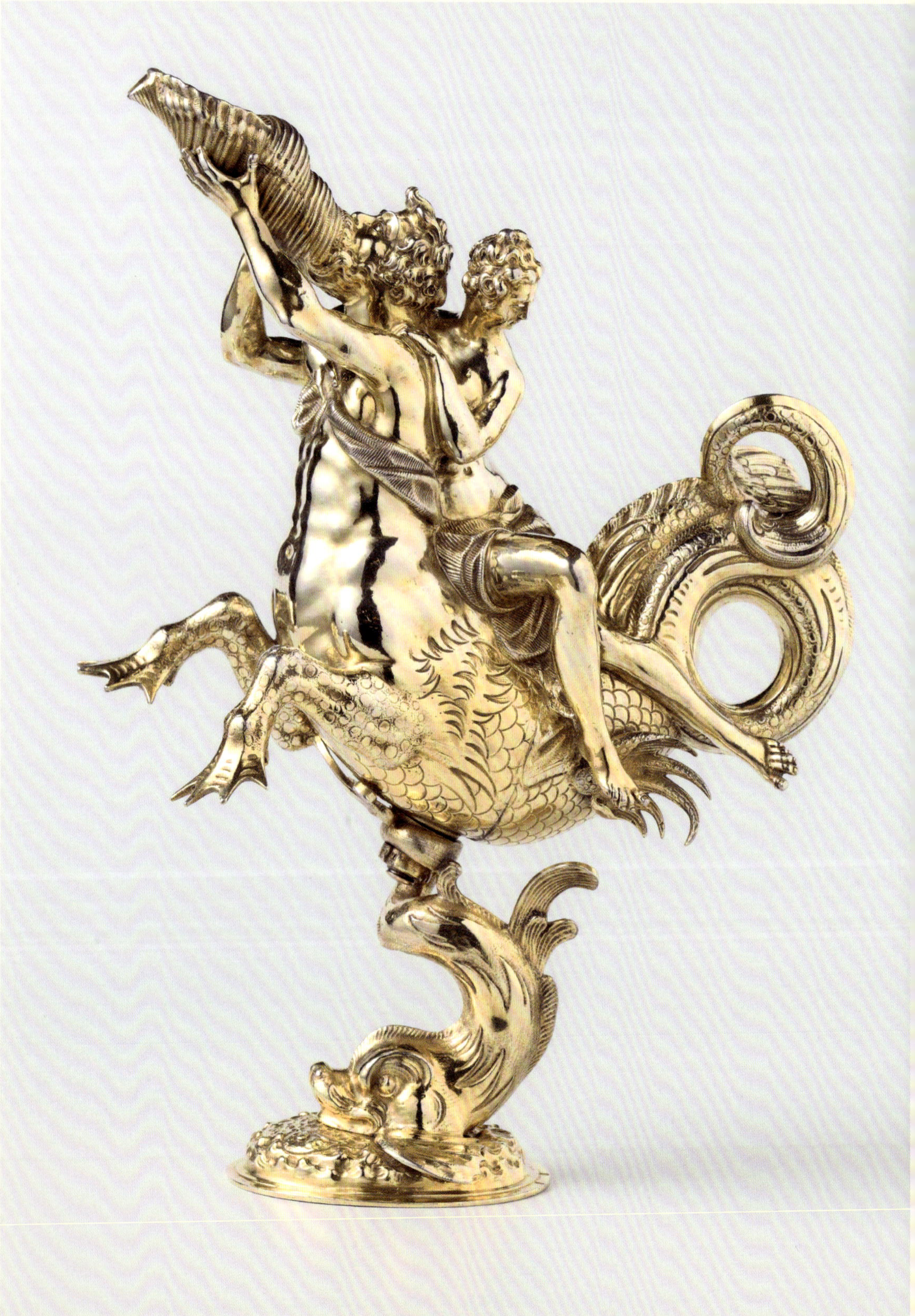

24
Ewer in the shape of a triton and a nereid, c. 1620
JOHANNES LENCKER (1573-1637)
Silver, gilded, c. 34.5 x 25.5 x 12.5 cm, Rijksmuseum, Amsterdam

---

One of the most extensive modern restitution claims for works from the NK Collection concerned nearly 100 works of art from Fritz Gutmann's former collection. In 2002, the Restitutions Committee advised granting the heirs' claim in full. Among the objects returned were several valuable art objects suitable for museums of international stature, such as this seventeenth-century ewer by Lencker. The ewer was acquired by the Dutch State for the Rijksmuseum in 2003.

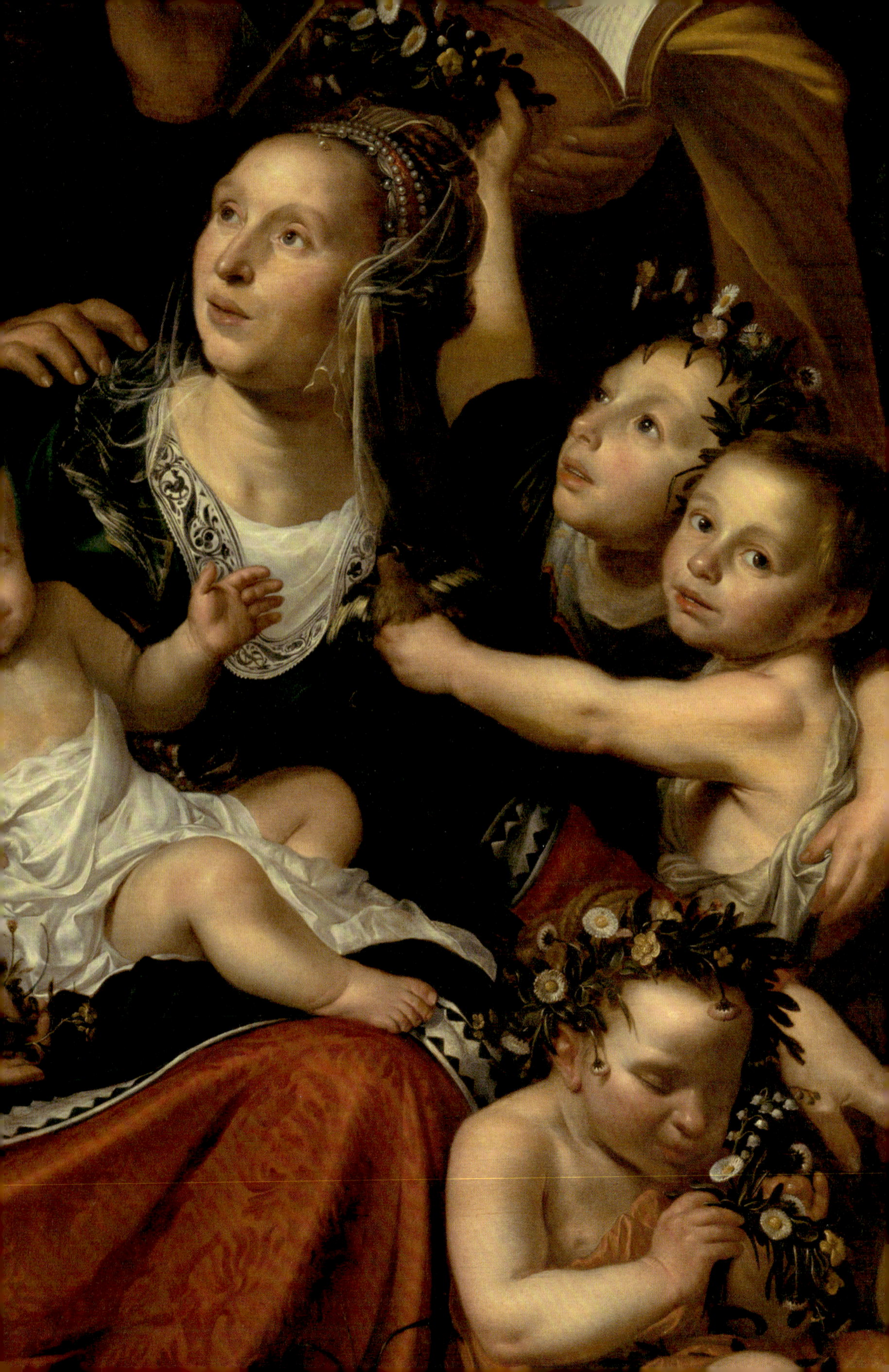

V GERMAN COLLECTORS

The most dominant players in the field of the Dutch art market were Adolf Hitler and Hermann Göring. Besides them, however, there were many other individuals and parties that operated on the Dutch market between 1940-1945. For instance, a series of German art dealers operated in occupied Holland and purchased, sometimes on commission but very often at their own risk, works of art of all kinds. Several museums also eagerly grabbed their chance to expand their collections, while numerous private collectors were also active during the wartime.

HITLER

Adolf Hitler had a personal affinity with art and architecture and considered them a means to drench his *Volk* with the glory of Germany's past and present. Already long before World War II, he fostered plans for a new museum and so collected paintings, with a strong preference for German and Austrian painting from the nineteenth century. Over time, these ideals took on more form and scope. In the late 1930s, Austria's Linz became the main focus of his cultural ambitions. He intended to transform this city, near his birthplace, into a new cultural

rchitectural model of the Führer-useum to be built in Linz to isplay the best old and modern asterpieces of European art

o furnish the museum, Hitler's col-ection was considerably expanded ith confiscaded works and objects urchased on the art market.

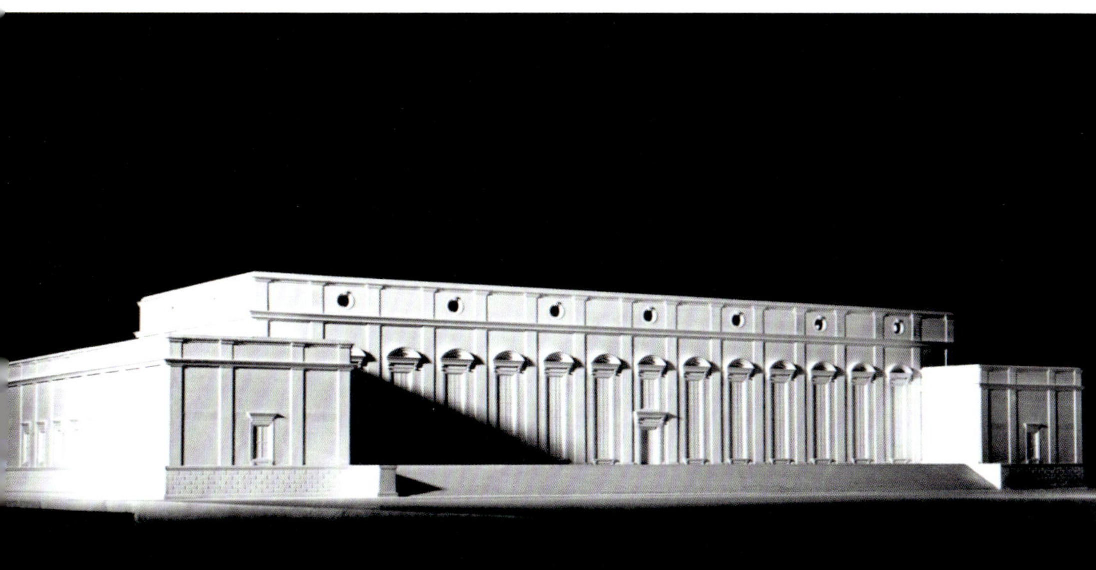

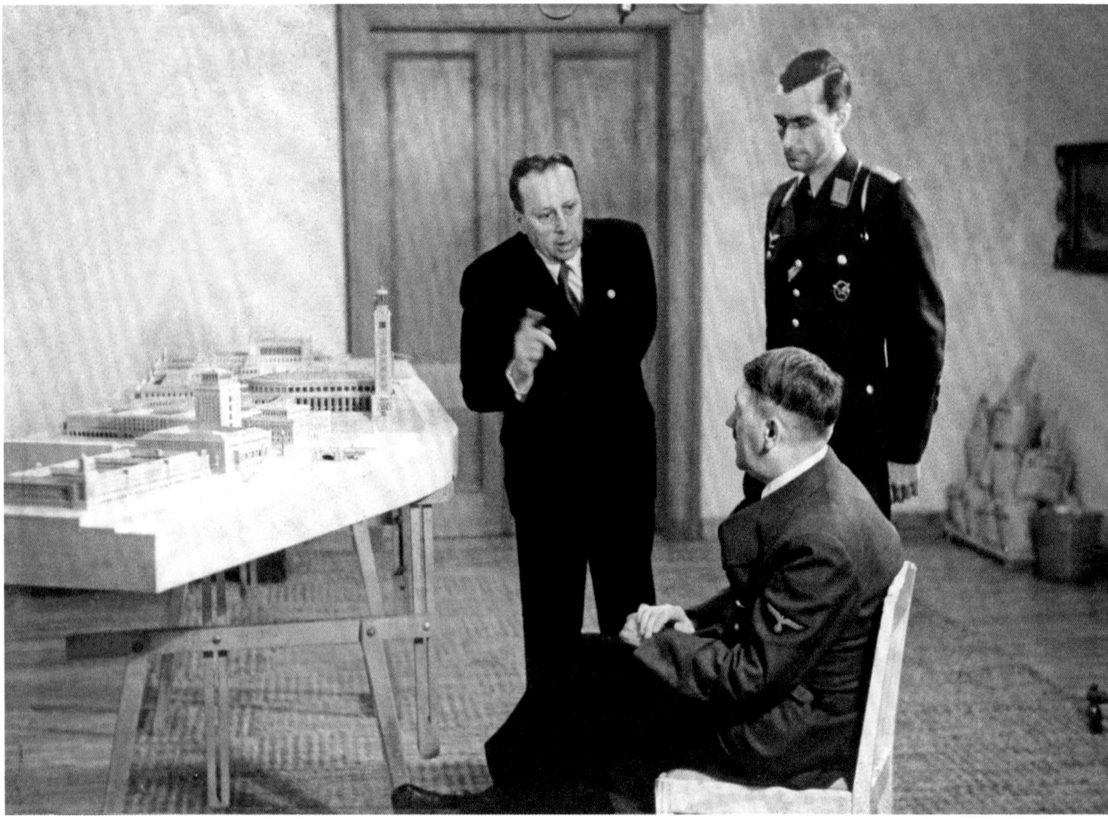

Adolf Hitler conversing with the architect Hermann Giesler beside an architectural model of the planned Führermuseum in Linz, Austria, 22 April 1944

Hitler planned to turn his 'Heimatstadt' into an economic and cultural metropolis. Among other structures, a new museum was to rise in the city's centre, to lead the public past the highlights of European cultural history.

capital in the Third Reich. The centre was to include a glorious museum with the best quality European artworks from multiple centuries. Hitler deemed this project to be of utter importance and devoted a great amount of time and energy to it. To implement his plans, he appointed art historian and museum director Dr Hans Posse as *Sonderbeauftragter des Führers* (Special Representative of the Führer) in 1939.

At first glance, Posse was not the most obvious candidate for this special assignment. As a result of his interest in contemporary art, Posse, who had been director of the Dresden museums since 1910, was controversial in National Socialist circles. This issue was one of the reasons why he had been refused membership to the Nazi party. Hitler, however, was impressed by his knowledge and professionality. In his new role, Posse's responsibilities included expanding the art collection for the future Führermuseum. To succeed in this, he headed a group of experts who mainly held office in Dresden. He also maintained contacts with various officials and advisers in the field to aid him with his task. The organisation became known as Sonderauftrag Linz.

The core of the collection consisted of works of art that Hitler himself had collected in the 1930s, mainly paintings by German and Austrian masters from the 19th century. Under Posse's professional influence, the focus of the collection shifted to old German, Dutch, French and Italian art (fig. 25-29). Posse was extremely aware of the seriousness of his assignment. In the first years of his tenure, he constantly travelled across Europe, tirelessly searching for masterpieces of European painting for the Führer's collection. Enormous funds were provided for this purpose. The estimates for the total size of the artworks collected vary. The database of the *Sonderauftrag*

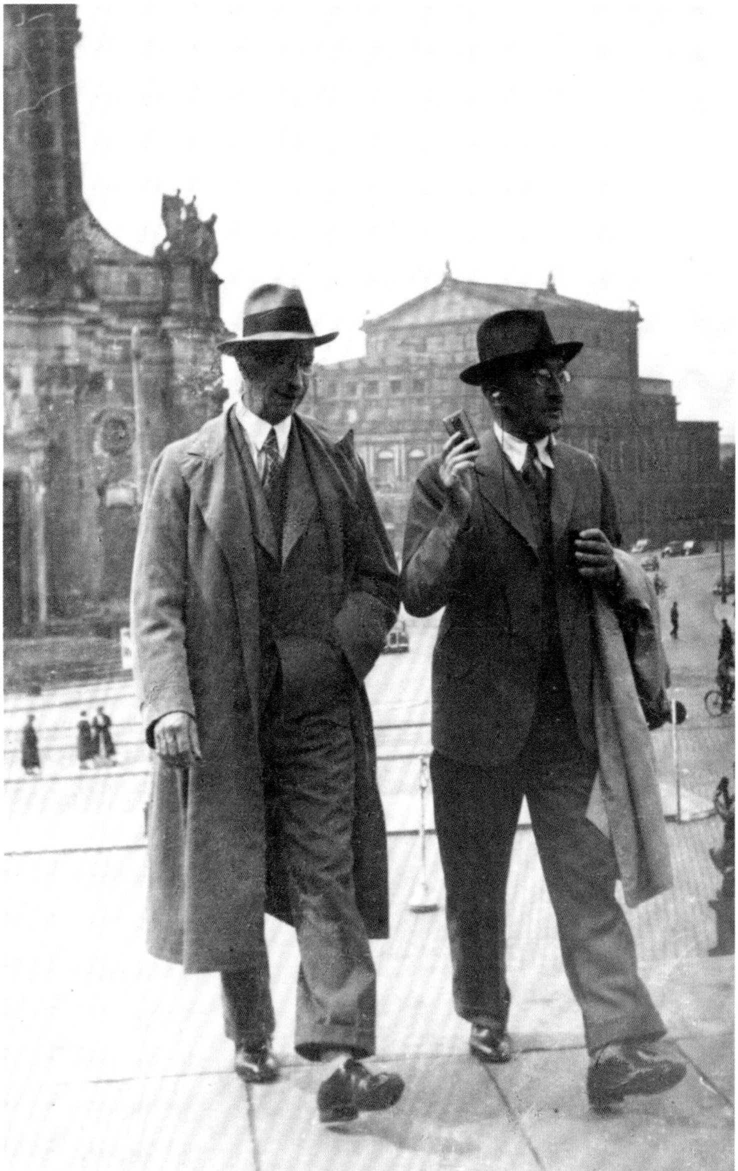

he German art historians Hans osse (left) and Eduard Plietzsch n front of the Hofkirche in resden, c. 1939

n the summer of 1939, Hitler ppointed the director of the Gemäldegalerie Dresden, Hans osse (1879-1942), as head of the onderauftrag Linz. This organisation was tasked with, among other things, uilding up the collection of the ührermuseum to be established n Linz. Posse died in Berlin in ecember 1942. His successor as onderbeauftragter des Führers was e art historian and museum director ermann Voss (1884-1969). duard Plietzsch (1886-1961) was an steemed art historian and dealer who already had many contacts in the Netherlands before the war. During e occupation, he became one of e key employees of the Dienststelle Mühlmann in The Hague. This official ody was charged with the acquisition f art for the Third Reich.

Linz of the Deutsches Historisches Museum in Berlin includes registrations of around 6,700 works, which were destined for the Führermuseum and for other collections. Some of these pieces were acquired through sale and others as a result of confiscations.

In the Netherlands, Posse was aided in his search by the *Referat Sonderfragen*, a civil service headed by Felix Wickel. This organisation prepared the transactions for art acquisitions so that Posse was able to operate at full efficiency on his travels. From May 1942, German art historian Dr Erhard Göpel became an indispensable aid for Posse, who was increasingly hindered by illness. Göpel had been dismissed from military service for this purpose and given a position at the *Referat*. Posse died in December 1942. In March 1943, art historian Hermann Voss succeeded him as leader of the *Sonderauftrag* Linz and director of the Gemäldegalerie Dresden. Voss travelled less than his predecessor. Göpel became the *Sonderauftrag's* representative in the Netherlands and remained Voss's contact for art acquisitions for the Führermuseum during the following years. Göpel had worked in the Netherlands before the war and had good contacts there. The Amsterdam art dealer Douwes characterised him as follows in his post-war report: 'Driven by his clients in Dresden who wanted results, he bought left and right, feared by the trade, pursued by dabblers, champion of auctions'.

GÖRING

An impressive rival to Hitler in skimming the Dutch art market was Reich Field Marshal Hermann Göring. The Nazi leader was obsessed with art and had a strong personal taste (fig. 30-31). His pace in collecting was initially low but increased as he moved up the political and social ladder. From the mid-1930s, he spent enormous amounts of money on his collection. His representatives criss-crossed Europe and he often travelled around himself to view potential acquisitions in various places Within a few years, Göring accumulated a collection of more than four thousand works, partly by 'regular' purchase, partly from looted Jewish property. In size and quality, it was the second largest National Socialist collection. Göring began his collecting activities based on artworks from old family property. Initially, the objects were intended to decorate his multiple residences. He therefore not only acquired paintings but also hunted for antiques and objects of applied art. As his ambitions grew, Göring concocted a plan to transform Carinhall, his country house on the Schorfheide Forest hunting estate, into a museum. The core of the collection was to consist of European works from the Middle Ages and Renaissance.

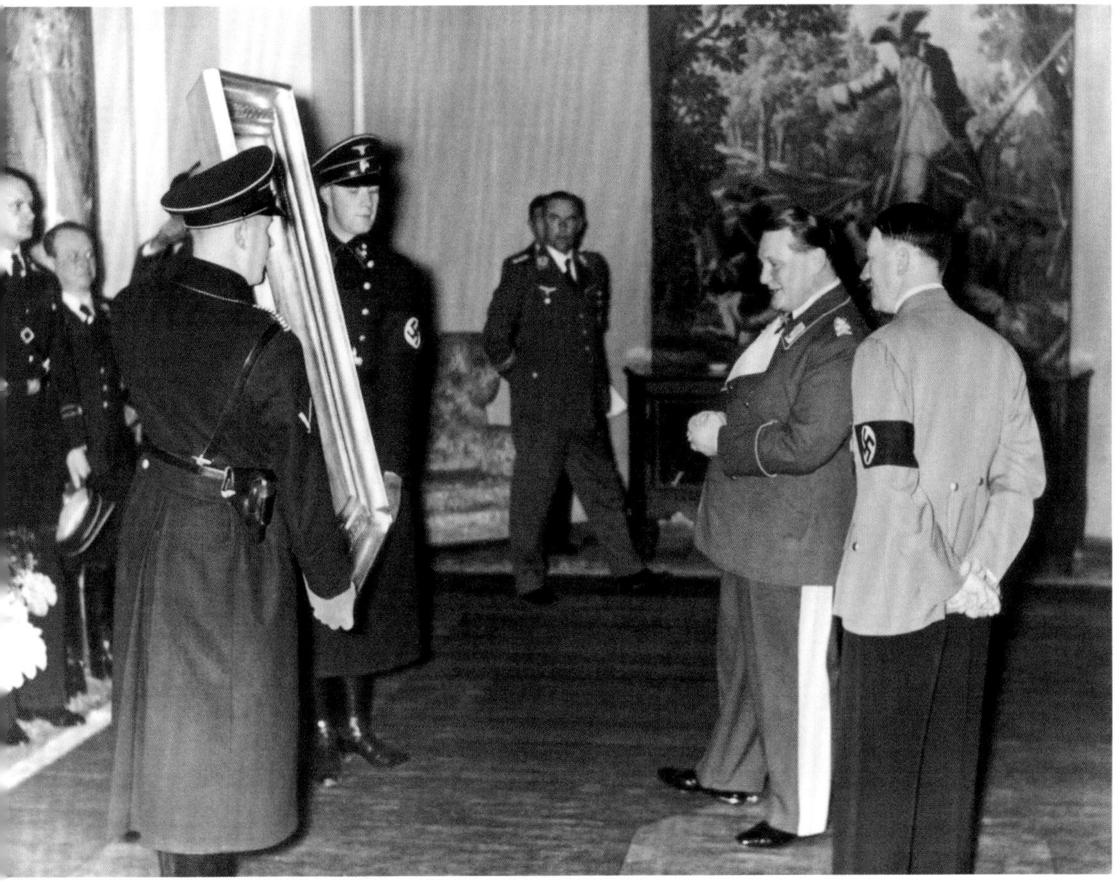

ermann Göring accepts a painting that was presented o him by Adolf Hitler on the ccasion of his 45th birthday on 2 January 1938.

he Nazi prominent Hermann Göring vas a passionate art collector who ımassed a collection of thousands of paintings and objects of applied art rom the late 1920s until 1945, partly hrough purchases and partly by the ıcquisition of confiscated property. nitially, these objects were supposed o furnish his residences, but were later primarily intended for a museum to pe built on Schorfheide near Berlin, he 'Norddeutsche Galerie'. This Nazi dream museum was never realised ither.

Göring also became interested in art from later periods, such as paintings from the Dutch Golden Age and works by 18th and 19th-century French artists. According to a post-war report by the United States Office of Strategic Services (OSS), the Netherlands was, after France, the second most important source of acquisitions for Göring's collection. When we exclude the confiscations and only consider the 'legal' purchases, the Netherlands would even rank first. Göring was keenly aware of the abundance of art available on the Dutch market. He had sent off a representative to scout works immediately following the Dutch capitulation. He visited the Netherlands in person shortly after, visiting various art dealers in search of appealing works of art. More trips to the Netherlands followed. According to the OSS, Göring was fond of the country and had friends there. Almost all of the most important works of art he obtained here were acquired on visits during the first year of occupation. Whoever Göring visited, according to the Amsterdam art dealer Douwes, had little say: 'The Reichsmarschall [visited] my colleagues at the most unexpected times, simply pointing to what he wanted to purchase, often completely indifferent to their claim to already be in negotiation with third parties for several works'. In the Netherlands, Göring's main representative was the German art dealer Walter Andreas Hofer. He had worked as Göring's personal art advisor since the second half of the 1930s and had already acquired art for him in the Netherlands during that time. Hofer had been director, and later procurator, of The Hague's Bachstitz Gallery in the 1920s, which provided him with good contacts in the Dutch art trade. His broad network also included Jewish art dealers and collectors. For example, Hofer played a prominent role in acquisitions from the Von Pannwitz and Gutmann collections during the occupation. The German-born banker and dealer Alois Miedl also rendered good services to Göring (fig. 32-33). Miedl had a Jewish wife, which did not prevent the Reichsfeldmarshall from doing business with him. After the flight and tragic death of the Jewish art dealer Jacques Goudstikker in May 1940, Miedl took over his Amsterdam art dealership. This transaction was a crucial source for acquisitions for Göring's collection. Other individuals and institutions also assisted Göring in combing out the Dutch art market, such as his chief of staff Erich Gritzbach.

THE INVOLVEMENT OF JEWISH DEALERS AND ART EXPERTS

Not every buyer for the Nazi elite was an inspired National Socialists or vicious anti-Semite. Several of them had contacts with Jewish art experts in the Netherlands that predated the war and were picked up again during the occupation. These buyers sometimes made use of their position in order to help or even save the lives of old and new relations. There was another side to such help. During the occupation, several Jewish art experts and dealers were employed to enrich the collections of the top Nazi hierarchy. They advised, scouted the market, purchased and consigned works, restored, provided their expert opinions or rendered other services for the collections of the Nazi patrons, primarily that of Hitler. They were offered protection in return for their services. For example, they received reprieves from deportation, and, in exceptional cases, were exempted from wearing the Star of David or were even granted permission to emigrate from the Netherlands. Individuals who survived the war in this manner include Kurt Walter Bachstitz, the brothers Nathan and Benjamin Katz, Abraham Nijstad, Otto Busch, Vitale Bloch and Max Friedländer. Protection was never assured and often only lasted as long as the individual seeking safety proved useful. Protective measures often had to be conquered by one German service over another. This became more and more difficult as the persecution of Jews intensified.

The acquisition method described above was not unique to the art trade. Jewish specialists were often used as agents or buyers. They were familiar with the local market and the Nazi's hoped their involvement would neutralize the resistance some sellers felt to do business with Germans. Lou de Jong, in his standard work on World War II, wrote the following about such practices: 'Jewish buyers would be better kept under their thumb, and if they were promised that they would be protected as much as possible from measures of persecution against Jews, they would surely also take action'. The exchange of art for human lives must often have engulfed those involved with aversion. Through extortion, Jews were forced to make themselves useful for the collecting activities of high-ranking Nazis. However, it also happened that their 'indispensability' for the collections of Nazi leaders was used as an excuse to save them from deportation. The line between practical motives and compassion is not always sharp among the German officials involved. Both dimensions are conveyed in a description of Göpel by Douwes: 'After Dr Posse died of cancer, the German authorities appointed Dr Göpel as his successor; not himself an overwhelming expert in our field, he let himself to be informed by several German Jews who had fled here, and who owed the preservation of their lives to this. [...] To be honest, I must say that he always used his influence, when asked, to try to help his fellow countrymen, whether Aryan or not'.

MÜHLMANN

Despite the heavy competition between German art buyers and art looters, numerous contenders also formed pacts in order to pass artworks to each other. One organisation that was particularly active in the Dutch art market was the agency of Austrian art historian Dr Kajetan Mühlmann. The Dienststelle Mühlmann in The Hague was responsible for collecting information on art and acquiring artwork for the Third Reich. Thousands of objects were transited to Germany and sold to a large number of diverse buyers, including prominent Nazis, museums and art dealers. Hitler and Göring were amongst Mühlmann's regular clients. The institution was firmly embedded in the German administrative structure. Eduard Plietzsch and Franz Kieslinger were close associates of Mühlmann's. The German art historian and dealer Plietzsch, who had previously been assistant to Cornelis Hofstede de Groot, had an excellent network and was especially respected for his knowledge of old Dutch painting. The Dienststelle Mühlmann's acquisition sources were diverse. The agency was

not exclusively focused on looted art but was also very active on the open market. In addition, the institution's exceptional authority gave it access to Jewish art property.
Seyss-Inquart had appointed Kieslinger as the *Sammelverwalte* (collective administrator) of art confiscated from 'enemy' (Jewish) property. The Dienststelle also combed through the confiscated art at various German administrative bodies, the trade stocks of Jewish art dealers placed under management and private properties in the custody of museums. Mühlmann, an SS officer himself, worked closely with a broad range of other agencies, such as the Sicherheitsdienst, the Devisenschutzkommando and the Abteilung Feindvermögen for example. Douwes sketched an unsympathetic picture of him in his post-war report. For instance, Mühlmann is said to have warned a dealer, who had, in his opinion, failed to comply with a 'request' that he had it in his power not only to destroy his business but also himself.

ERR

Another organisation that was active in appropriating cultural property in the Netherlands was the Einsatzstab Reichsleiter Rosenberg (ERR). This looting taskforce was led by Alfred Rosenberg and was authorised by Hitler to confiscate property belonging to 'enemies of National Socialism'. In France, the ERR impounded numerous collections belonging to Jewish owners, such as the renowned De Rothschild collection. The Einsatzstab's focus on art in the Netherlands was limited in comparison. According to the historian Gerard Aalders, Albert Schmidt-Stähler, leader of the ERR's Hauptarbeitsgruppe Niederlände, felt that Dutch Jews were inferior as art collectors, especially when compared to France. In the Netherlands, he therefore targeted other cultural objects, including those in archives and libraries. Another factor in this choice would have been that Schmidt-Stähler had to compete in the Netherlands against, among others the Dienststelle Mühlmann with which Reich Commissioner Seyss-Inquart was personally involved. In the Netherlands, the ERR confiscated property from Masonic lodges, the International Institute of Social History (IISG), the Portuguese-Israeli Seminarium Ets Haim and the Bibliotheca Rosenthaliana. In 1942, the Einsatzstab was given additional tasks. From then on, the ERR systematically seized complete household furnishings left behind by Jews who had been deported or had fled (see also Chapter IV).

he Austrian art historian and S officer Kajetan Mühlmann 1898-1958) (right) with Hans rank (1900-1946), governor eneral of Poland from 1939

n 1938, Kajetan Mühlmann participat-d in the Anschluss of Austria. He was ppointed various positions in the new overnment and, among other things, vas closely involved in the confiscation f Viennese Jewish art collections. After the German invasion of Poland, e led a unit that was responsible or large-scale looting of Polish art property. Mühlmann was summoned o the Netherlands by Arthur Seyss-nquart in 1940. During the occupation, is agency, the Dienststelle Mühlmann, lso played an important role in the arge-scale confiscation and looting of ultural property in this country.

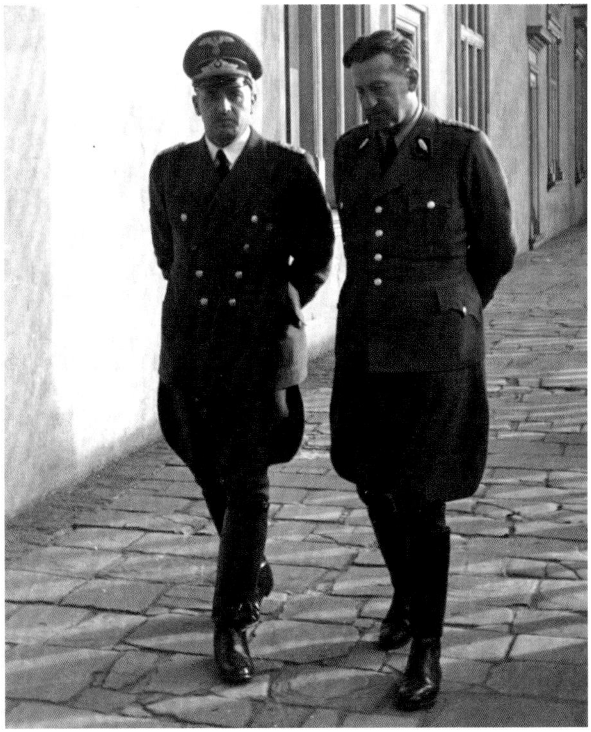

GERMAN MUSEUMS AND OTHER BUYERS

The Dutch art market was dominated by representatives of prominent Nazis who raked in the best pieces. A flood of German buyers with smaller budgets followed in their wake, including art dealers, administrators, officers, entrepreneurs, wholesale buyers, pedlars and hawkers (fig. 34). In addition to decent people, according to Douwes, 'many came here of an entirely different disposition [...], scouring the premises with more or less arrogance.' One important category of buyers was represented by German museums, some of them expanding their collections significantly (fig. 35-37). These acquisitions included paintings as well as numerous other art objects, such as ethnographic pieces. According to Max J. Friedländer, a renowned art historian and former museum director of German-Jewish origin who resided in the Netherlands during the occupation, mainly municipal museums seized the opportunity to complement their collections with new acquisitions: 'The State Museums in Berlin, Munich, Dresden and Cassel were not enriched, but cities grabbed the opportunity to expand their municipal art collections, such as Düsseldorf, Bonn, Cologne, Gdansk, Wroclaw, Hamburg'. Reportedly, the municipal collection of Düsseldorf in particular was proficiently enriched by 'shrewdly picked out 17th-century Dutch paintings by smaller masters'.

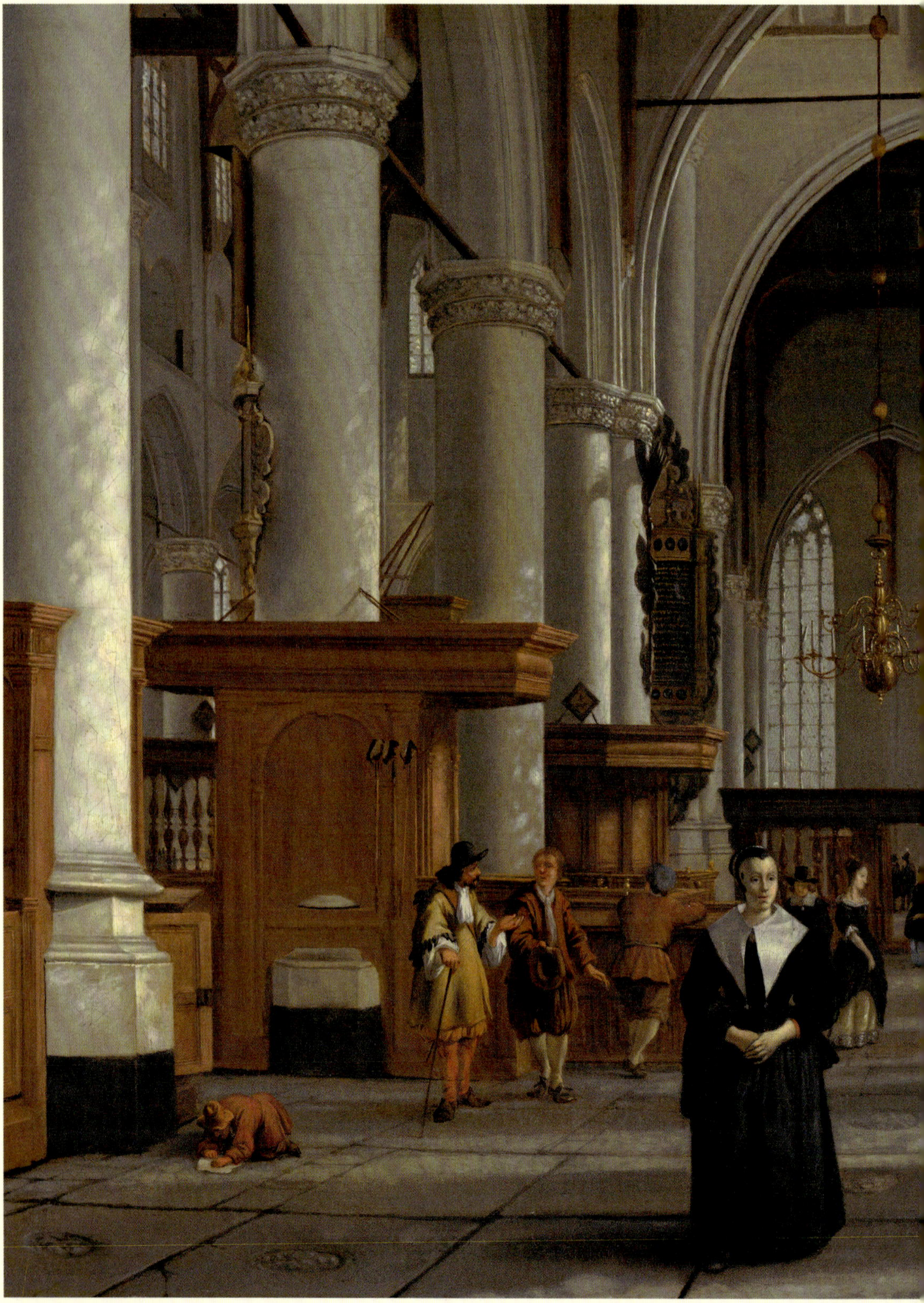

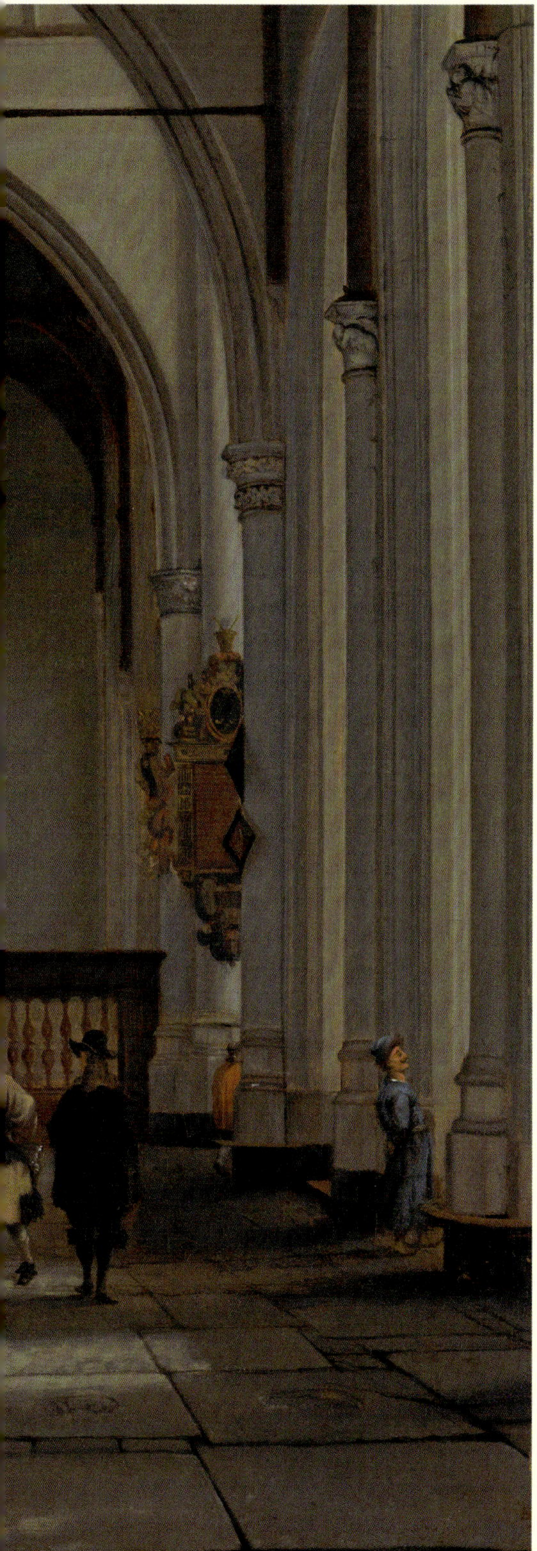

25
Interior of the Laurenskerk in Rotterdam, c. 1665-1667
CORNELIS DE MAN (1621-1706)
Canvas, 39.5 x 46.5 cm, Koninklijk Kabinet voor Schilderijen Mauritshuis, Den Haag

---

In the 1930s, the Katz art gallery in Dieren purchased this church interior from a private collection in England. Katz sold it in August 1940 to Hans Posse, who acquired the painting for the Führermuseum in Linz.

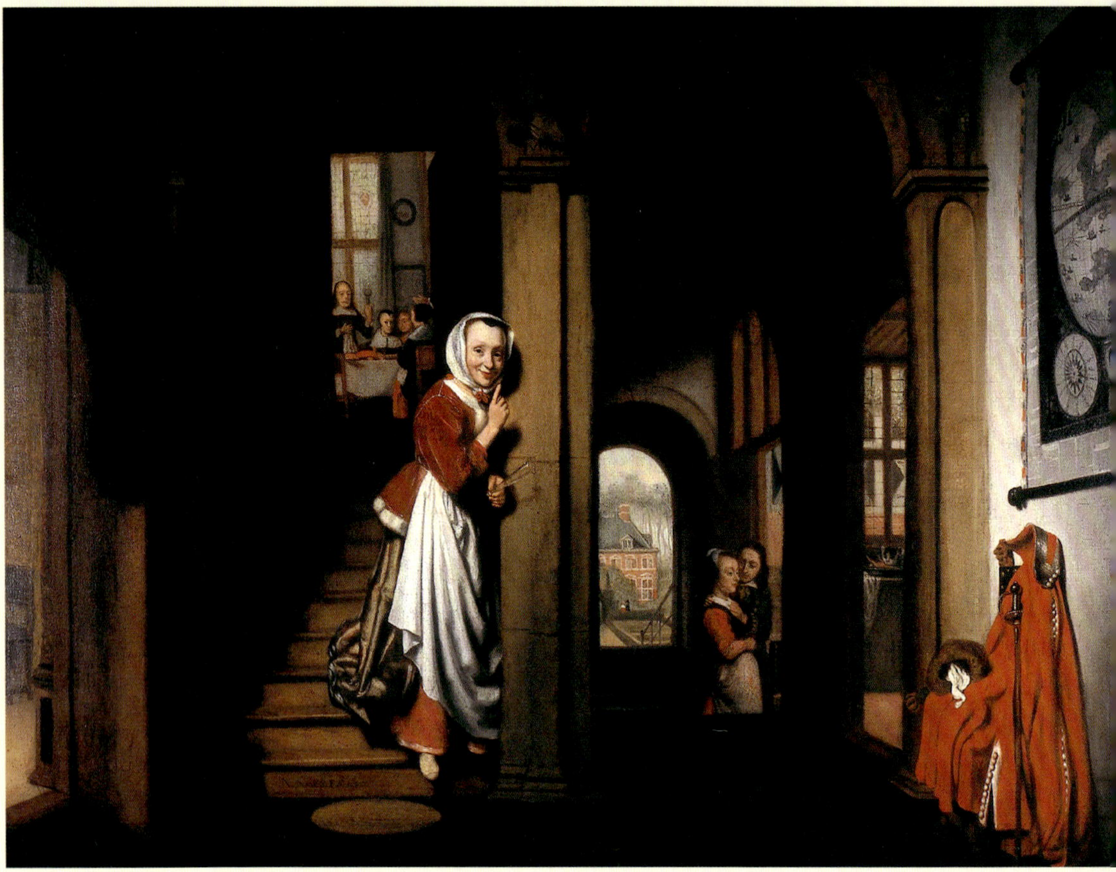

26
The Eavesdropper, 1657
NICOLAES MAES (1634-1693)
Canvas, 92 x 121 cm, Dordrechts Museum, Dordrecht, on loan from RCE, NK2560

This famous genre scene by Nicolaes Maes was part of the renowned Six collection in Amsterdam from the nineteenth century onwards. It was sold on the Dutch art market in 1928 and was the property of the Katz art gallery during the war. In 1941, Posse purchased the painting on behalf of the Führermuseum in Linz. Works by the Rembrandt pupil Nicolaes Maes were highly coveted by German collectors and the Führermuseum's collection featured several paintings by this Dutch master. These mainly included portraits of well-to-do burghers, the genre in which Maes was mainly active after 1660.

27

The Standard Bearer, 1660
JACOB OCHTERVELT (1634-1682)
Canvas, 65 x 57 cm, Museum Rotterdam, on loan from RCE, NK2374

This painting was purchased from a private Dutch owner in 1941 by Hans Posse, the head of the Sonderauftrag Linz. The sale was conducted through Gustav Cramer, an art dealer of Jewish origin who had fled to the Netherlands from Germany in 1938. He ran an art gallery on the Javastraat in The Hague. During the war, Cramer was granted protection from Posse and his associate Erhard Göpel as the art dealer's services were greatly beneficial for the Sonderauftrag Linz. Cramer survived the war; his art gallery was later continued by his son Hans Cramer.

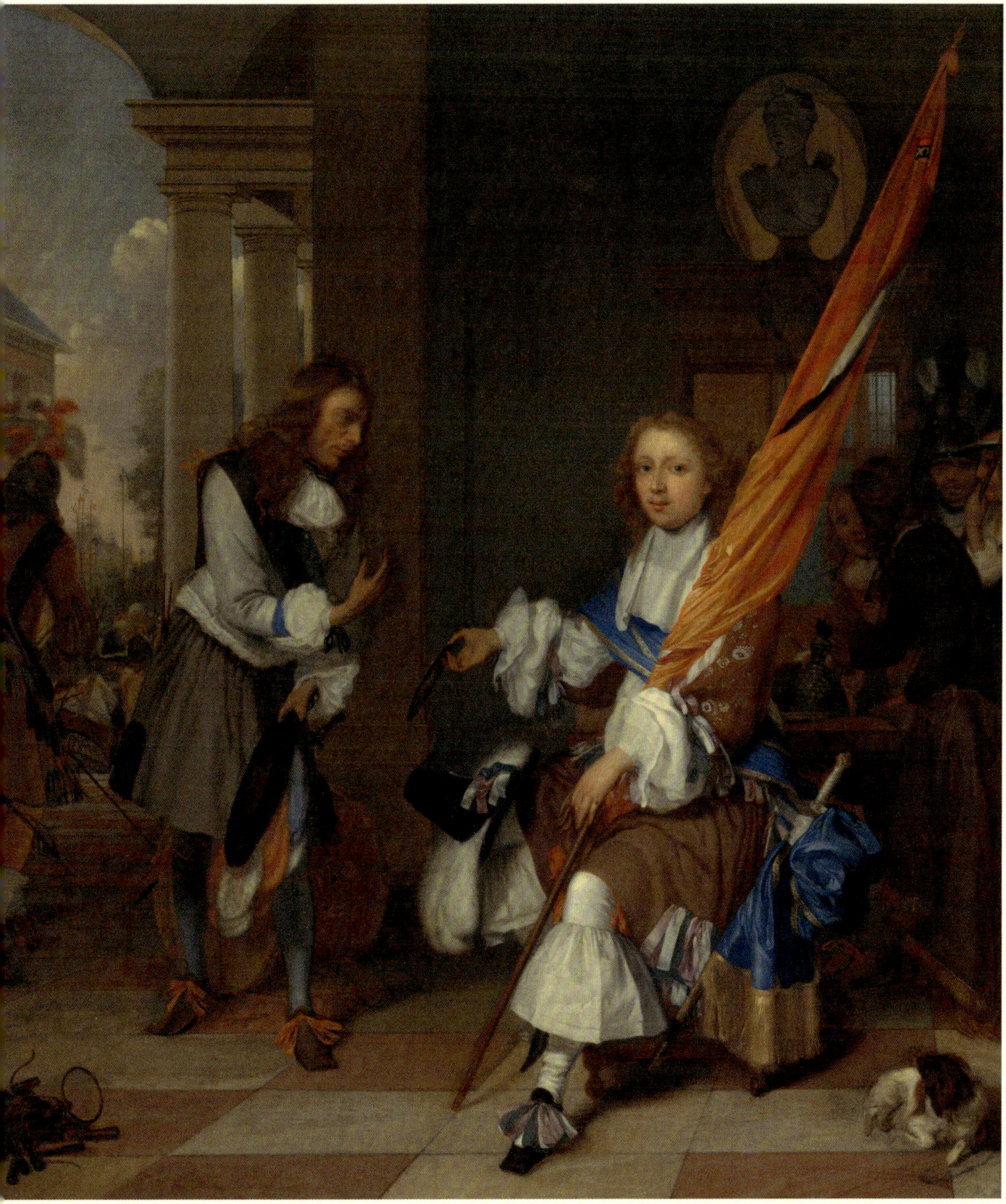

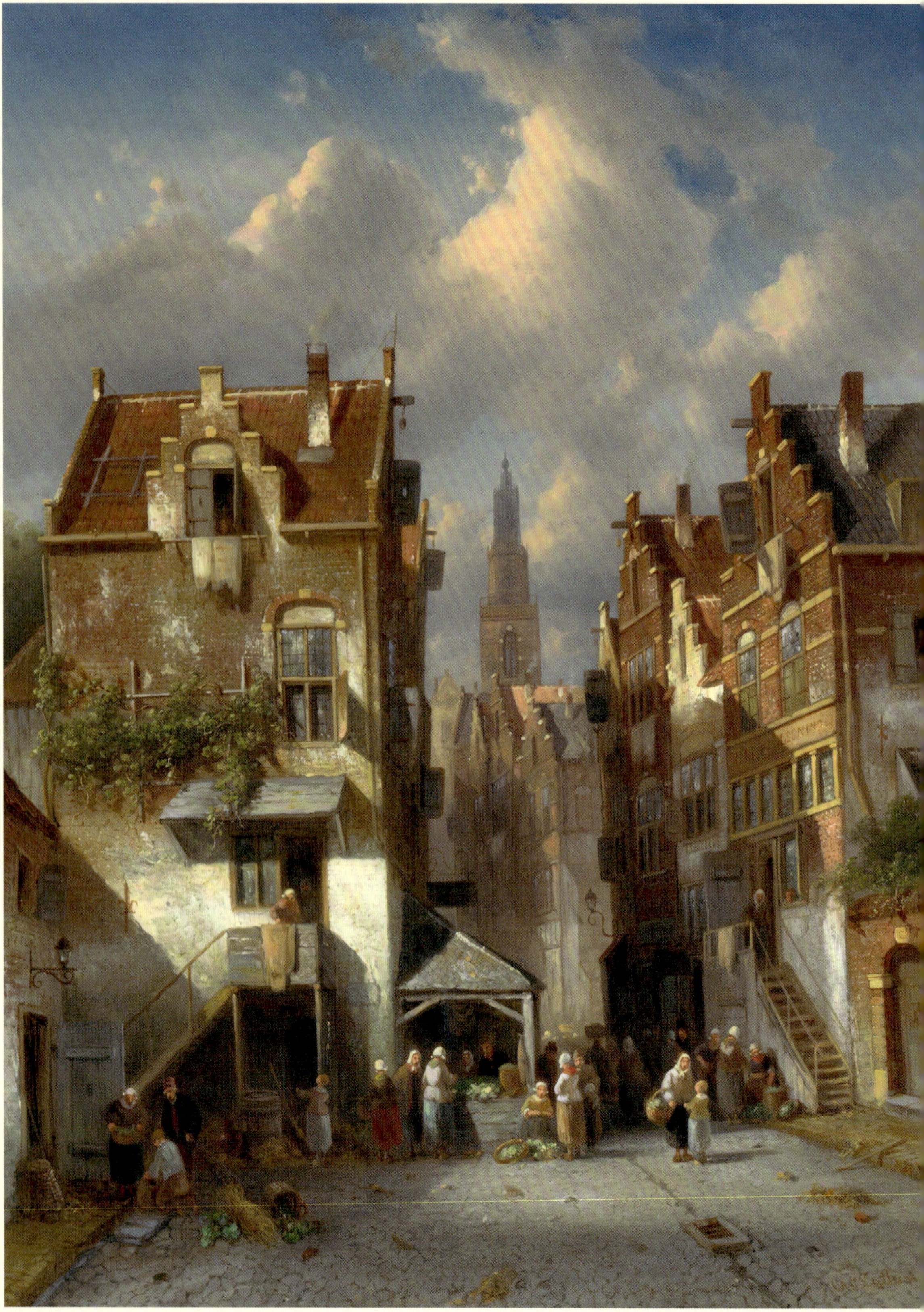

28
A View of Nijmegen
CHARLES LEICKERT (1818-1907)
Canvas, 84 x 64 cm, Rijksdienst voor het Cultureel Erfgoed, NK1869

This nineteenth-century view of Nijmegen was owned by a private collector of Jewish descent in Amsterdam. During the war, she gave it to the art dealer De Boer for safekeeping to protect it from being confiscated by the German authorities. When the owner needed currency to go into hiding, De Boer sold the painting for her. It was acquired for the collection of the Führermuseum in Linz. Leickert's work was recovered from Germany after the war. The daughter of the original owner wrote to the legal recovery authorities that her mother did not wish to claim the painting because she had been reasonably compensated for it.

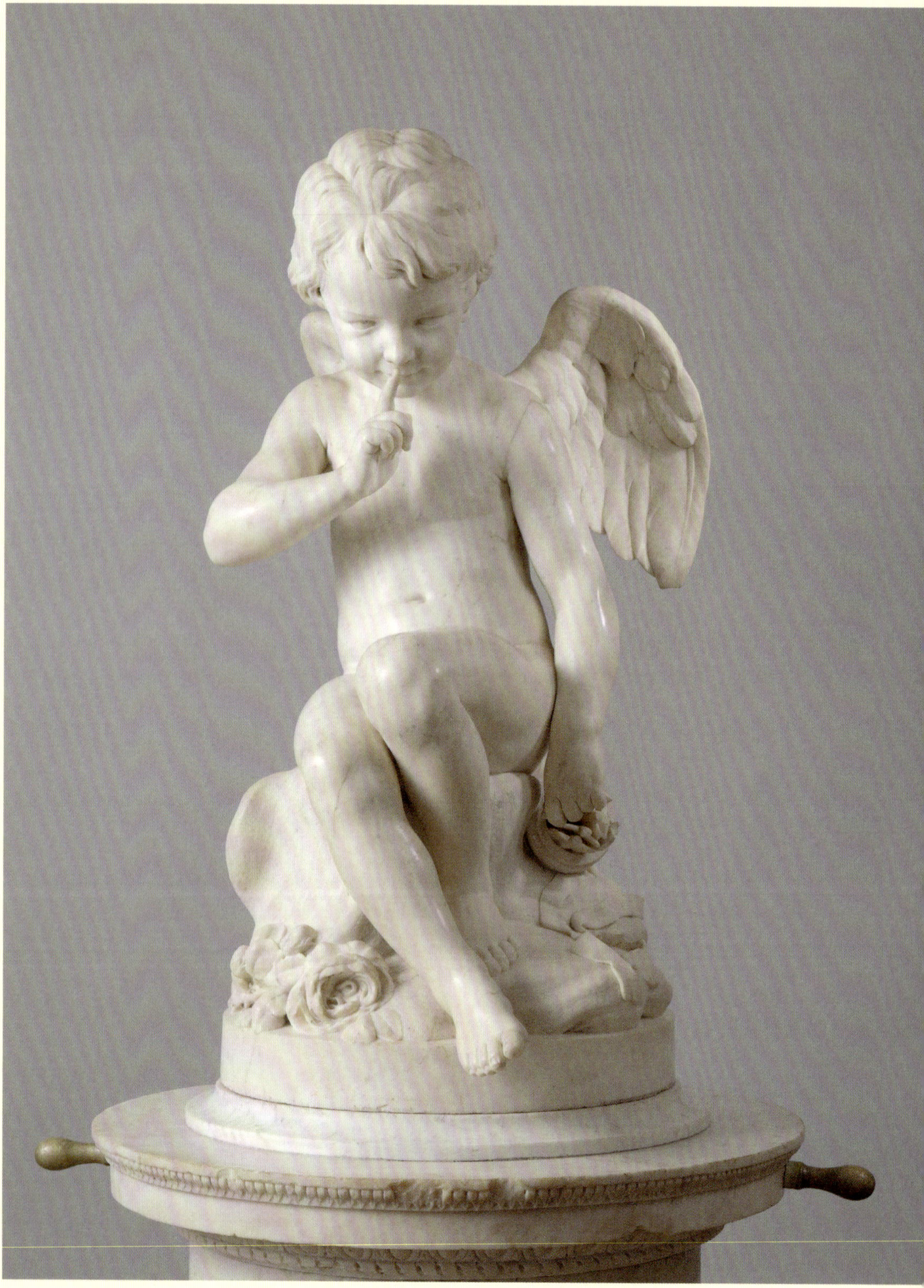

29

Seated Cupid: 'L'amour menaçant', 1757
ÉTIENNE-MAURICE FALCONET (1716-1791)
White marble and copper, 185 x 47.5 x 68.5 cm,
Rijksmuseum, Amsterdam, on loan from RCE, NK3119

This famous sculpture was created by Falconet for Madame de Pompadour, the mistress of King Louis XV. It was later kept in the Hermitage in St. Petersburg but was sold by the Soviet government in the 1930s. The Seated Cupid was then acquired by Fritz Mannheimer (1890-1939), a successful and high-profile banker of German-Jewish descent. His collection of international stature decorated his luxurious home at the Hobbemastraat 20 in Amsterdam, nicknamed 'Villa Protsky'.
Mannheimer's zealous passion for collecting was partly to blame for the financial problems he had as early as the first half of the 1930s. As soon as arrangements were made to cover his debts, Mannheimer incessantly continued to buy art. He died in 1939, two months after his marriage to the Brazilian Marie Annette Reiss (1917-2004). During the occupation, the collection was purchased by the German organisation Dienststelle Mühlmann on behalf of the Sonderauftrag Linz. Protests by the curator of Mannheimer's bankrupt estate were to no avail. The collection was recovered from Germany after World War II and came into the custody of the Dutch State. Some of the objects were auctioned off, while many hundreds of other works of art were retained. Most of these are now kept at the Rijksmuseum in Amsterdam.

30

Hunting Scene with a Rabbit Caught by a White Falcon
FRANZ DE HAMILTON (before 1640-after 1702)
Canvas, 88 x 111 cm, Rijksdienst voor het Cultureel Erfgoed, NK2872

This seventeenth-century German hunting scene was gifted to Hermann Göring by the Austrian authorities in 1938. The painting's theme well represented one of Göring's greatest passions – hunting. In numerous photographs, he can be seen posing with game and other hunting trophies. He built the Carinhall hunting lodge north of Berlin, where he organised driving hunts for high-ranking Nazi guests. In 1944, Göring sold dozens of works of art, including this hunting scene, to obtain the painting *Christ and the Woman Taken in Adultery* (fig. 33), which was then attributed to Vermeer. After the war, the Austrian government claimed De Hamilton's work from the Dutch authorities but this did not result in a return.

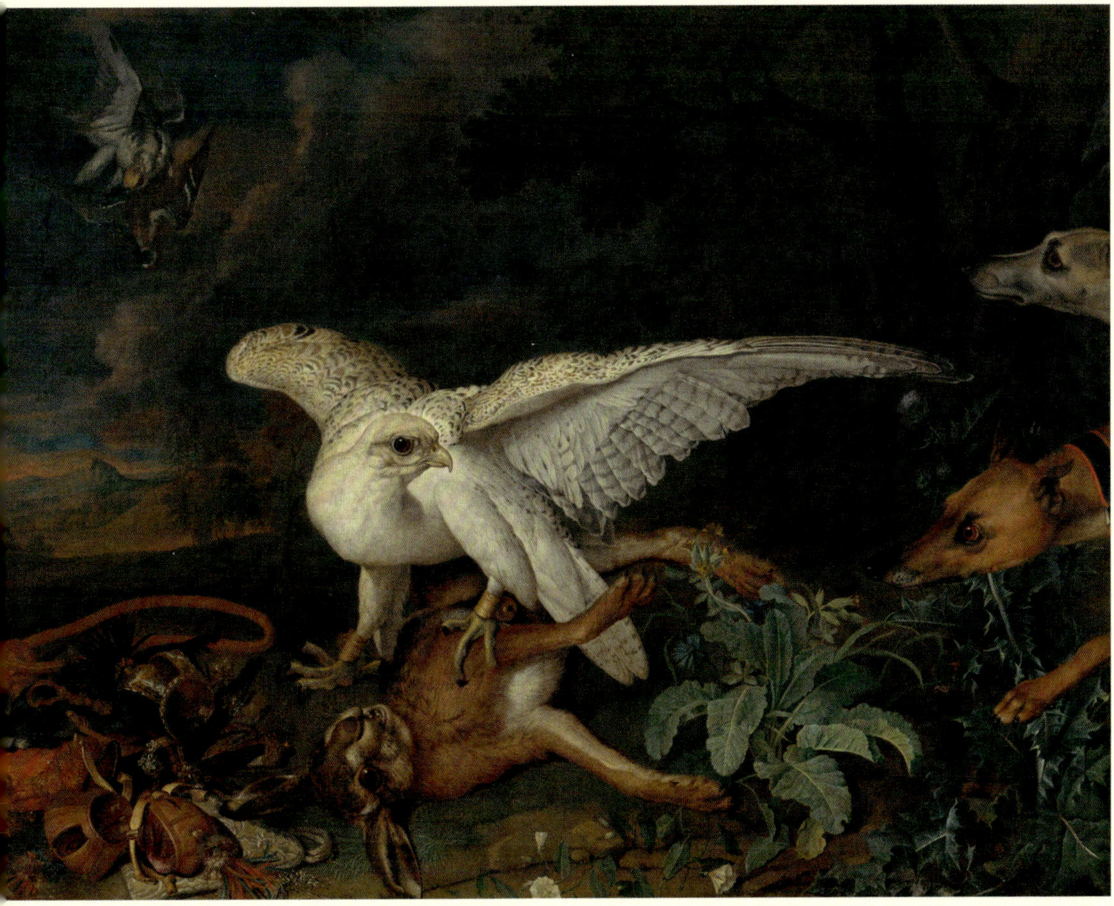

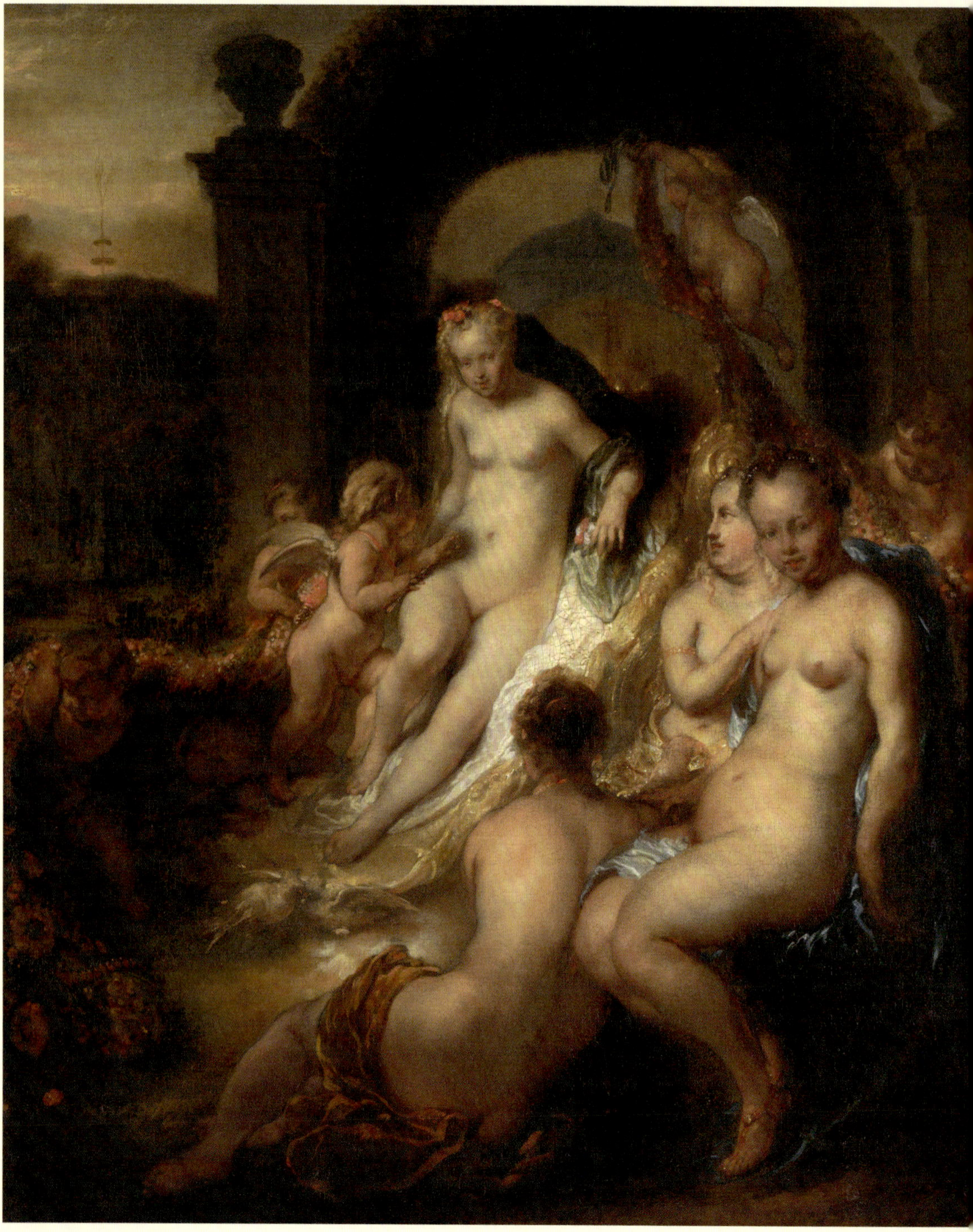

31
enus and the three Graces, c. 1655
AN VAN NOORDT (1623/1624-1676)
anvas, 79 x 65.5 cm, Rijksdienst voor
et Cultureel Erfgoed, NK1697

Valter Andreas Hofer was one of Hermann Göring's main art agents. In June 1940, he urchased this painting from the art dealer . de Boer in Amsterdam, who had acquired : before the war from a private collection in The Hague. According to Hofer, the Reichsfeldmarschall was quite fond of erotic themes in art. This scene filled with female nudes will have well befitted Görings 'goût érotique'.

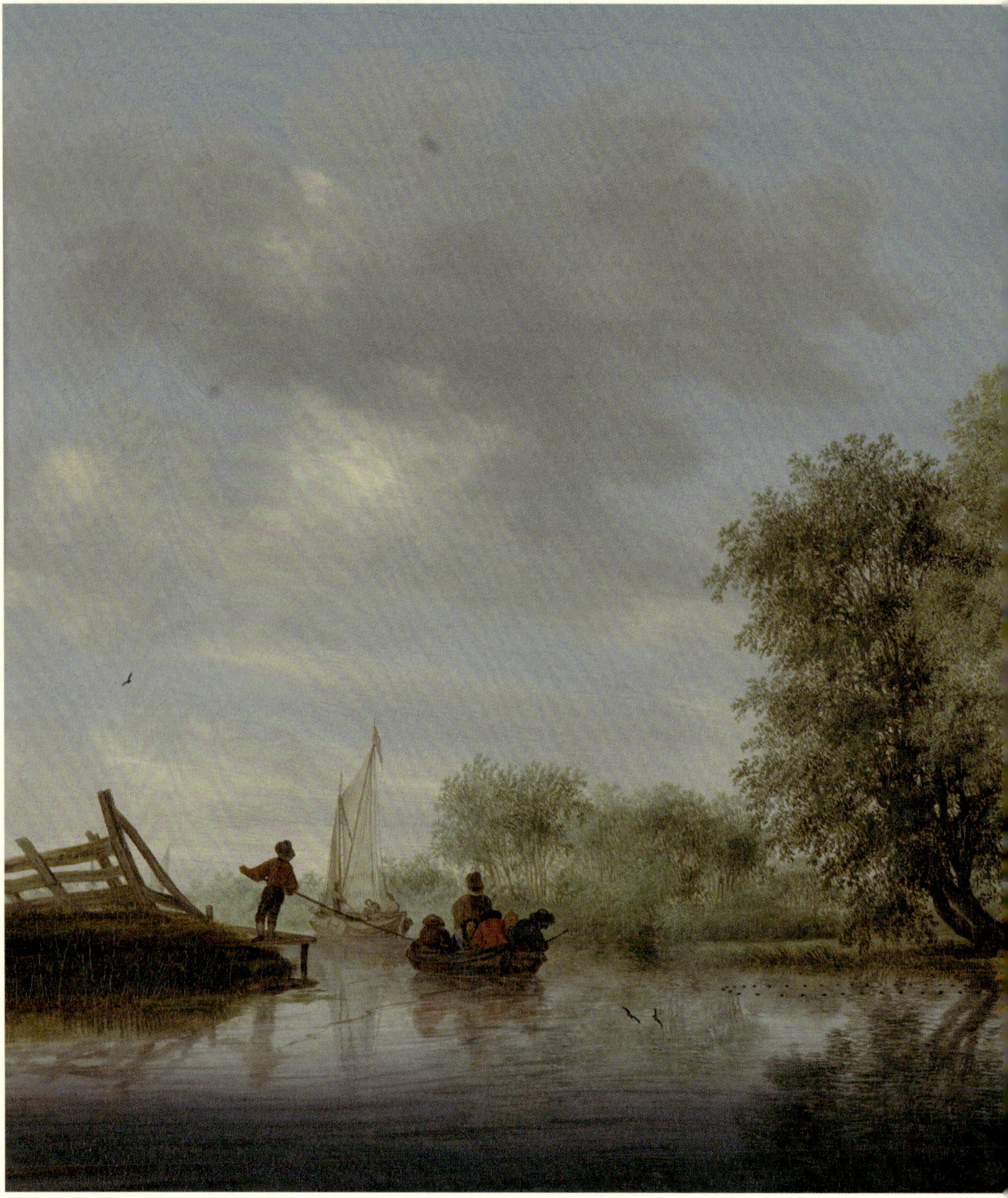

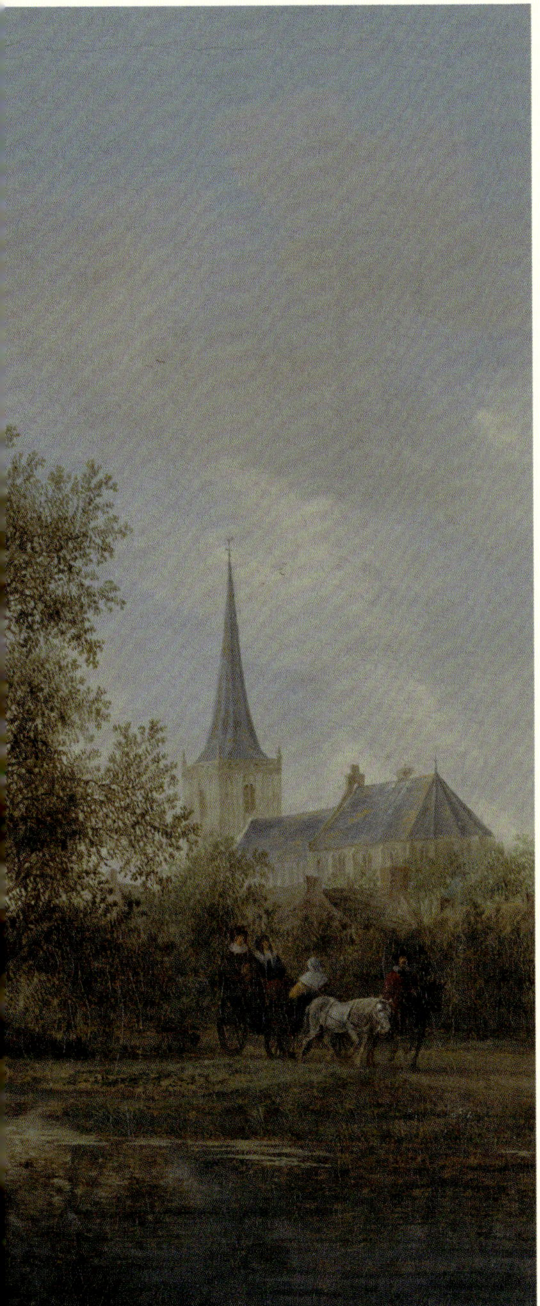

32
River View with travellers, 1645
SALOMON VAN RUYSDAEL (c. 1600-1670)
Canvas, 61 x 85 cm, Rijksdienst voor het Cultureel Erfgoed, NK1823

In October 1940, Erich Gritzbach (1896-1968) purchased this painting from Kunsthandel Goudstikker-Miedl for Hermann Göring's collection. Gritzbach was Göring's chief of staff and played an important role in many of his art acquisitions. In 1937, he wrote the biography *Hermann Göring. Werk und Mensch*, a propaganda book on the life of the Nazi leader. The biography was translated into Dutch and published in 1943.

33

Christ and the Woman Taken in Adultery, 1942
HAN VAN MEEGEREN (1889-1947)
Canvas, 100 x 90 cm, Museum De Fundatie, Heino, on loan from RCE, NK3394

In February 1944, Hermann Göring managed to top off his collection by the acquisition of a previously unknown work by Johannes Vermeer of Delft. He was able to purchase it from a private collection via Alois Miedl. The work's high price forced the Reichsfeldmarschall to relinquish dozens of artworks from his collection. Towards the end of the war, when the German defeat became clear, Göring gifted this painting to his wife Emmy. He was confident that this would be enough to provide her and their daughter with financial security. However, the work was confiscated by US troops in May 1945 and transported to the Netherlands that October. By then, Han van Meegeren, who was suspected of collaboration because he let a unique work by Vermeer slip into German hands, had already confessed that not Vermeer but he himself was the maker of this painting as well as a series of other 'Vermeers that had surfaced in the previous nine years.

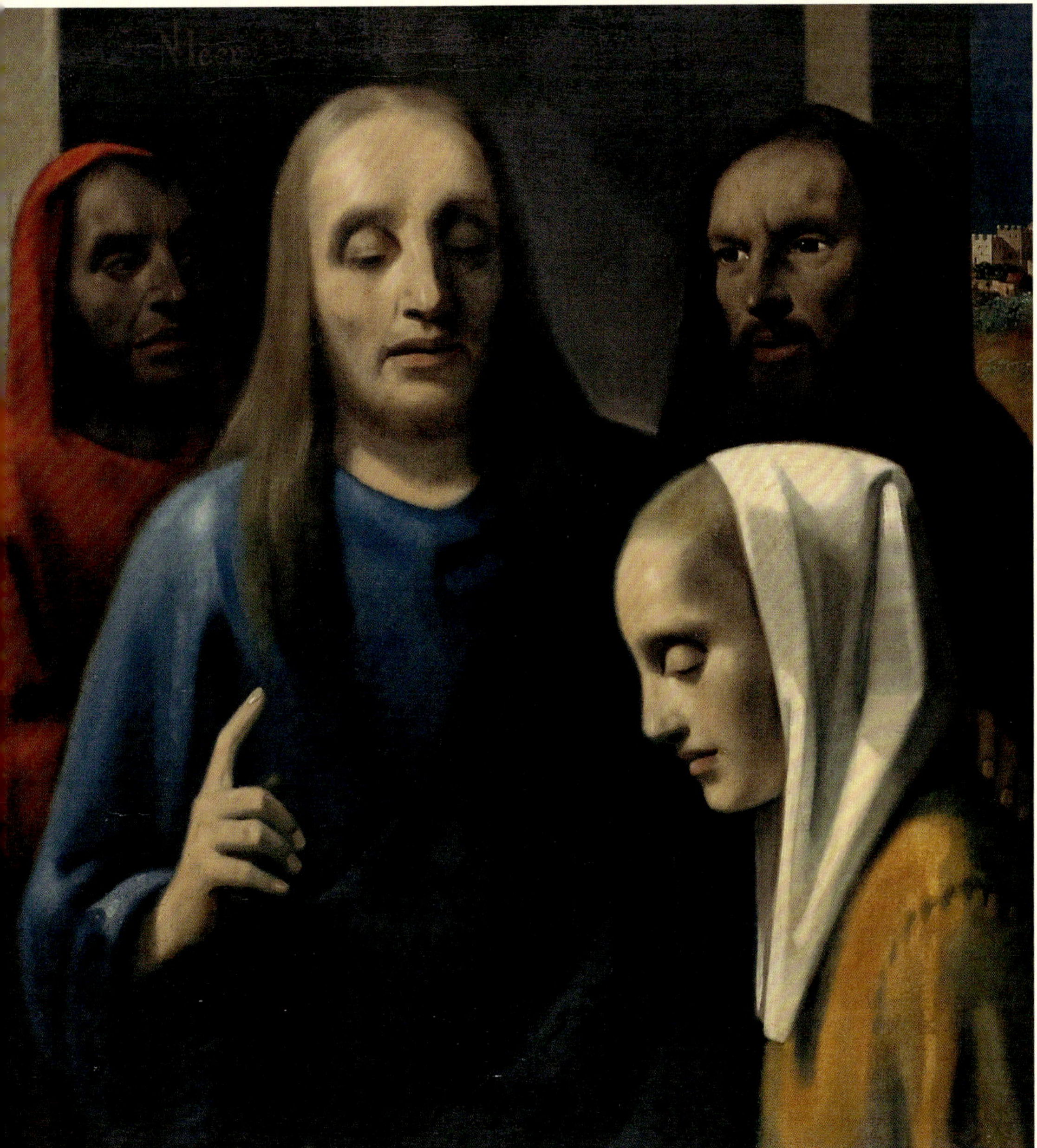

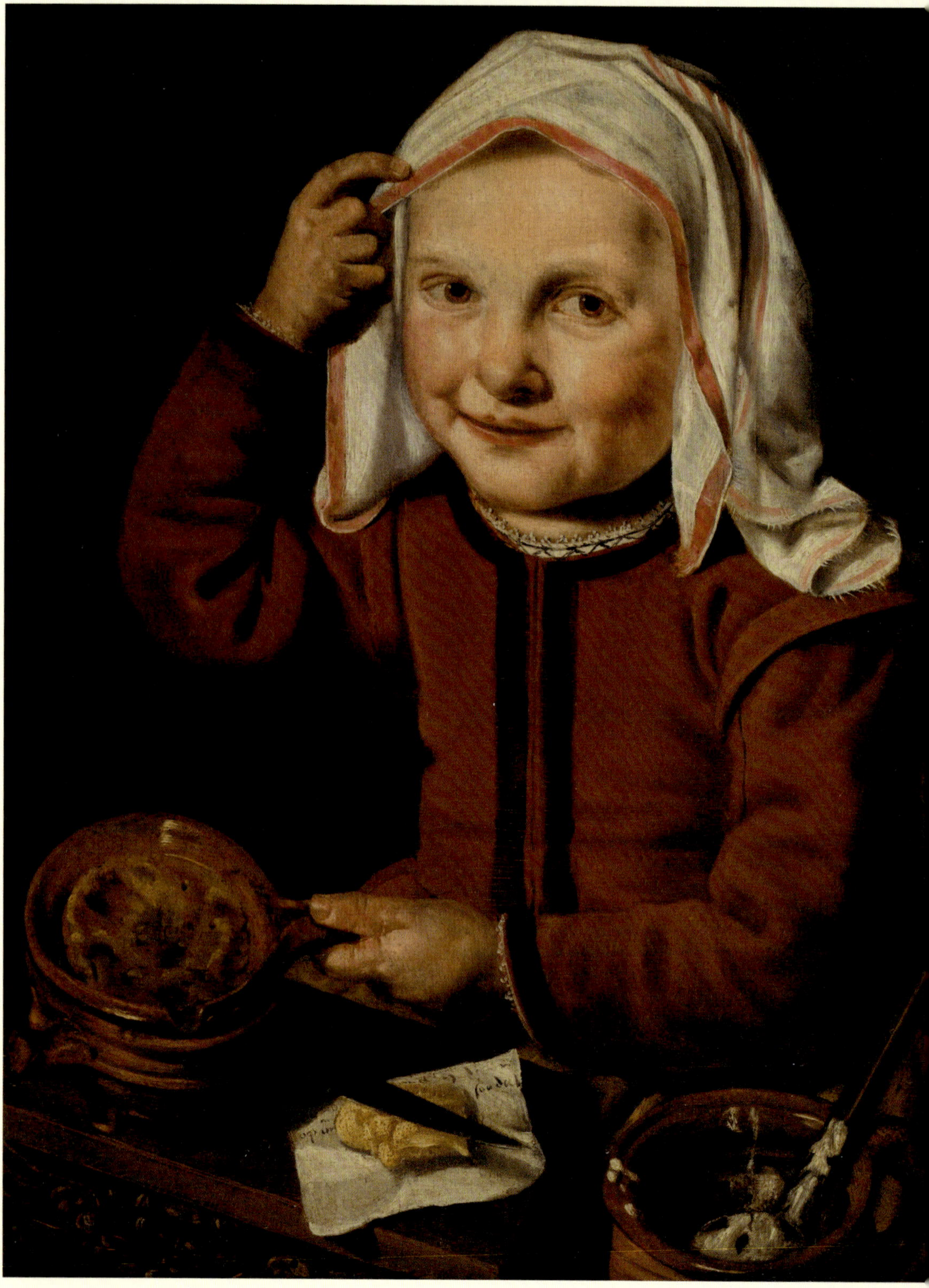

34
A Child with a small Pan
JAN WOUTERSZ. STAP (1599-1663)
Panel, 54 x 33 cm, Rijksdienst voor het Cultureel Erfgoed, NK3758

This painting was at the P. de Boer art gallery before the occupation and was acquired by the German collector E. Kummerlé at Kunsthandel Goudstikker-Miedl in Amsterdam during the war. It was later added to the collection of the Museum der Bildenden Künste in Leipzig. In 2012, the painting was recovered to the Netherlands from Germany, along with several other works from the Kummerlé collection. These paintings were brought under in the NK Collection and a few of them have been returned to heirs of former owners since then.

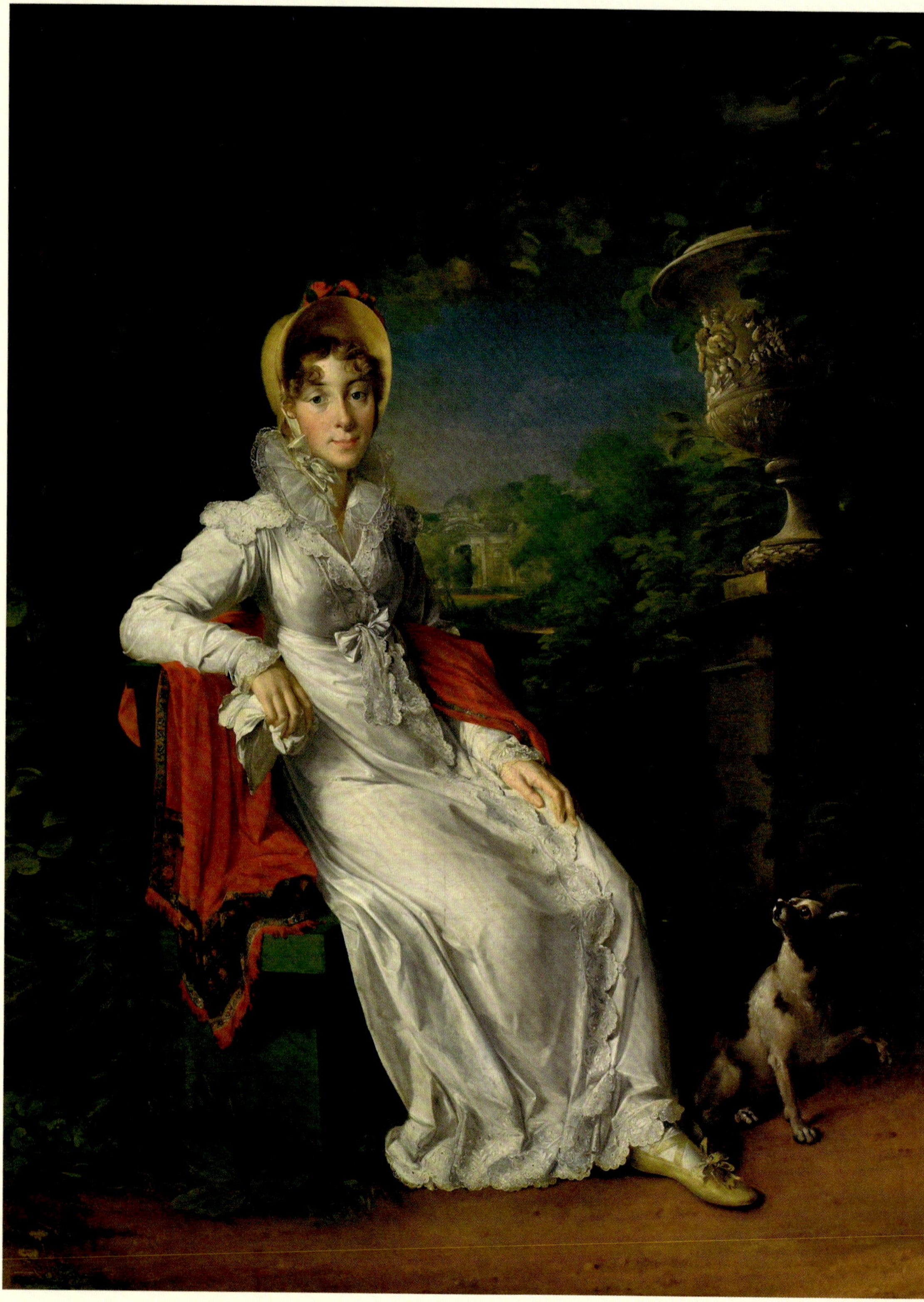

35

Portrait of Carolina Ferdinanda Louisa of Sicily, duchess de Berry, c. 1820
FRANÇOIS PASCAL SIMON BARON GÉRARD (1770-1837)
Canvas, 194.5 x 142.5 cm, Rijksmuseum, Amsterdam, on loan from RCE, NK3406

This painting was purchased in 1926 by Jacques Goudstikker in joint ownership with the Berlin art dealer Rathgeber. It remained unsold for many years and was acquired in 1940 by Alois Miedl along with Goudstikker's further stock. Miedl sold the portrait to the Wallraf-Richartz Museum in Cologne in 1943. After the war, the piece was recovered to the Netherlands. It was among the works of art that Dési Goudstikker relinquished in a 1952 settlement with the Administrative Department of the Council for the Restorations of Rights (NBI).
In 2005, the Restitutions Committee advised that this relinquishment should be considered final.

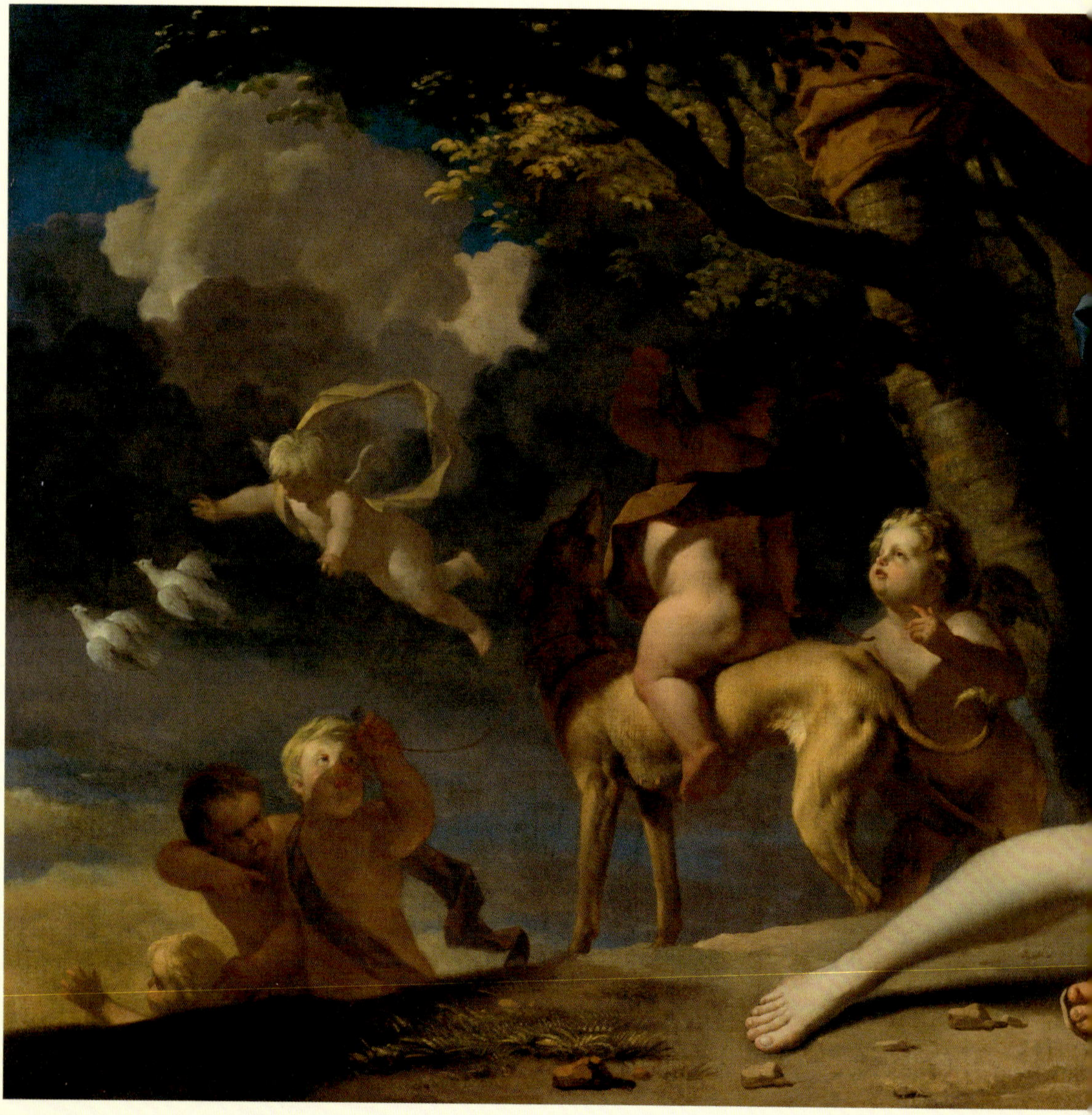

36

'enus and Adonis, c. 1665-1667
KAREL DUJARDIN (1622-1678)
Canvas, 87 x 180 cm, Rijksdienst voor
et Cultureel Erfgoed, NK2386

'his painting by Karel Dujardin was the roperty of the art gallery Hoogendijk in msterdam from the late 1930s. In December 940, Hoogendijk sold the work to Hans Vilhelm Hupp, who was the director of the Kunstmuseum der Stadt Düsseldorf. It is one of the many high quality works that Hupp acquired on the Dutch art market during the war for his museum.

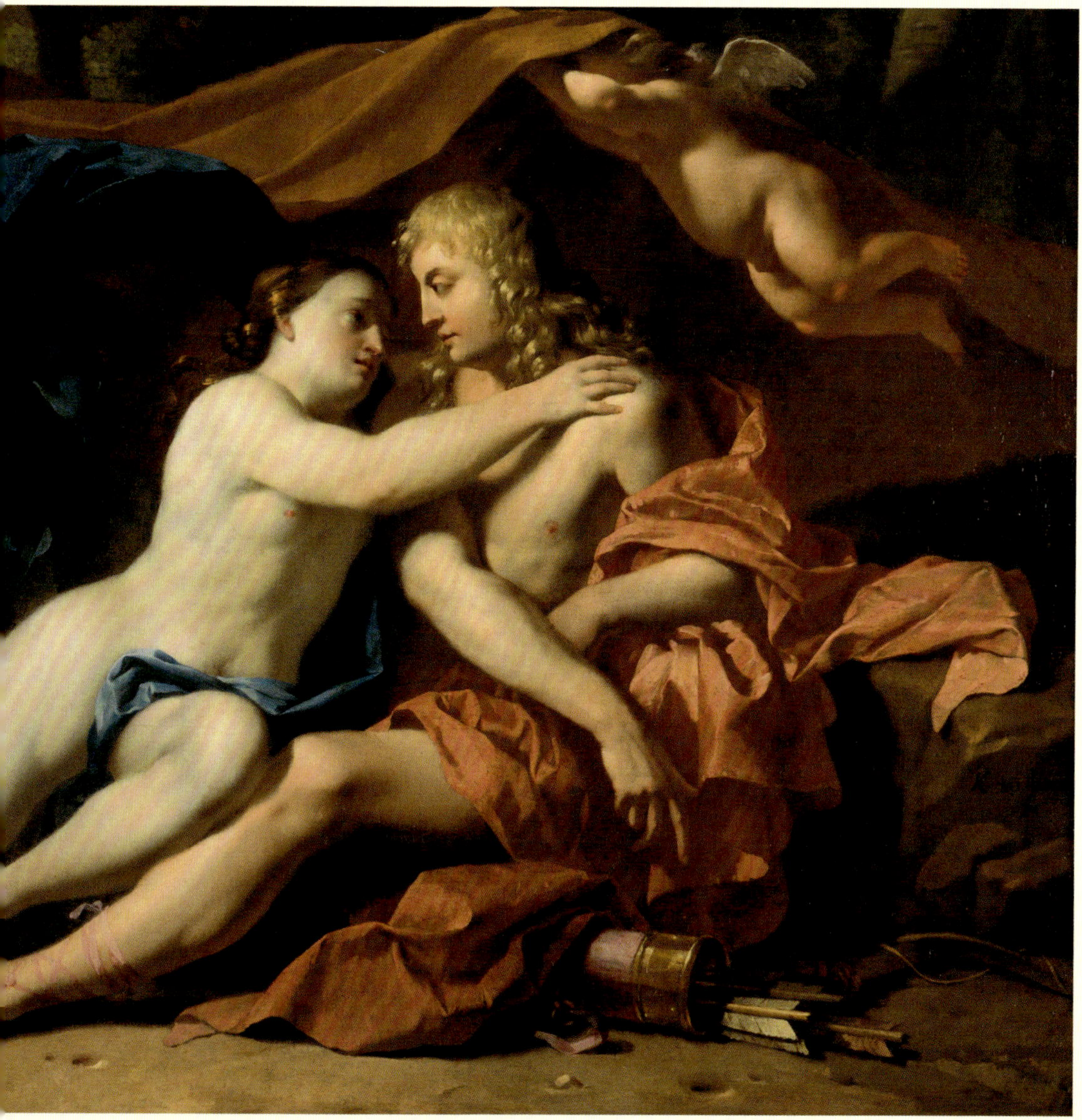

37

Family group as Caritas, 1623
WERNER VAN DEN VALCKERT
(c. 1580-after 1627)
Panel, 162 x 125.5 cm,
Rijksdienst voor het Cultureel Erfgoed,
NK1785

Walter M.H. Paech (1890-1974) was born in Berlin and settled in the Netherlands in 1925, where he initially worked as a restorer for the art dealer Douwes in Amsterdam. In 1929, he opened his own art gallery on the Rokin, where he mainly dealt in old master paintings. In 1939, he acquired the Dutch nationality. After the war, he was convicted for his activities during the occupation by the tribunal in Amsterdam. He modestly resumed dealing in art after serving his priso sentence from 1945 to 1946.

This monumental *portrait historié*, depicting family with the woman in the role of Caritas, was sold by Paech to the Kunstmuseum der Stadt Düsseldorf in 1942. He had purchased the painting, as so many of the pieces from hi stock, in Belgium.

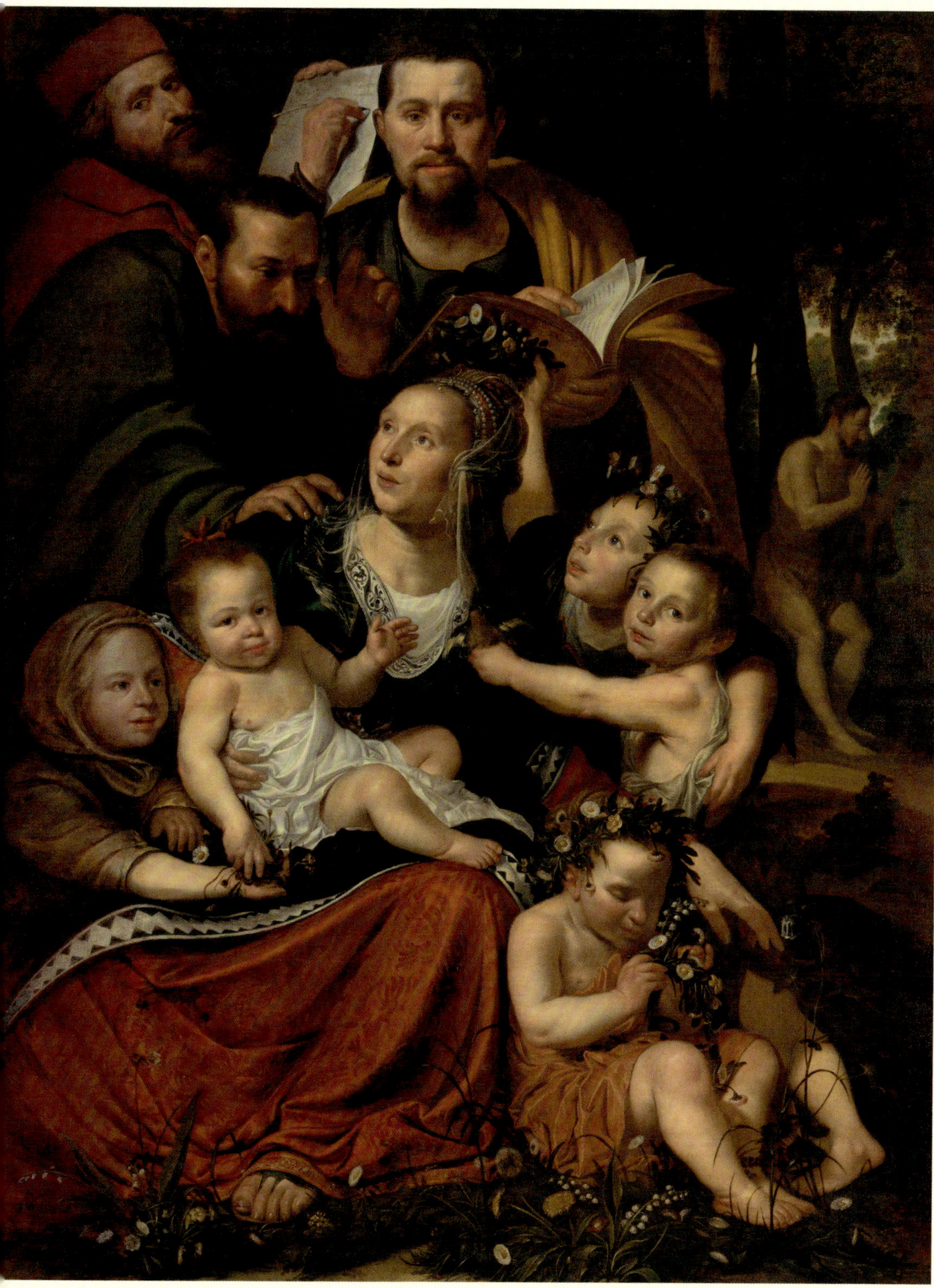

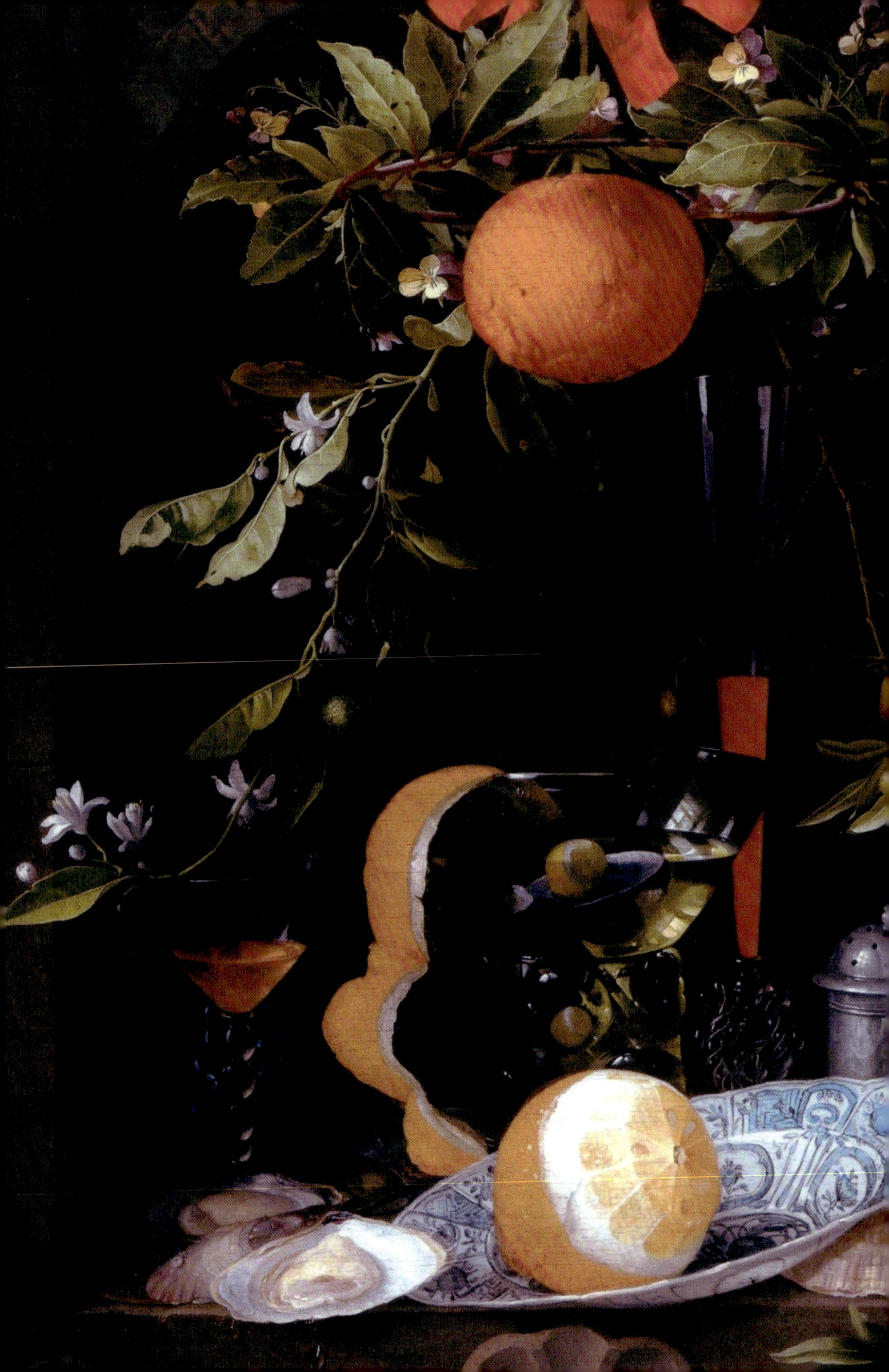

VI RECOVERY, RETURN AND RESTITUTION

The fall of the Third Reich presented the allies with a task that was unprecedented in history – the appropriation of staggering numbers of art treasures that Nazi Germany had acquired during the war and their repatriation to the formerly occupied countries from which they had been taken. Advances through enemy territory led to the discovery of many hundreds of makeshift art depots in the most diverse and often unexpected locations, such as salt mines, trains, old barns and castles. During the war, the Americans and their allies had made thorough preparations to salvage the cultural heritage of Europe. In accordance with agreements made beforehand, the works of art would be recovered to their countries of origin. The Soviet occupation authorities were the only parties not to comply. In the Netherlands, the Netherlands Art Property Foundation (Stichting Nederlandsch Kunstbezit, SNK) had a pivotal role in efforts to restore the cultural losses that had been sustained. The staff worked on the return of art from Germany with great diligence and results were speedily achieved thanks to sound preparations and effective organisation. On 8 October 1945, a plane full of seventeenth-century masterpieces landed at Schiphol Airport, where it was welcomed by a reception committee of dignitaries. Many thousands of works of art were recovered to the Netherlands in the years that followed, ranging from famous paintings by Rembrandt and Rubens to toy harlequins and fake armour.

The artworks and valuables that were recovered were mostly voluntarily sold during the occupation by the original owners. As a result of anti-Jewish measures, there were also many other objects that had fallen into German hands. It was up to the Dutch state to return the recovered works, if the objects were eligible, to the original owners or their heirs. However, this post-war restitution process initially proved difficult and would take several years to lead to more results. This chapter offers an overview of both the art recovery from Germany and the restitution process in the Netherlands.

THE PREPARATIONS DURING THE WAR

After World War II broke out, it soon became clear that the Nazi were looting possessions on a massive scale in the occupied countries. In London, on 5 January 1943, the allies signed the Inter-Allied Declaration, rejecting the German dispossession methods in the occupied areas. This was a warning that the allies were opposed to overt theft or plundering and also to apparently legal, voluntary agreements. This declaration of January 1943, together with the later Bretton Woods Conference and the Paris Agreement on Reparation from Germany, formed the basis for the post-war recovery of art. The underlying principle was that items of cultural value were to be returned from Germany to the formerly occupied countries, irrespective of the circumstances in which possession had been lost. It was then the task of the receiving countries to develop a restitution policy through which the artworks would return to possible rightful owners. During the course of 1943, there was a sharp rise in the number of reports regarding the expropriation of art. Moreover, committees were established to implement the objectives of the Inter-Allied Declaration, for example in the United States, England and France. In addition to these national committees, there was also a need for an international consultation forum and looted art information point. This was set up in April 1944 in London and was to become known as the Vaucher Commission.

A major part of the inventory of war damage to European cultural heritage was conducted under the supervision of allied armed forces. A system was constructed in the autumn of 1943 under which art experts joined the Monuments, Fine Arts and Archives (MFA&A) programme and served in uniform in military units. A number of these so-called Monuments Men, usually young art historians and museum curators, joined troops at the front in order to protect and inspect monuments and cultural objects.

Early on in the war, the Dutch government in exile made a stand against Nazi dispossession methods by introducing emergency legislation. On 7 June 1940, for instance, Dutch nationals were prohibited from participating in contracts or agreements with the enemy. Concern about harm to cultural heritage also gradually increased. At the end of 1943, the art historian J.G. van Gelder, acting director of the Netherlands Institute for Art History (Rijksbureau voor Kunsthistorische Documentatie, RKD) in The Hague, was instructed to make preparations for the post-war recovery of items of cultural value that had disappeared to Germany. He chaired a newly formed committee consisting of representatives of museum circles and the art trade as well as several lawyers. In addition, the Dutch Ministery of Education, Arts and Sciences in London established a small art recovery department. F.E.G. Nilant was assigned to this department in July 1944. He was a young art history student who had abandoned his studies in South Africa to join the Royal Netherlands Motorized Infantry Brigade, later known as the Princess Irene Brigade (P.I.B.). From the very beginning, as a recovery officer, Nilant organised the accumulated documentation, he represented the Netherlands in meetings of the Vaucher Commission and he helped make the department's office a hub of information on looted art. Shortly after Nilant's arrival, the department was reinforced by the art historian A.B. de Vries, who was to play a leading role in the return of art treasures to the Netherlands. In November 1940, De Vries had been dismissed from the Rijksmuseum because of his Jewish descent. He had managed to flee to safety in Switzerland with his family. Between December 1944 and mid-February 1945, he worked in London, where he represented the Netherlands in the Vaucher Commission, and on 17 January 1945 he became chairman of the Provisional Committee Regarding Recovery of Art Treasures, Libraries and Archives Originating from the Netherlands (Voorloopige Commissie inzake Terugverkrijging van Kunstschatten, Bibliotheken en Archieven uit Nederland afkomstig), which was established by minister Bolkestein.

he salt mines at Altaussee in ustria, where US forces found housands of art treasures in May 945, including those from the ollection of the Führermuseum to e built in Linz

nmediately after the fall of the Nazi egime, allied authorities began eizing art that had been transported om the occupied territories to Germany and Austria during the war.

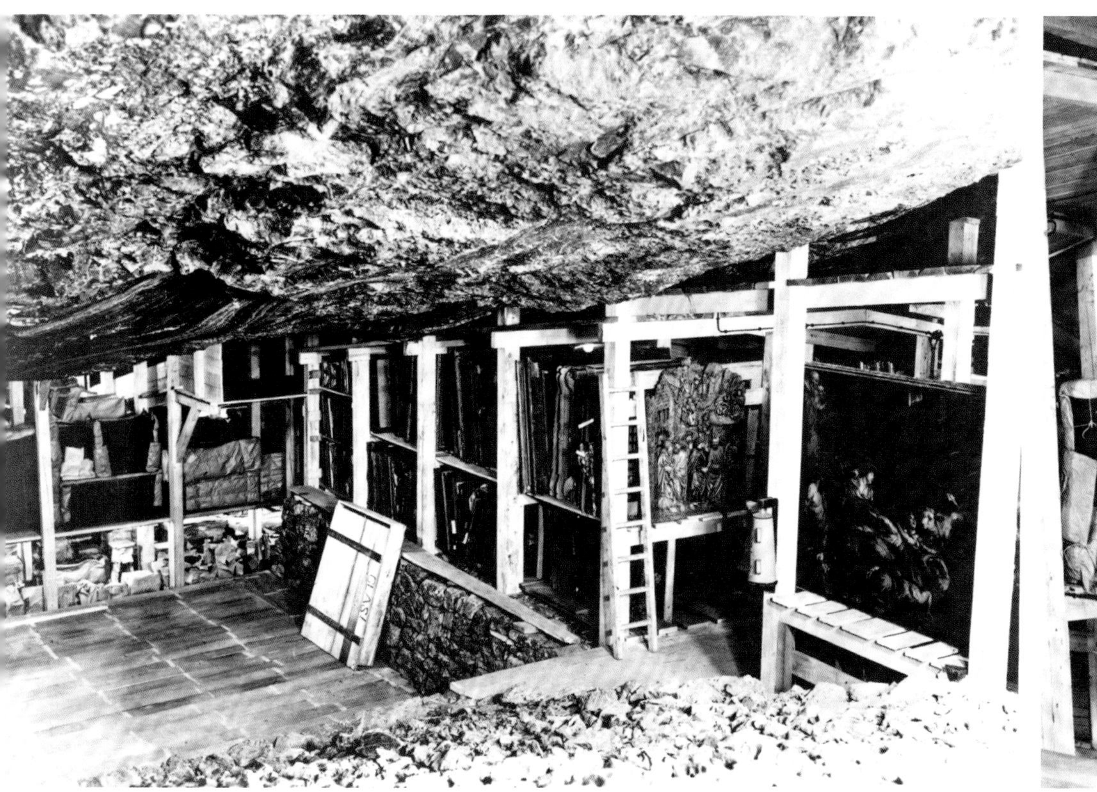

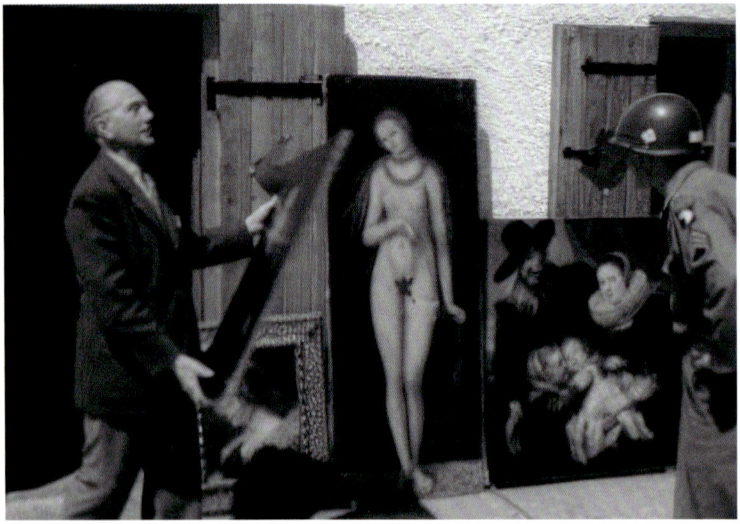

The recovery and registration of Hermann Göring's collection by the 101st Airborne Division of the US Army, 1945

The US forces were assisted by Görings former art agent Walter Andreas Hofer in the survey of the collection. The photograph features Hofer with several recovered paintings that were later returned to the Netherlands. In the centre the *Venus* by Lucas Cranach the Elder, to the left the *Portrait of Hélène Fourment* by Peter Paul Rubens from Franz Koenigs' collection (NK1409) and on the right the *Portrait of Cornelis de Vos and his Family* by Anthony van Dyck, which had been sold by the Katz gallery to Göring in 1940.
These works were among the thousands of works of art that allied troops brought to safety as they advanced through Germany. US troops found them in Hermann Göring's collection in May 1945.

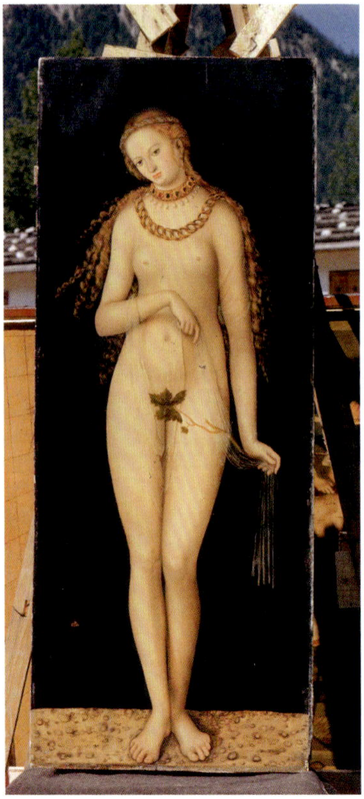

The painting *Venus* from around 1518 by Lucas Cranach the Elder, as illustrated in the previous image, after recovery by US troops

The work was the property of the German banker Ernst Proehl (1885-1973), naturalised to Dutch citizenship. He had acquired it from Kunsthandel Goudstikker in 1924 and sold it to Göring under duress in 1940.
The *Venus* was brought back to the Netherlands and returned to its original owner in 1952. Today, the painting is part of the collection of the National Gallery of Canada in Ottawa. These days, Venus' nudity is no longer covered by a fig leaf.

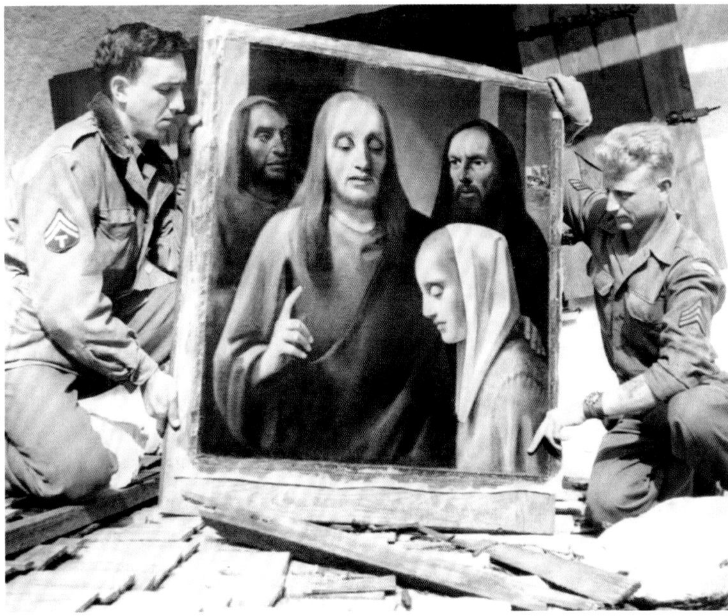

he recovery of the painting *Christ* nd the *Woman Taken in Adultery*

he painting acquired by Hermann öring in 1944 was one of his most rized possessions (see fig. 33). It as considered a previously unknown, enuine masterpiece by Johannes ermeer. The selling price was so high at Göring paid for it partly with orks from his own collection. After the ar, it turned out that the painting was forgery by the master forger Han van Aeegeren (1889-1947).

RECOVERY AND RETURN AFTER THE WAR

It was not until the spring of 1945, when the allies advanced into Germany, that the full extent of art looting by the Nazis became evident. The allies discovered many hundreds of art depots, full of inconceivable quantities of cultural goods stolen from all over Europe. There was a race against time to retrieve these art treasures from mines, bunkers, churches and countless other storage places as quickly as possible. The Monuments Men played a key role in this. They had to see to it that the artworks were protected, inventoried and relocated.

The biggest art storage facilities were to be found in the American zone. In May 1945, American forces made one of the most sensational discoveries in Altaussee in Austria. They found an enormous depot in a complex of salt mines. The works of art included thousands of objects that were destined for the Führermuseum, which was to be constructed in Linz. Among them were many works of Dutch origin, such as numerous pieces belonging to the Mannheimer and Lanz collections. These art treasures nearly got lost forever. The local *Gauleiter* had issued an order to blow up the mines when the allied troops approached but the order was never carried out. There was another important discovery near Berchtesgaden, where the US 101st Airborne Division, known as the Screaming Eagles, found over a thousand paintings, sculptures and other valuables from Hermann Göring's collection. This also included many works from the Netherlands, for example, the best quality works from the

Goudstikker collection, such as *Landscape with an Episode from the Conquest of America* by Jan Mostaert and *Adam and Eve* by Lucas Cranach the Elder. Art depots of significance were also discovered in Neuschwanstein Castle, Siegen, Merkers and elsewhere. The major storage facilities contained only a part of the stolen art. Many objects had been distributed all over Germany and beyond. These had to be tracked down through careful investigations of museums, art dealerships and private residences.

After the German capitulation, in the summer of 1945, the allies decided that Germany would be governed by the Allied Control Council and that the country would be divided into American, British, French and Soviet occupation zones. Berlin, which was in the Soviet zone, was also divided into four sectors. Attempts to implement a joint recovery policy in all four zones failed as a result of growing tensions between the allies. Consequently, each of the occupying authorities became responsible for taking measures in their own national zone. The allies set up various art depots, to which traced objects were transported. The Americans established four central collecting points (CCPs), in Marburg, Wiesbaden, Munich and Offenbach. The depot in Munich was supervised by the art historian Craig Hugh Smyth. This was where Hitler's and Göring's collections were brought together, for example. Envoys of the formerly occupied countries were welcome to inspect the cultural works in the CCPs and submit restitution requests if they recognized objects from their countries.

Views on restitution differed substantially within the Allied Control Council. A key issue was whether restitution was applicable to all goods exported to Germany or only to goods that were obtained under duress. In 1947, the Americans and the British decided that all items of cultural value taken to Germany were eligible for recovery, regardless of how the Germans had obtained them. This principle had already been applied in the French zone right from the beginning.

The Federal Republic of Germany was established in 1949 by combining the American, British and French militarized zones. The occupying authorities supervised the political development of the new republic through the Allied High Commission (1949-1955) and the occupation of West Germany formally ended in 1955. These political events did not put an end to the process of the restitution of art, however. The western occupying authorities saw to it that the German Federal Republic made provisions for the mission and the allied recovery measures were confirmed in the *Überleitungsvertrag*. On the grounds of this treaty, the Netherlands was able to submit applications until 8 May 1956 for the restitution of items of cultural value to the Bundesamt für äussere Restitutionen. By no means could all of the looted art be traced. West Germany also provided financial compensation for stolen possessions in addition to the restitution of cultural goods.

Virtually no privately owned art was recovered from the German Democratic Republic (DDR), the former Soviet occupation zone. Measures concerning such art were provided for in the 1990 *Gesetz zur Regelung offener Vermögensfragen*.

ESTABLISHMENT OF THE NETHERLANDS ART PROPERTY FOUNDATION, 1945

The Dutch government in London laid the basis for its post-war restitution policy through emergency legislation. After the liberation, the Council for the Restoration of Rights (Raad voor het Rechtsherstel) was established in August 1945. The objective was to compensate the losses that had been sustained during the German occupation as much as possible. This concerned 'the expropriation and liquidation [...] of assets of people and institutions'. The council had a jurisdiction division, to which claims could be submitted until 1 July 1951.

Formally speaking, the practical implementation of recovery was the task of the Office of the Commissioner-General for the Commercial Interests of the Netherlands in Germany (Commissariaat-Generaal voor de Nederlandsche Economische Belangen in Duitsland, CGR, 1945-1949). This government agency assembled items of cultural value from the collecting points in Germany and had the objects transported to the Dutch border. Here, they were handed over to the SNK, which had been established specifically for this purpose.

The SNK's founding act was signed on 11 June 1945 by J.G. van Gelder, as representative of the Ministries of Education, Arts and Sciences (OK&W) and Finance. According to its statutes, the foundation's aim was 'to assist in all activities relating to art treasures, libraries and archives that are or have been in enemy hands and to carry out all the actions associated therewith in the broadest sense...'. The SNK would gain custody of the recovered works of art awaiting any claims. The SNK was run by a management board, which was chaired by D.C. Röell, director of the Rijksmuseum. Van Gelder was the secretary. Van Gelder and De Vries were appointed directors at the SNK's constituent meeting on 18 June 1945. They were tasked with the foundation's day-to-day management. The preliminary guidelines for the future policy were also discussed at the meeting. Those guidelines were changed a number of times later on. Moreover, they were never formally adopted by the responsible ministries. Over the years this situation sometimes led to uncertainty and problems. The SNK consisted of two departments: a Domestic Department and a Foreign Department. The vast majority of the current NK Collection comprises works of art that came into state custody via the Foreign Department.

The Foreign Department was responsible for the recovery, management and restitution of cultural objects that had been removed or exported from the Netherlands during the war. Two offices were set up to carry out these tasks, one in Amsterdam and the other in The Hague. This soon proved rather impractical and the Hague office was soon dissolved. For the first few years, the Foreign Department was mainly financed by state subsidies, while the foundation's work was actually intended to be budget neutral. The SNK charged fees to the original owners to whom works of art were returned. This initially generated little income, however. It was not until the sales of recovered art and the restitution process started taking off, that debts began to subside in 1949.

The Domestic Department was set up to keep and manage items of cultural value that were confiscated in the Netherlands after the war. These included the properties of enemies, political offenders, absentees and unknown owners. The foundation hoped that such works of art could be added to the public art collections but the result was disappointing. Meanwhile, the Foreign Department's portfolio far outgrew its capacities. Serious errors were made in the management of the objects and criminal offences were even committed. In August 1948, a government agency, the Administrative Department of the Council for Restoration of Rights (Nederlands Beheers-instituut, NBI), took over the activities of the Domestic Department.

DECLARATION AND RECOVERY

Assembling information pertaining to art that had been taken out of the country was an important task for the SNK. Under a regulation issued by the military authorities in July 1945, everyone who had sold or handed over a work of art to the enemy during the war was obliged to submit a declaration to the foundation. Radio announcements, newspaper advertisements and posters were used to publicise this. These declarations did not provide a complete picture of course, one reason being that many original owners did not survive the war. The SNK therefore supplemented the data on the basis of other sources, such as the records of auction houses, transport companies and the looting organisation Liro, which in the meantime had been put under administration. This all generated a huge number of forms that could be used to identify and claim art objects in Germany. By the 1st of

Poster for the tracing of missing Dutch art treasures in Germany, 1945

On 24 July 1945, the military authority in the Netherlands issued a decree stipulating that anyone who had voluntarily or involuntarily sold or handed over cultural property to the enemy during the occupation had to report those goods to the Stichting Nederlands Kunstbezit ('Netherlands Art Property Foundation'). Thousands of completed declaration forms were submitted. The registrations were far from complete, however. This was partly because there was rarely any immediate family of the former owners of vanished art still alive. The SNK itself therefore also filled out declaration forms based on various administrative records, such as those of the Liro bank and the art gallery Kunsthandel Goudstikker-Miedl. Through these so-called 'internal declaration forms', great effort was made to get the records as complete as possible. Visiting the allied Collecting Points, SNK employees used the data from these forms to recover as many objects originating from the Netherlands as possible.

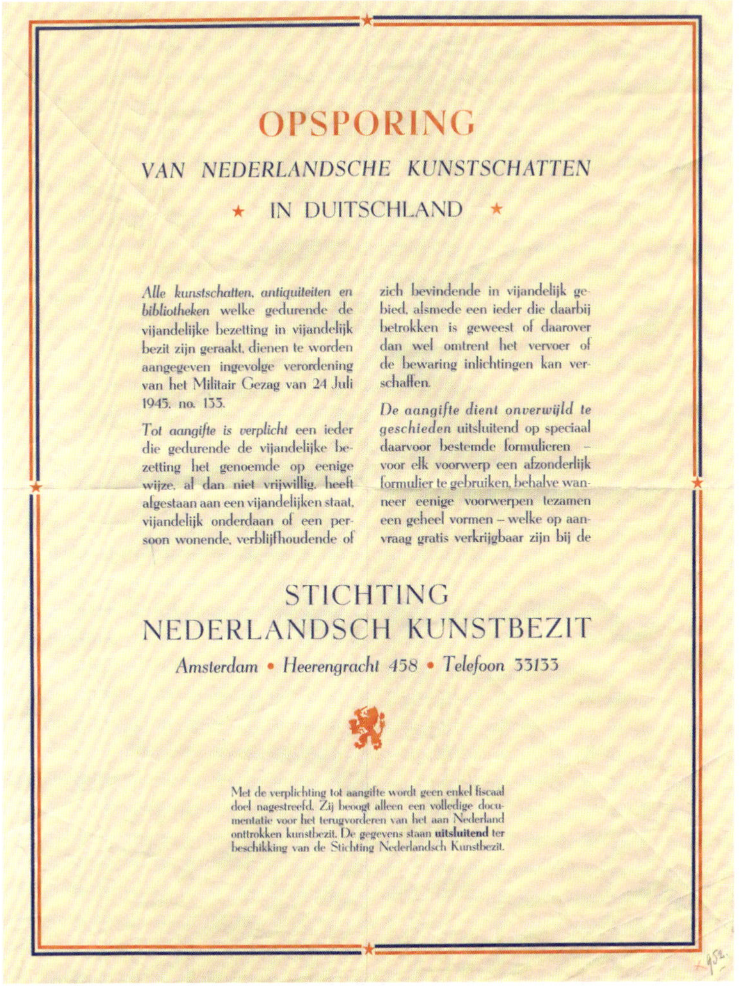

OPSPORING

VAN NEDERLANDSCHE KUNSTSCHATTEN

★ IN DUITSCHLAND ★

Alle kunstschatten, antiquiteiten en bibliotheken welke gedurende de vijandelijke bezetting in vijandelijk bezit zijn geraakt, dienen te worden aangegeven ingevolge verordening van het Militair Gezag van 24 Juli 1945, no. 133.

Tot aangifte is verplicht een ieder die gedurende de vijandelijke bezetting het genoemde op eenige wijze, al dan niet vrijwillig, heeft afgestaan aan een vijandelijken staat, vijandelijk onderdaan of een persoon wonende, verblijfhoudende of zich bevindende in vijandelijk gebied, alsmede een ieder die daarbij betrokken is geweest of daarover dan wel omtrent het vervoer of de bewaring inlichtingen kan verschaffen.

De aangifte dient onverwijld te geschieden uitsluitend op speciaal daarvoor bestemde formulieren – voor elk voorwerp een afzonderlijk formulier te gebruiken, behalve wanneer eenige voorwerpen tezamen een geheel vormen – welke op aanvraag gratis verkrijgbaar zijn bij de

STICHTING
NEDERLANDSCH KUNSTBEZIT

Amsterdam • Heerengracht 458 • Telefoon 33133

Met de verplichting tot aangifte wordt geen enkel fiscaal doel nagestreefd. Zij beoogt alleen een volledige documentatie voor het terugvorderen van het aan Nederland onttrokken kunstbezit. De gegevens staan **uitsluitend** ter beschikking van de Stichting Nederlandsch Kunstbezit.

January 1947, almost 18,000 objects had been registered. This calculation does not include the church bells, libraries, archives and thousands of works from a number of major collections (Mannheimer, Lanz, Gutmann and Goudstikker) that had left the country. According to an estimate by De Vries, ultimately eighty percent of the art objects that had disappeared were registered.

The European recovery system was a military matter and the SNK was therefore not permitted to send civilian personnel to Germany. As a result of this, art experts were first commissioned as officers and then sent to the different occupation zones, where they assisted allied forces in tracking down and identifying art with a Dutch origin.
Much of the infrastructure had been destroyed during the acts of war and it consequently took some time before the transport of consignments of art to the Netherlands could actually begin. The American occupation zone proved to be the most effective

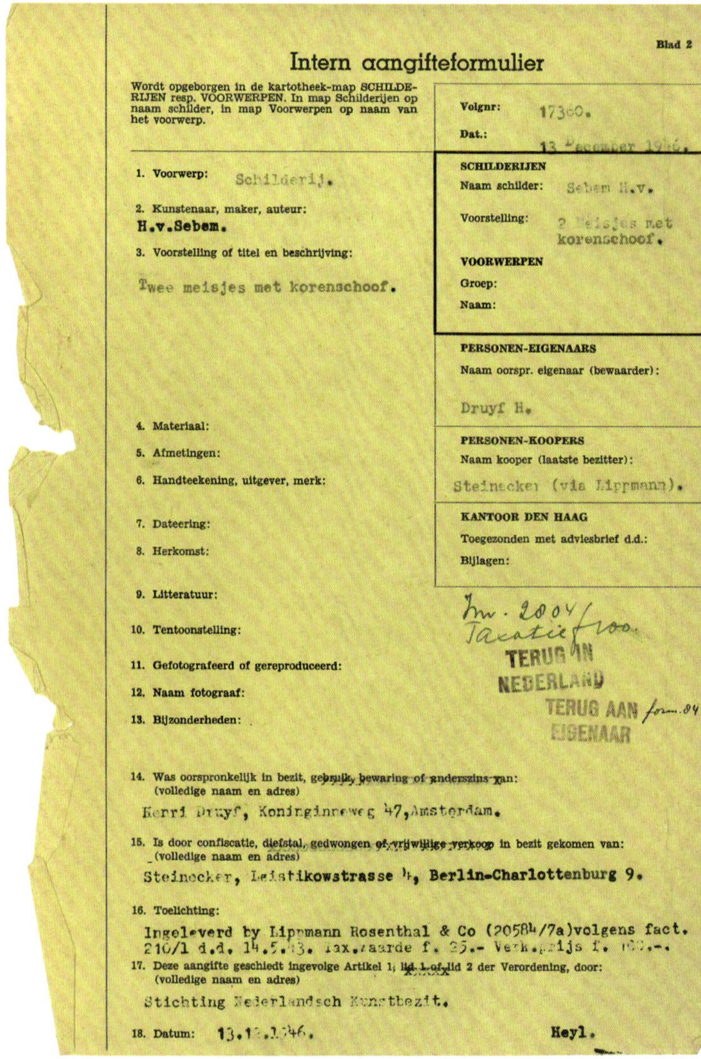

Blad 2

Intern aangifteformulier

Wordt opgeborgen in de kartotheek-map SCHILDERIJEN resp. VOORWERPEN. In map Schilderijen op naam schilder, in map Voorwerpen op naam van het voorwerp.

Volgnr: 17360.
Dat.: 13 December 1946.

1. Voorwerp: Schilderij.
2. Kunstenaar, maker, auteur: H.v.Sebem.
3. Voorstelling of titel en beschrijving: Twee meisjes met korenschoof.
4. Materiaal:
5. Afmetingen:
6. Handteekening, uitgever, merk:
7. Dateering:
8. Herkomst:
9. Litteratuur:
10. Tentoonstelling:
11. Gefotografeerd of gereproduceerd:
12. Naam fotograaf:
13. Bijzonderheden:

SCHILDERIJEN
Naam schilder: Sebem H.v.
Voorstelling: 2 meisjes met korenschoof.

VOORWERPEN
Groep:
Naam:

PERSONEN-EIGENAARS
Naam oorspr. eigenaar (bewaarder): Druyf H.

PERSONEN-KOOPERS
Naam kooper (laatste bezitter): Steinecker (via Lippmann).

KANTOOR DEN HAAG
Toegezonden met adviesbrief d.d.:
Bijlagen:

Inv. 2004 / Taxatie f 100.
TERUG IN NEDERLAND
TERUG AAN EIGENAAR [illegible]

14. Was oorspronkelijk in bezit, ~~gebruik, bewaring of anderszins~~ van: (volledige naam en adres)
Henri Druyf, Koninginneweg 47, Amsterdam.
15. Is door confiscatie, diefstal, gedwongen ~~of vrijwillige verkoop~~ in bezit gekomen van: (volledige naam en adres)
Steinecker, Leistikowstrasse 4, Berlin-Charlottenburg 9.
16. Toelichting:
Ingeleverd by Lippmann Rosenthal & Co (20584/7a) volgens fact. 210/1 d.d. 14.5.43. Tax.waarde f. 25.- Verk.prijs f. [illegible].-.
17. Deze aangifte geschiedt ingevolge Artikel 1, ~~lid 1 of~~ lid 2 der Verordening, door: (volledige naam en adres)
Stichting Nederlandsch Kunstbezit.
18. Datum: 13.12.1946. Heyl.

An example of an SNK internal declaration form concerning a work of art confiscated by the occupying forces

The stamps on this form indicate that the artwork in question was recovered from Germany to the Netherlands.

in this regard. The first Dutch representative in Germany was the art historian Professor A.P.A. Vorenkamp, who was given the rank of lieutenant colonel and sent in October 1945 to the CCP in Munich, where he identified a large number of works of art.

It was an unforgettable moment when an American military aircraft from Munich landed at Schiphol in October 1945 with twenty-six important paintings, including masterpieces by Rembrandt, Rubens, Van Dyck and Steen. It was a carefully orchestrated flight, which had been organised on the orders of General Eisenhower, who ceremonially brought these works back to the Dutch people. Over the next few years this was to be followed by dozens of transports by road from Munich. Nilant was one of those in charge. A satisfied De Vries wrote the following in a 1946 mission report:

'Thanks to the good organisation of the American MFA&A officers in Munich, and no less importantly the excellent work done by Lieutenant Colonel Vorenkamp for our country, between October 1945 and today the Netherlands has in relative terms achieved the best results with regard to the restitution of artworks.' It was pointed out in a meeting of the SNK's Management Board that same year that 'at least 80% of what has to be classified as the most valuable art has been returned from Munich'.

Another important Collecting Point in the American zone was at Offenbach. The largest collection of Jewish cultural objects in the world was assembled at this depot. Staff was faced with the Herculean task of establishing the origins of millions of stolen archives, books, letters and Judaica from all over Europe. D.P.M. Graswinckel, who later became the State Archivist, and Lion Morpurgo, the first post-war curator of the Jewish Historical Museum, played a key role at Offenbach in the identification of cultural items from the Netherlands. Their efforts also contributed to the return of most of the Bibliotheca Rosenthaliana, the Ets Haim Library and the Jewish Historical Museum collections to the Netherlands.

The return of items of cultural value from the British zone, in the northwest of Germany, got underway more slowly.

The first transport to the Netherlands of works of art recovered from Germany, 1945

On 8 October 1945, 26 paintings, mainly by old Dutch and Flemish masters, were flown into Schiphol Airport from Munich in a US army plane. This ceremonial air delivery was a 'token shipment to the Netherlands' at the initiative of General Eisenhower. It marked the beginning of the large-scale art recovery from Germany and Austria.

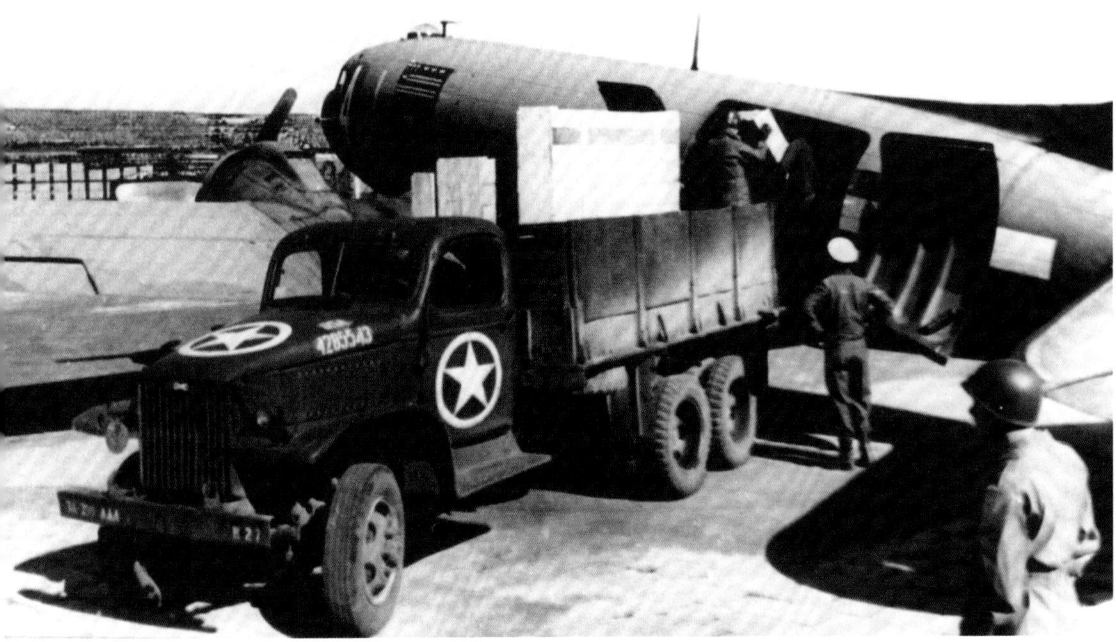

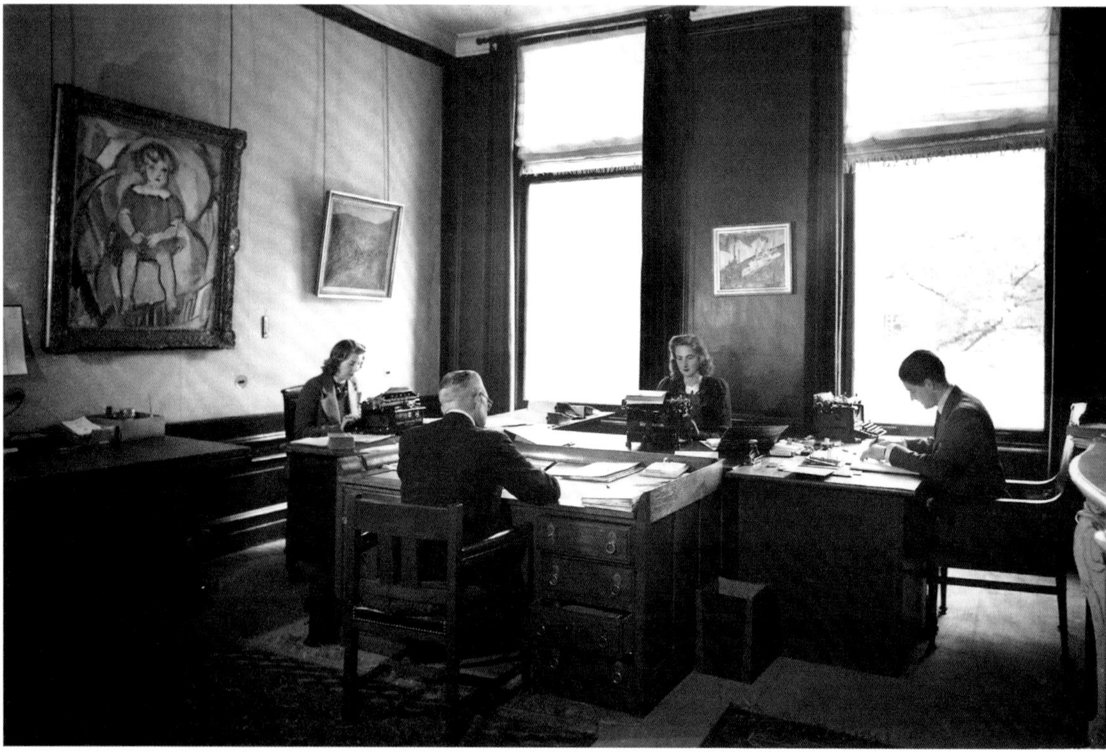

SNK employees at work

The SNK's Amsterdam office was located on the premises of the former Goudstikker gallery at Herengracht 458. On the wall on the left a children's portrait by Jan Sluijters, which came from Kunsthandel Goudstikker stock (fig. 38). The SNK also held office in The Hague, which was housed at the Rijksbureau voor Kunsthistorische Documentatie (RKD), at Korte Vijverberg 7, but this office closed as early as 1945. In the summer of 1946, the SNK moved to Keizersgracht 105 in Amsterdam. From 1 February 1949, it was accommodated by the Ministry of Finance's *Bureau Herstelbetalings- en Recuperatiegoederen* (Agency for the RecoveryFunding and Repossession of Goods), which was located at Mauritskade 37 in The Hague.

Fewer Nazi art depots were discovered there after the war than in the American zone and intensive investigations were needed in order to recover objects. Moreover, the British authorities were initially unwilling to return art that had been sold voluntarily. This policy was changed in 1947. Despite all possible cooperation, the search for objects proceeded with difficulty in the French zone, in the southwest of Germany.

The SNK gave priority to the recovery of works of national importance, but it realised that attention had to be paid to less important objects. From 1947 onwards, the number of works of art being returned decreased and progressively more research was necessary to trace objects. By the end of the year, the SNK concluded that its recovery task was as good as over. It reported in June 1952 that 'over 4,000 paintings, approximately 400 tapestries, thousands of pieces of furniture, several tens of thousands of decorative art objects as well as several barge and lorry loads of books, were in the foundation's custody'. This calculation did not include the several thousand objects that belonged to the Mannheimer, Gutmann and Lanz collections.

RETURNED ART IN MUSEUMS

In 1946, the SNK and the RKD organised the exhibition *Art Treasures Regained (Herwonnen kunstbezit)* in order to display the treasures that had been brought back from Germany.

It was held first in the Mauritshuis in The Hague, followed by the Centraal Museum in Utrecht and the Van Abbemuseum in Eindhoven. In 1947 the SNK organised a travelling exhibition of forty-eight returned paintings that toured the United States and Canada. With this gesture, the Netherlands wished to show its gratitude for the efforts of the MFA&A branch in the recovery of art. This exhibition, entitled *Pictures Looted from Holland, Returned Through the Efforts of the United States Armed Forces*, visited a number of American and Canadian cities and was a big success.

In addition to these temporary exhibitions, the SNK had more far-reaching plans for the returned art. A guiding principle relating to the return of art was that the objects concerned could enhance the national art heritage if they were placed in museums and public buildings. In April 1947, Dutch museum directors were invited to the Rijksmuseum to view around 1,200 recovered artworks and itemise wish lists for loans. However, the viewing took place before thorough research had been conducted into whether or not the works concerned were eligible for restitution to their original owners or their heirs. This is how it came to pass that a collector who had submitted a declaration to the SNK about a stolen painting, found that work of art hanging on a museum wall, where it had been on view at the initiative of the SNK. The greatest number of loans of recovered objects went to the Rijksmuseum. Among other things, this museum houses hundreds of works of art from the Mannheimer collection. Most of these pieces are not included in the present inventory of the NK Collection.

RESTITUTION POLICY 1945-1948

The SNK was responsible for both the recovery of cultural objects and its restitution to the original owners or their heirs. This restitution had to correspond with the general restoration of rights. What happened in practice, however, is that during the initial post-war years the SNK concentrated on bringing back items of cultural value from Germany, and little attention was given to the actual restitution task. The need for appropriate regulations for the restitution of recovered goods became more and more pressing as the number of claims mounted. The first guidelines stipulated that the foundation had to examine whether the recovered artworks originally belonged to 'owners who had to surrender them under duress or not'. 'Duress' was therefore the key concept here. The SNK refined the restitution criteria in later guidelines. Restitution required determining who the original owner of the claimed object was and it had to be beyond doubt that the loss of

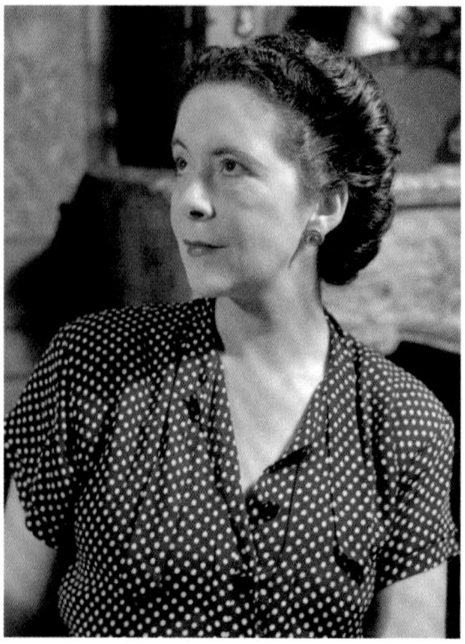

Portrait of Désirée (Dési) Goudstikker-von Halban (1912-1996)

After the war, the administrators of Kunsthandel Goudstikker-Miedl found several hundreds of works of art from Kunsthandel Goudstikker's old trading stock in the art gallery's buildings. These works were transferred to Desi Goudstikker in 1949, in advance of the formal settlement. That formal settlement, finalized three years later, provided in the restitution of the pieces of the old trading stock that were found in the Netherlands. However, it did not lead to the restitution of several hundred works of art recovered from Germany after the war. Some of these returned objects were sold at auction by the Dutch state between 1950 and 1952. Other works of art were added to the national collection and were returned to the Goudstikker heirs in 2006.

possession was involuntary. Any sum of money received by the original owner as a 'compensation' for the loss of a work of art had to be paid back. Objects could furthermore only be returned to the owner after payment of 2.75% of the assessed value to the SNK, as a contribution towards the general costs of restitution and management as well as a reimbursement for the transport and insurance costs.

A 1949 report by the Central Audit Department (Centrale Accountantsdienst) on the SNK reveals that the foundation handled over forty restitution cases between June 1945 and September 1948 (fig. 39-40). The authors were critical about the SNK's restitution policy and they asserted that the guidelines for restitution cases were seldom complied with.

SNK REORGANISATION, 1948

In the spring of 1948, the Central Property Investigation Department (Centrale Vermogensopsporingsdienst) of the Ministry of Finance launched an investigation into irregularities resulting from the activities of an SNK employee. The SNK's records were seized for investigation because suspicion arose that others were also responsible for irregularities. During this investigation suspicions arose regarding De Vries, including possible preferential treatment of the art dealers Nathan and Benjamin Katz by the restitution of paintings claimed by them. This resulted in the arrest of De Vries and Benjamin Katz on 8 July 1948. The arrests attracted ample attention in the press. It was eventually decided to not press any criminal charges against Katz and, in 1951, the charges against De Vries were dropped because of insufficient evidence of misconduct.

L.F. Otto was appointed as acting director of the SNK during De Vries's absence. An official report was drawn up as a result of the foundation's instability. Among other things, the report concluded that the SNK's management was weak because the day-to-day management had been entrusted to an art historian. It would be advisable to put someone with 'commercial, legal and administrative experience' in charge of dealing with recovered art objects. Jolle Jolles, head of the Bureau for Restoration Payments and the Restoration of Property (Bureau Herstelbetalings- en Recuperatiegoederen, HERGO) from 1948 to 1953, was subsequently appointed director. D.F. Lunsingh Scheurleer, head of the State Inspectorate for Movable Monuments (Rijksinspecteur voor Roerende Monumenten), was appointed acting director. He acted as a replacement for De Vries, who remained director in name until his dismissal on 1 July 1950. Practical management of the NK Collection was entrusted to the Department for

Dispersed Government Artworks (Dienst voor 's Rijks Verspreide Kunstvoorwerpen), which was headed by Lunsingh Scheurleer.

When Jolles and Lunsingh Scheurleer took office, they were confronted with grave administrative chaos. They also observed that until then 'practically nothing' had been done about the restitution of recovered artworks. There was a great deal of catching up to do in these areas. In addition to active research into original ownership, it was decided to exhibit recovered objects so that original owners would be able to identify their lost artworks themselves. Altogether, the foundation organised three such 'claim exhibitions'. The

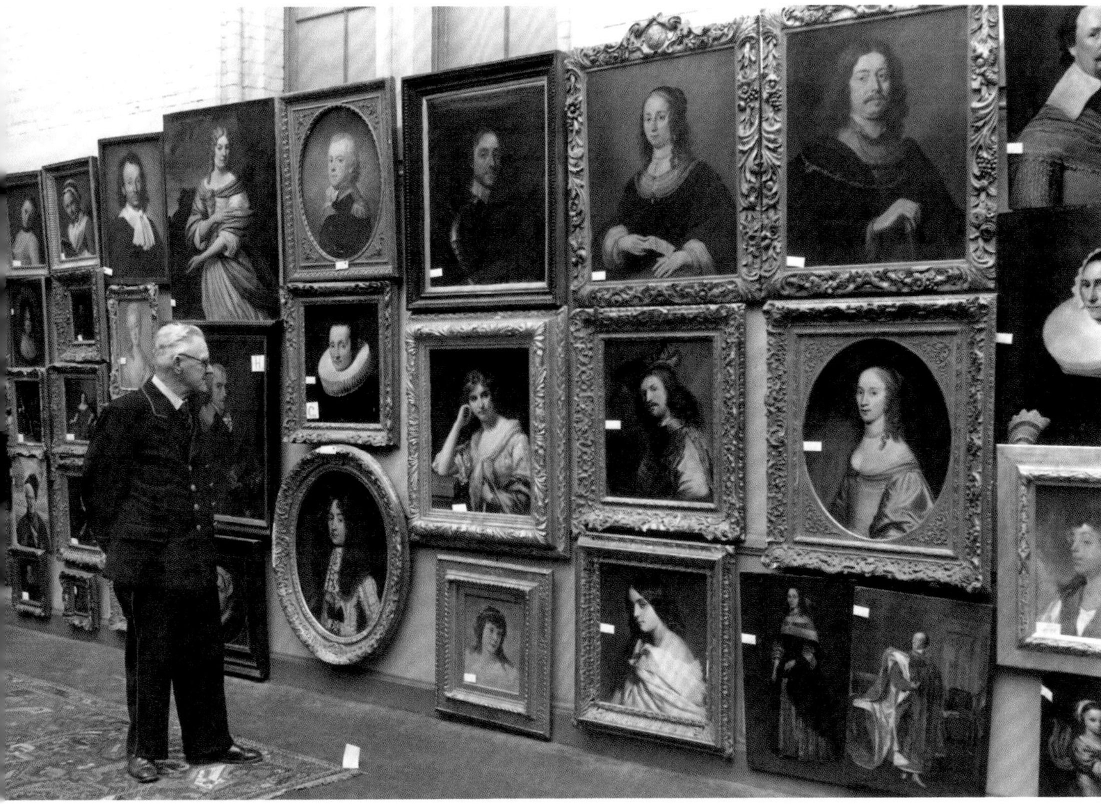

laim exhibition of paintings, rawings and tapestries at the ijksmuseum in Amsterdam, 0 April-9 June 1950

he SNK was tasked with managing e artworks that were recovered from ermany and returning them to their riginal owners or their next of kin. his restitution process got off to a low start but gained momentum after reorganisation of the SNK in 1948. The organisation strove to track down rightful owners and organised three claim exhibitions in 1949 and 1950 for those who missed artworks. To be eligible for restitution, it had to be confirmed that the applicant was the original owner or his heir; involuntary loss of possession had to have occurred, and any amount received had to be repaid. Another condition was the payment of the expenses for the recovery and management of the required object. This fee was set at 2.75 per cent of the artwork's appraised value. The claim exhibitions were regarded by the Dutch authorities as the last opportunity for rightful owners to apply for the return of artworks.

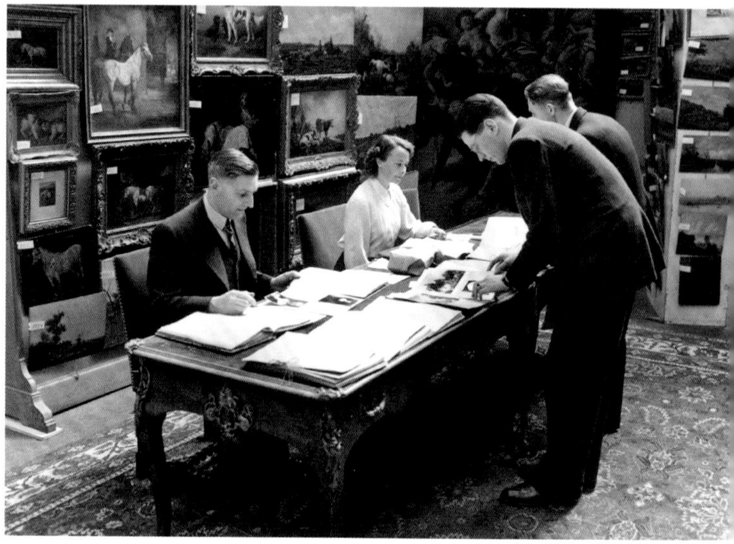

Members of the SNK staff during the claim exhibition of paintings, drawings and tapestries at the Rijksmuseum in Amsterdam, 20 April-9 June 1950

first of these was held in The Hague in 1949. The following two exhibitions took place in the Rijksmuseum in Amsterdam in 1950. Works of art that were not identified at the claim exhibitions could then, according to SNK management, be considered as 'not eligible for restitution of rights, therefore available to the State'. In practice, however, those who requested the restitution of works of art were often confronte with major difficulties. Proving former ownership could be particularly difficult. In many cases owners of Jewish descent had been robbed of all their possessions and were unable to produce any written evidence. Jolles was of the opinion that leniency was appropriate: 'It is often not possible to provide legally valid proof of ownership and/or duress. In practice, it will therefore be necessary to not set requirements that are to stringent.' Many claims were nevertheless rejected, primarily i cases concerning furniture and decorative arts objects, where one artwork was identified and claimed by multiple claimants, for example. The SNK files contain poignant examples of correspondence about such rejections.

The vast majority of claimants stated that they lost the claimed objects through confiscation, looting or theft, for instance because their home had been plundered on the orders of the occupying forces. In many cases, they did not need to produce further evidence. More information was asked of the much smaller group of claimants who declared that their loss of possession had been through an involuntary sale. Recurrent themes in the relevant SNK files are the compensation received during the war and the question to what extent the transaction had involved duress. Few claims were rejected on the grounds of doubt about the forced nature of the sale. It has become clear, however, that policy on the criterion of duress was not always consistent.

Numerous original owners accepted their loss of possession because they were unwilling or unable to pay the sum they received as a compensation during the war. Some people were simply unable to come up with the required amount because they were left destitute by the war. In a few cases, the problems were caused by the collapse of the art market after the war, when the financial value of many artworks plunged.

The SNK tried to settle as many claims as possible without judicial intervention. One case that was put before the restoration of rights court, however, was the restitution application submitted by the Gutmann heirs. In this case the SNK doubted whether there had been involuntary loss of possession. The court ruled in favour of the Gutmann heirs and opened the door to restitution of the artworks concerned.

Something had to be done with the art stock that remained because no claim had yet been submitted. The ministries responsible disagreed about which interests should have the greatest weight – those of the Dutch treasury or those of the public art stock. The Ministry of Finance wanted a massive sale of the recovered art. The Ministry of Education, Arts and Science (OK&W) and the SNK were opposed to the idea. A compromise solution emerged. The stock was to be split between a part that would remain and a part that would be sold.

THE TASK HANDOVER TO HERGO, 1950

From the disarray he observed at the SNK, Jolles concluded that the Management Board was not up to its task. He denoted a 'complete lack of understanding of the government tasks assigned to the foundation'. In 1949 it was decided that the Bureau of Reparation Payments and Recoveries (HERGO) should take over the responsibilities of the SNK. In response, five of the seven board members, including chair Röell, stepped down. The handover to HERGO was finalised in 1950. After that, the SNK existed only in name until it was dissolved in 1951. HERGO set up an art department, with restitution as one of its tasks along with the liquidation of the artworks that were not eligible for restitution. The recovered objects that were of value to museums were transferred to the Ministry of OK&W. The other artworks were sold at auction between 1949 and 1953, with proceeds going to the Dutch treasury. These sales were conducted by various Dutch auction houses. A painful detail is that some of the sold works were confiscated Jewish possessions that had already been auctioned off during the war and now these objects were used once more as a source for profit for others. The lists of the sold recovered objects show great variety. In addition to the large numbers of everyday items and curiosities, artworks from well-known collections, such as those of Goudstikker, Lanz and Mannheimer, also went under the hammer. As a rule, the artistic quality of the objects was low but some works were acquired by museums during the sales or later on. There was an unknown amount of looted art among the cultural items that were sold. For instance, several of the object's inventory cards feature indicative terms such as 'Jewish property Amsterdam', 'Unknown confiscated by Mühlmann Agency (Dienststelle Mühlmann)' and 'Unknown appropriated by Lippmann'. The sale results for many of the works were terribly disappointing. This was not only caused by the sharp drop in art prices after the war but also by the fact that the State sold the objects without a reserve price. Furthermore, there were cases in which original owners chose to buy back their lost objects at auction instead of submitting a restitution application to the SNK. This could be less costly for them since an acquisition at a public sale did not entail reimbursement expenses, and the payment of any compensation received during the war was not necessary.

The HERGO organisation was dissolved on 1 February 1953. Its tasks were transferred to the Ministry of Finance's Administration Directorate (Directie Bewindvoering). Meanwhile, the stock of recovered art had been largely liquidated, so that handling claims became the primary remaining task. Restitution applications were still submitted on an incidental basis.

Jolles was of the opinion that 'the primary task of the Netherlands Art Property Foundation and later of the Bureau [HERGO] was to realise an amicable restoration of rights'. It is difficult to calculate how often these two organisations succeeded in this task. An indication is offered by the internal declaration forms and inventory cards, which recorded the restitution of, among other objects, hundreds of paintings, many hundreds of decorative art objects, many hundreds of crates filled with libraries, archives, books and so on. The future digitisation of these and other sources can offer a clearer picture of what was returned to the rightful owners or heirs and what was sold for the benefit of the Dutch treasury.

The key motives behind the recovery of art objects to the Netherlands were the concerns regarding the cultural bloodletting of the devastated country as well as the desire to employ the returned art treasures for the benefit of the national cultural heritage and to restore the morale of the Dutch people. The recovered artworks represented a golden opportunity to give the general public access to a large number of objects and to form a national collection of art. Another driving factor, which was equally focused on the national interest, was based on the monetary value of the recovered objects. If the art stock was sold, it would generate many million guilders, which could supplement the decrepit Dutch treasury.

During the years immediately after the war, the interests of the individual bereft citizens appeared to have been almost an afterthought. As the pile of artworks rose higher and higher in the SNK's depots, the task of restitution to the original owners or their heirs was neglected. For them, the emotional significance of the recovered art treasures was far greater than their monetary and artistic value. For example, one applicant described a painting that he hoped to have returned to him as '...a memory from a beautiful past, a painting that was also loved by people who were dear to me, whose lives were snuffed out by the hand of tyrants. Not material considerations, but rather purely spiritual motives make the painting desirable to me' ('eine Erinnerung aus einer schönen Vergangenheit, ein Bild, das mit mir Menschen liebten, die mir lieb und teuer waren, deren Leben die Hand des Tyrannen ausgelöscht hat. Nicht materielle Erwägungen, sondern rein seelische Motive sind es, die mir das Bild begehrenswert machen').

After a slow start, the restitution process received great stimulus following a drastic reorganisation of the SNK in 1948. With a new director in function, the foundation actively strove to track down owners. These efforts included organising three exhibitions in The Hague and Amsterdam for people who had lost possession of art. Possible restitution required establishing the ownership and the involuntary loss of possession of the claimant. Any compensation received for the artwork was to be paid and costs for the procedure had to be reimbursed. These requirements could obviously form an insurmountable obstacle for war victims who had lost everything.

Despite the SNK's restrictive restitution policy, thousands of works were returned to the original owners or their heirs after World War II. In the early 1950s, the Dutch government decided that the task was fulfilled and the SNK was dissolved. However, something had to be done with the remaining stock, which amounted to thousands of objects. Works that were deemed less important were sold off. The remaining items were transferred into the custody of the Ministry of Education, Arts and Sciences so that they could be loaned to museums or used to adorn the interiors of public buildings. This large number of objects became the present Netherlands Art Property Collection (Nederlands Kunstbezit-collectie, NK Collection). Currently the collection contains over 4,000 artworks.

38

Girl in a Red Dress, 1913
JAN SLUIJTERS (1881-1957)
Canvas, 106 x 85 cm,
Collection Stichting Hannema-de Stuers,
Museum De Fundatie, Zwolle/Heino

This children's portrait by Jan Sluijters was the property of the Amsterdam art dealer Jacques Goudstikker. The work was left behind when Goudstikker attempted to flee from the Netherlands in May 1940 and was found in one of the Goudstikker-Miedl firm's business premises after the war. It was returned to the Goudstikker gallery in 1949. The portrait was acquired by former Boymans Museum director Dirk Hannema in 1962 on behalf of the Hannema-De Stuers Foundation, which later became Museum De Fundatie.

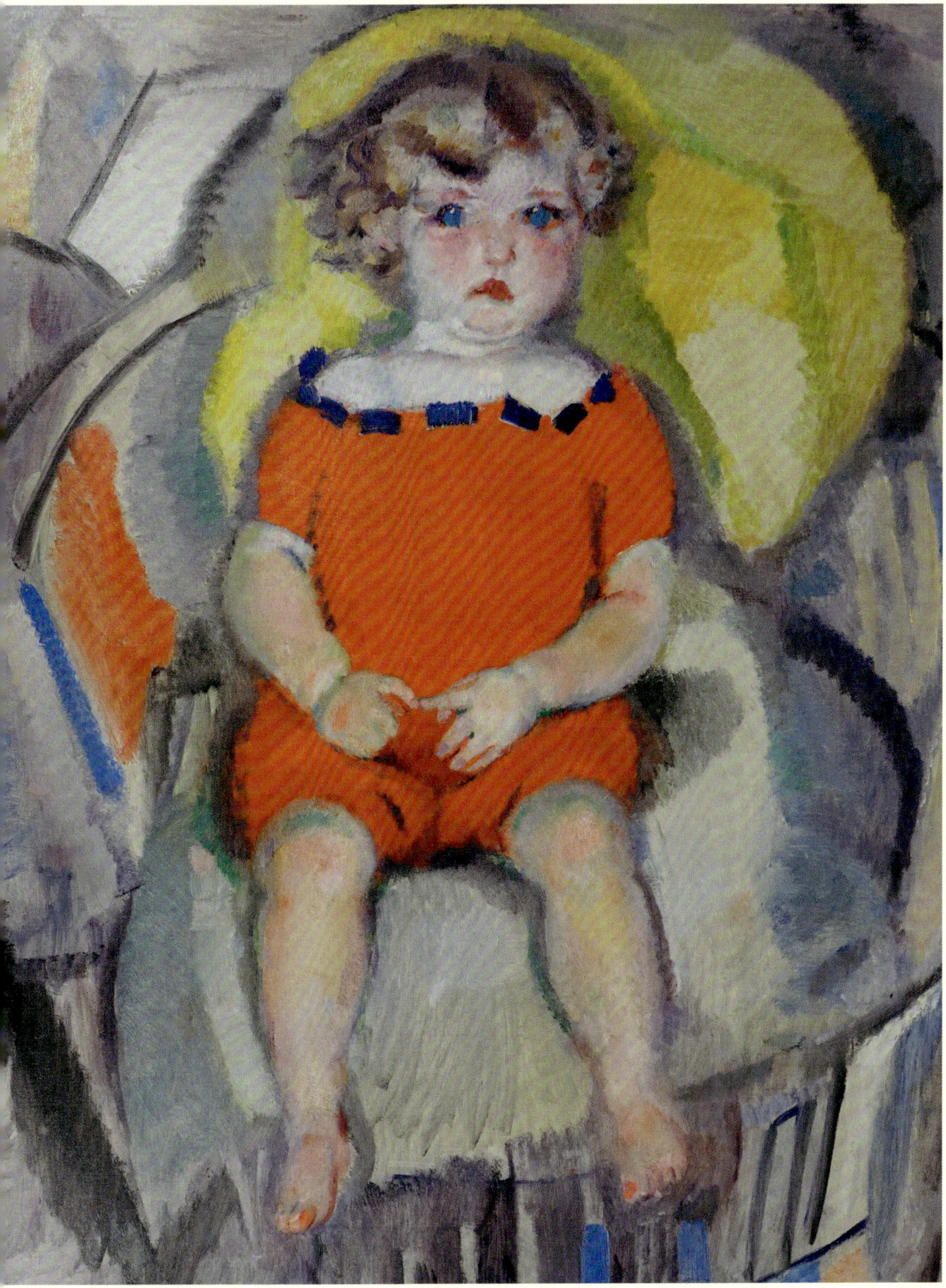

39

Portraits of Willem Everwijn and Johanna Kelffken, 1653
GERARD TER BORCH (1617-1681)
Panels, 28.5 x 22 cm each, Brantsen van de Zyp Stichting, Arnhem

---

These two portraits were the property of entrepreneur and art collector Arthur Hartog (1891-1986), of Jewish descent. Hartog was director of N.V.H. Hartog's Fabrieken, which merged with a predecessor of Unilever in 1930. He lived with his family on the Backershagen estate in Wassenaar, but had already left the Netherlands before the German invasion. During the occupation, the two paintings were confiscated as enemy assets and added to the collection for the Führermuseum in Linz. After the liberation, the two works were recovered in the first art transport to the Netherlands on 8 October 1945. In 1948, they were officially returned to Hartog, along with several other paintings from his collection. Through time, they eventually ended up in a private Dutch collection. In 2010, the effigies were gifted to the Geldersch Landschap en Kasteelen Foundation. There they were reunited with the collection of Gelderland portraits of the Brantsen family, to which they had belonged in the past. The companion pieces are now kept at Huis Zypendaal in Arnhem.

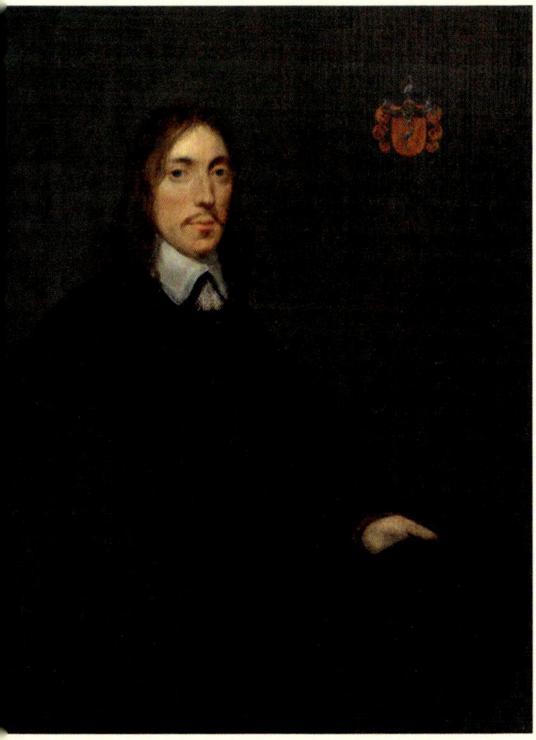

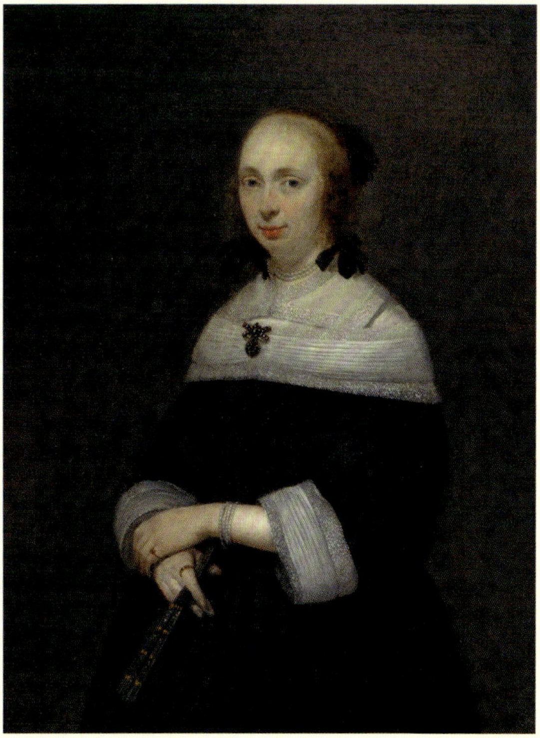

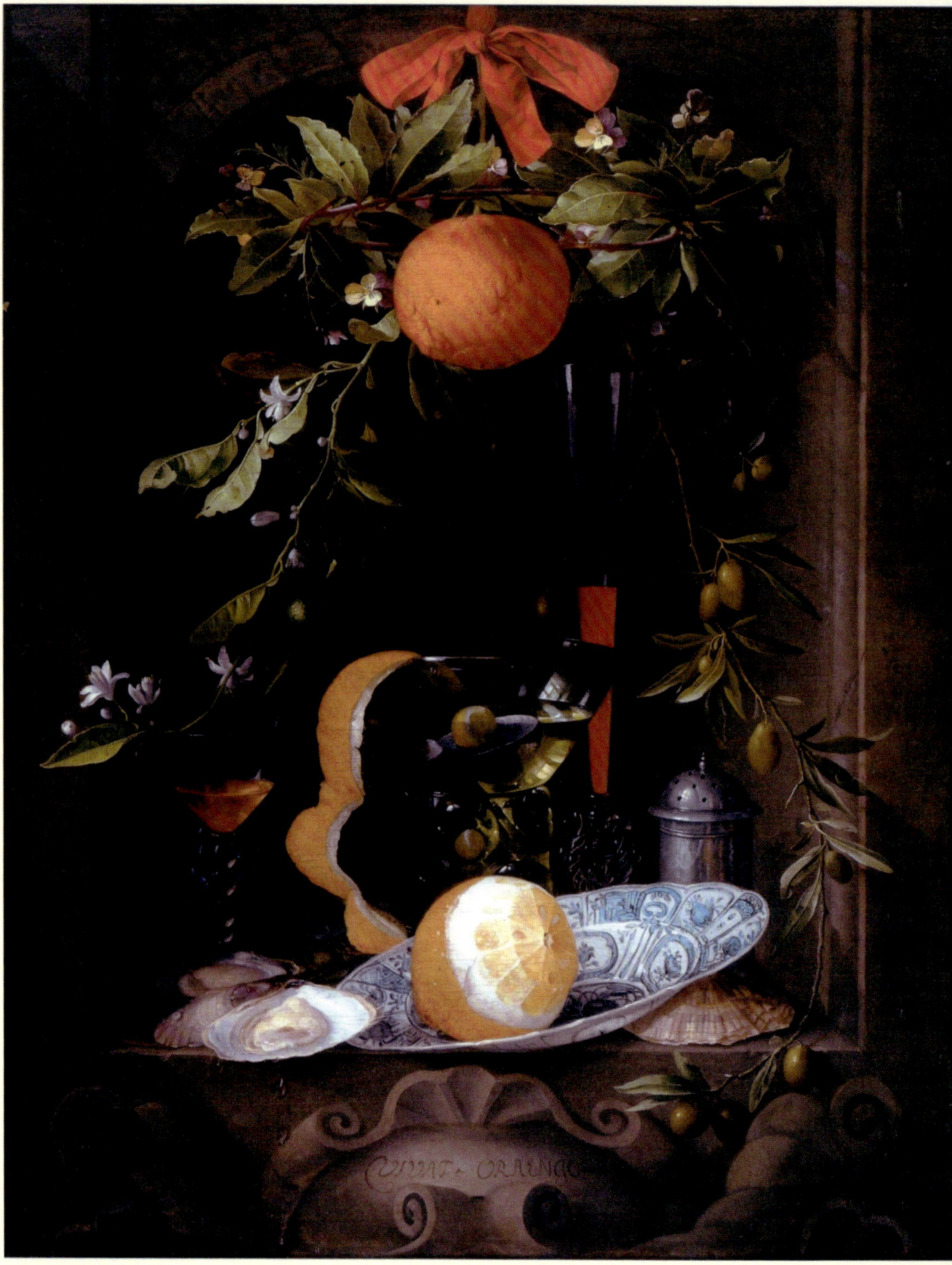

40
Vivat Oraenge, c. 1670
JAN DAVIDSZ. DE HEEM
(1606-1683/1684)
Canvas, 63 x 49 cm, National Museum Paleis het Loo, Apeldoorn

In 1941, the Jewish collector Alfred Cohen managed to obtain an exit visa from the Netherlands for himself and his family in return for the surrender of a collection of 16 paintings from his estate. One of those artworks was this still life by Jan Davidsz. de Heem, which Cohen had acquired a few years earlier from the Katz gallery in Dieren. In 1946-1947, the work was the subject of heated discussions between the SNK, the Council for the Restoration of Rights and its Administrative Department (NBI) over whether the 1941 surrender should indeed be considered an involuntary transaction, as the SNK assumed. Eventually, this painting and a numerous other recovered works were returned to Cohen. In 2005, De Heem's still life was later presented to the National Museum Paleis het Loo on the occasion of Queen Beatrix's silver jubilee.

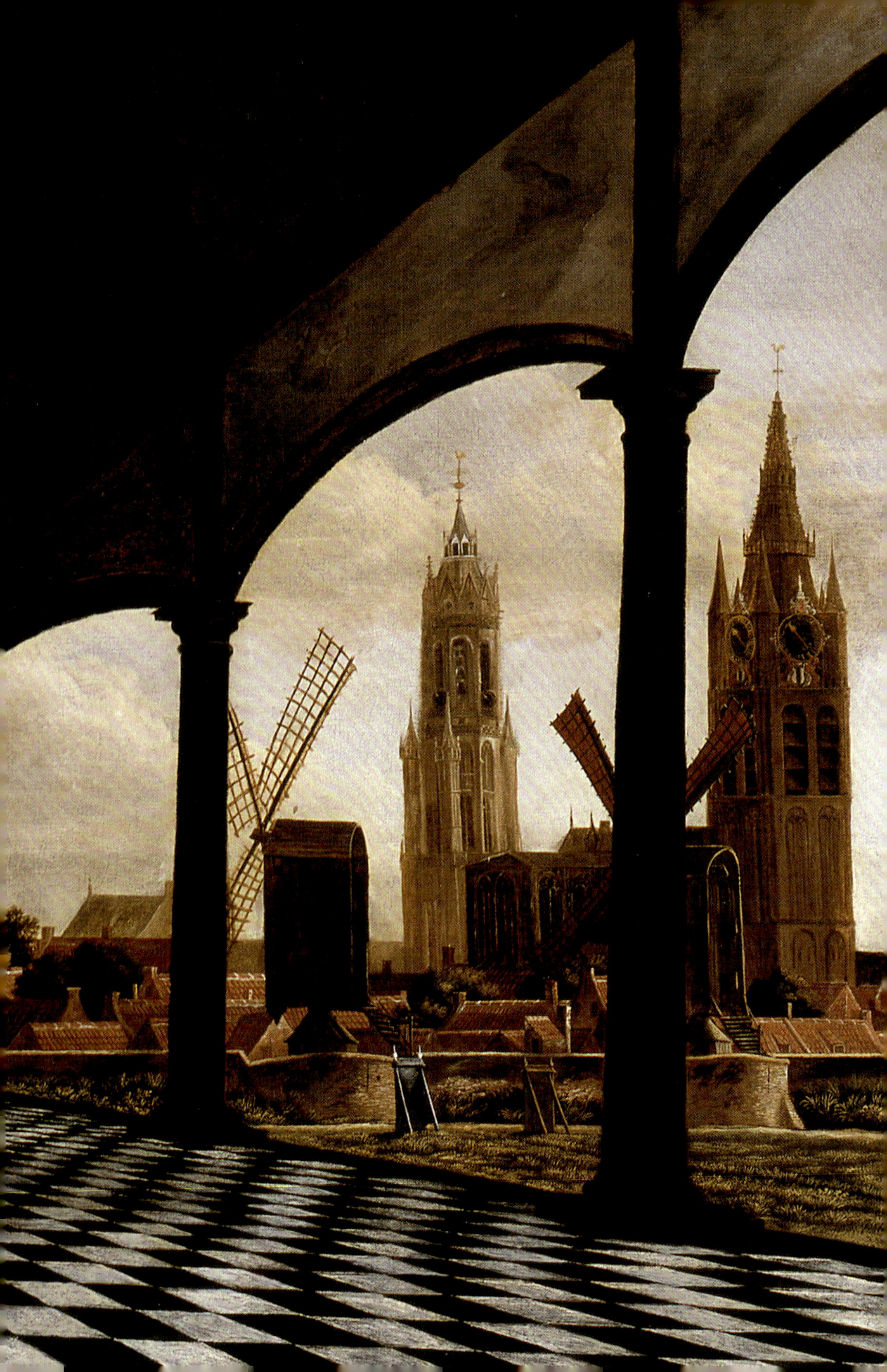

VII A NEW RESTITUTION POLICY

After the termination of the SNK (Stichting Nederlands Kunstbezit), a core collection of remaining artworks were transferred to the Ministry of Education, Arts and Sciences and objects of low interest were sold off at auction. Subsequently, it became fairly quiet on the front of restitution for many years. Several further restitutions were realised in the first years after 1951, including, for example, 59 works of art returned to the heirs of the collector Fritz Gutmann. Occasionally, a few more requests for restitution trickled in. However, the knowledge by the receiving end of how to deal with them became increasingly scarce, making the results of claims rather erratic. The oblivion into which the provenance details of the NK Collection had fallen becomes clear when we consider that, despite all of the publicity surrounding Pieter Menten and his art collection in 1976 and subsequent years, no attention was paid to the fact that the NK Collection included artworks belonged to Menten and his brother. Occasional publicity did rear its head regarding various old cases, such as in 1990 when Ageeth Scherphuis wrote an extensive article for the weekly *Vrij Nederland* on the elderly widow of art dealer Jacques Goudstikker, Dési Goudstikker. After her death in 1996 and the decease of her son Eduard von Saher later that year, the Goudstikker case was reopened by Eduard's widow Marei von Saher and her two daughters. The three women formally laid claim on the original trading stock of the art dealership's artworks, which were still kept by the state. After this claim was rejected by State Secretary Nuis in 1997, Marei von Saher turned to the Dutch courts. The Hague Court of Appeal ruled in December 1999 that it did not have jurisdiction, thus preventing a substantive ruling. Meanwhile, in the preceding years, the press had been giving worldwide attention to Jewish war victims and, especially, to the various material and immaterial consequences of World War II for them. Reports about Jewish gold assets kept in Swiss banks played a central role here. Within this context, newspaper articles were also published reporting about Dutch museums keeping numerous artworks that had been looted during the war. In particular, the article by Lucette ter Borg (*Overheid bezit grote collectie oorlogskunst*; 'Government owns large collection of looted art'), published in the *Volkskrant* on 23 May 1997, caused concern and led to questions in the Lower House to the then State Secretary of Culture, Aad Nuis. The words 'large collection of looted art', referred to the so-called NK Collection, which was under the management of the ICN (Netherlands Institute of Cultural Heritage) and the former state museums. In his first reply to these parliamentary questions, the state secretary stated that he intended to commission an investigation into the provenance of the art brought back to the Netherlands after World War II. Immediate steps were taken to examine how such an investigation should be conducted.

SAMPLE RESEARCH IN A PILOT STUDY

On 2 October 1997, State Secretary Nuis informed the Lower House that he had just commissioned a pilot study into the provenance of the so-called NK Collection. The analysis, which was to be completed within a few months, was to be carried out by the Netherlands Institute of Cultural Heritage, together with the Cultural Property Inspectorate. The responsibility would lie with a seven-person supervisory committee, which was to include two employees of the Ministry of OCW, the director of the Netherlands Institute for Cultural Heritage, the head of the Cultural Property Inspectorate, two representatives of the Jewish community in the Netherlands and an independent chairman. This first Ekkart Committee was given three main questions to consider. First, which objects from the NK Collection lack any information about their former owners in the available collection documentation? The second issue focused on whether it was possible to find more data about original owners with the help of additional sources. In particular, the commission was referred to the Rijksbureau voor Kunsthistorische Documentatie (RKD), the Rijksinstituut voor Oorlogsdocumentatie (RIOD) and the archives of the above-mentioned SNK for such sources. The third task for the committee, partly based on the results of the two previous topics, was to answer the question of whether further research would be necessary. A sample case was formed using 113 artworks from the collection. As it had been evident from the start that the possibilities for further provenance research could vary by the type of the object, it was agreed to divide the total collection into four categories (paintings and drawings; prints and reproductions; ceramics; other applied arts) and to select a proportional sample from these four groups. On the first of November 1997, the project group commenced with the study and the report was completed in April 1998. This report and the government's decision to implement its recommendations were published on

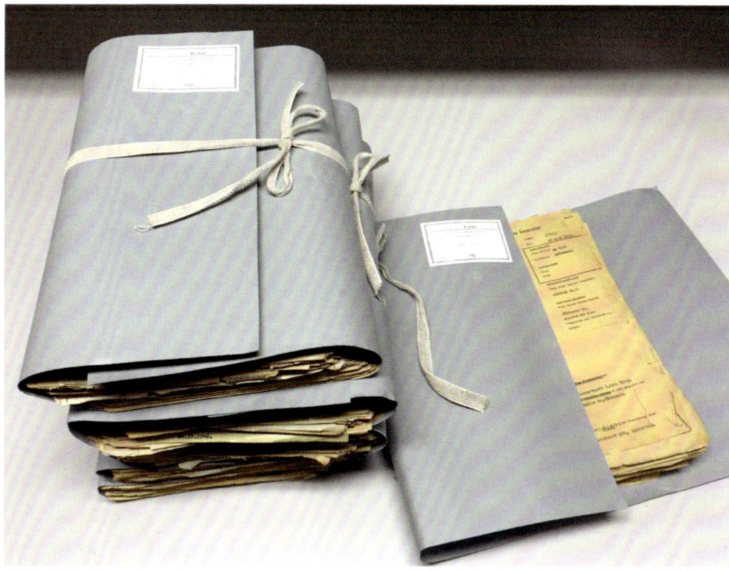

The report of the pilot study on works of art from the NK Collection, April 1998

In October of 1997, State Secretary Nuis commissioned a pilot study of the provenance of works of art in the so-called NK Collection. The report stated in April 1998 that an extensive investigation into the provenance of the entire collection was necessary and that a new restitution policy needed to be developed. These recommendations were subsequently adopted by the Dutch government.

Files from the SNK documentation at The National Archives in The Hague

The SNK archive forms an essential source for research into the NK Collection. Its files register which works of art were signalised the SNK after the war, which objects were returned from abroad to the Netherlands and the later history of the recovered art. The archive also holds a large number of declaration forms for works of art that are still missing today.

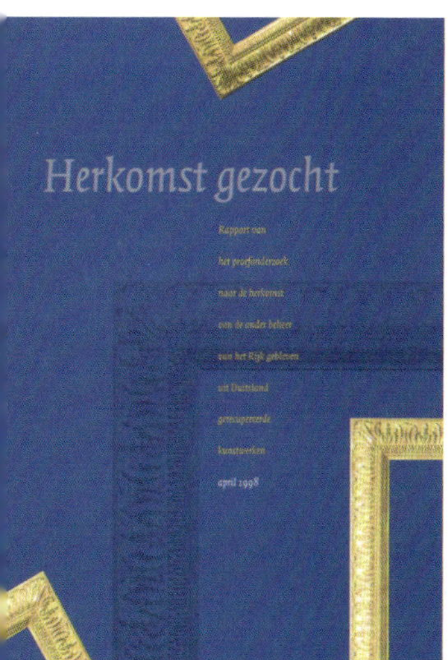

18 May. The committee concluded that the information at hand regarding the provenance of the NK Collection was entirely inadequate, that far more provenance information could be retrieved through research, especially for individual objects with a unique recognisability, and that further research was urgently needed. Based on these conclusions, the committee recommended a systematic examination of the SNK archives for all NK objects, and to extend research to other sources on the basis of the information assembled. If indications of previously unidentified third-party rights to works from the NK Collection were to emerge, active follow-up research should be carried out and, if necessary, the rights-holders traced. In terms of the implementation of the tasks at hand, it was recommended that a project agency be established at the Cultural Heritage Inspectorate. Additionally, a supervisory

File cabinets with provenance research results at the Origins Unknown Agency

For the benefit of the provenance research, a separate analogue file was created for each work of art in the NK Collection. All relevant data on that particular work was assembled in the file folder. The conclusions for the data collected in these folders were processed in a database, which formed the basis for the editions of the reports as well as for the Origins Unknown website. Since then, the folders are kept in archive boxes, which, depending on the quantity of documents per inventory number, each contain about ten to twenty file folders.

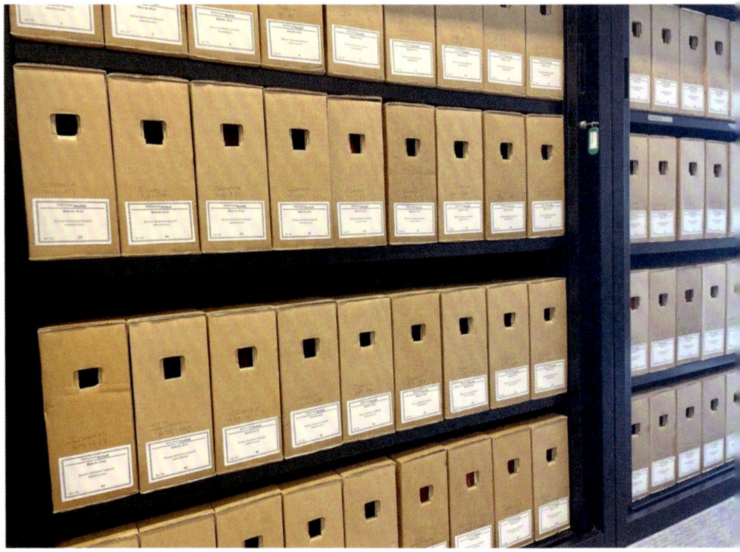

committee was to be appointed to oversee the study and also provide advice on the basis of the study results. With the full acceptance of the recommendations, the Netherlands took a leading role in the international developments of restitution policy. It was not until 3 December 1998 that a large number of countries at an international conference in Washington agreed on active policies regarding Jewish losses during the Nazi period. Moreover, what had already been mobilized in the Netherlands at that time and what was further developed in subsequent years went beyond the obligations set out in the Washington Principles.

THE TASKS OF THE ORIGINS UNKNOWN AGENCY

Preparations for the extensive investigation of the NK Collection were taken up swiftly. As early as 3 September 1998, the kick-off meeting was held for the project team, which initially consisted of six employees and the head of the Cultural Heritage Inspectorate. The chairman of the first Ekkart Committee acted as a replacement for the as yet unappointed new supervisory committee. A new committee had not yet been appointed due to the change of government that summer. Outgoing State Secretary Aad Nuis preferred to leave the project to his successor of the new cabinet, which would not be sworn in until August of 1998. Apart from the supervision of the study's implementation, the new committee would also have the task of drafting up proposals for a new restitution policy. The culture portfolio had in the meantime been taken over by State Secretary Rick van der Ploeg, who was actively involved with the progress of the project in the following years

The research undertakings of the Origins Unknown Agency proved more time-consuming than originally estimated and, during the years after 1998, the team grew to a maximum of twelve employees in 2002. The first interim report with results was published in October 1999 and the sixth and last one was presented in September 2004. These results were also available on the internet from April 2001. By now, the dividing up of the compiled inventory numbers had revealed that the total number of individual NK objects was circa 4,800. The second task assigned to the project office – historical research into the SNK and the restitution of looted art after 1945 – was also taken up. This specific task was carried out by two staff members of the Origins Unknown Agency, Eelke Muller and Helen Schretlen, and led to the book *Betwist Bezit*. This 2002 publication has in the meantime become a widely consulted handbook on Dutch recovery and restitution. Shortly after publishing, an exhibition of artworks from the NK Collection was organised in collaboration with the Fries Museum in Leeuwarden. This exhibition was on view from February to

'açade advertisement for the xhibition *Origins Unknown* 'Herkomst Gezocht') at the Fries Auseum in Leeuwarden, 2003

he exhibition *Origins Unknown* was joint project of the Fries Museum nd the Origins Unknown Agency. A election from the NK Collection was isplayed, highlighting the significance f this collection and illustrating the roblems of provenance research. The xhibition ran from 18 February to 31 ugust 2003 and drew much attention.

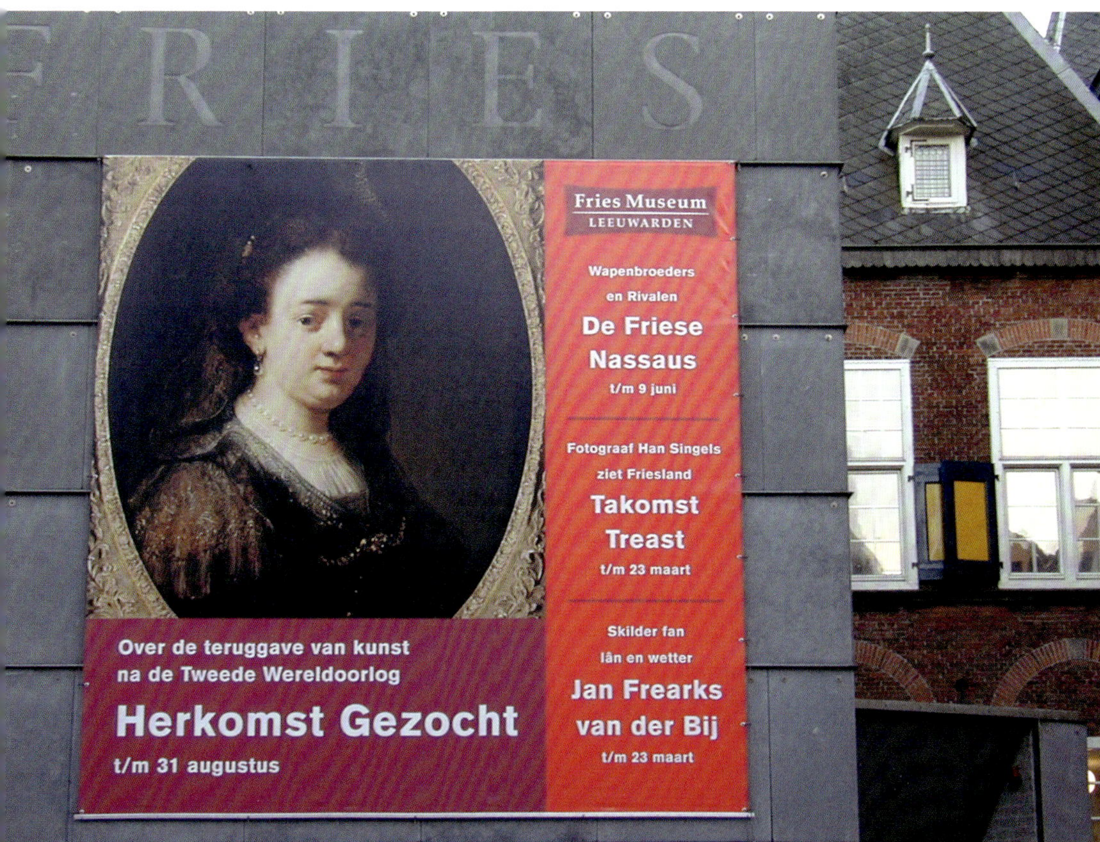

August 2003 and presented the issues of restitution for the benefit of a wider audience and also catalysed general interest in the subject.

THE RECOMMENDATIONS ON RESTITUTION POLICY

The Origins Unknown supervisory committee was also tasked with advising the government on a renewal of the restitution policy, making use of the research results. Due to the Origins Unknown Agency's slower progress, the realisation of a new restitution policy was in danger of being seriously delayed, which was considered highly undesirable. In 2000, in consultation with State Secretary Van der Ploeg, the decision was therefore made to advise on the new policy in three stages. The first stage would consist of advice on lost private property, a topic on which such an abundance of information had already been gathered in the first years of the study that there was a reasonable overview of the different types of problems at hand. A much more complex topic, for which more information was needed to be able to come to a responsible policy opinion, was the issue of voluntary and involuntary sales by the art trade. These problems were therefore postponed to the second set of recommendations. Conclusively, a third tranche, more or less coinciding with the completion of the research, was stipulated with final recommendations that addressed the remaining issues regarding restitution procedures. This phasing guaranteed that a new policy could fully benefit from the study of the mistakes made in the restitution policy of the first post-war period. Moreover, the instalment of a new policy would not be delayed any longer than strictly necessary. The first set of recommendations, which dealt with private art property, was presented to the State Secretary on 26 April 2001. Based on the study, it was concluded that post-war restitution policy should generally be characterised as 'formalistic, bureaucratic, cold and frequently even heartless'. The new policy recommendations advocated limiting the term 'settled cases' to those cases in which a decision by the court had been issued in the past or in which a settlement had been achieved between the interested parties and the Council for the Restoration of Rights or the Netherlands Property Management Institute and signed by both parties. Decisions reached by or settlements with the SNK did not qualify as settled cases. Further recommendations mainly concerned a more elaborate definition of the terms 'voluntary sale' and 'involuntary sale.' Sales by Jewish private owners in the Netherlands between 10 May 1940 and the end of the war were to be considered involuntary unless the contrary could be proven. The same had to apply to sales by

Jewish private individuals in Germany from 1933 and in Austria from 1938. A reversal of the burden of proof was therefore suggested here. It was further advised that, in the absence of hard evidence regarding the right of ownership, a high degree of probability should suffice. The repayment of sales proceeds could only be brought into the case if the seller or his heirs had actually received those proceeds at their own free disposal. On 29 June 2001, the State Secretary informed the Lower House that the government intended to follow the committee's proposals and that a detailed response would follow about a few details. It was also announced that a committee would be established to advise the government on the submitted individual restitution claims. After intensive discussions with the various ministries involved (OCW, Finance, Justice and Foreign Affairs), the state advocate and the chairman of the Origins Unknown Committee, the conclusions were sent to the Lower House on 16 November 2001. On the same day, a decree was published establishing the Advisory Committee on the Assessment of Restitution Applications for Items of Cultural Value and the Second World War. This committee took up its duties on 1 January 2002. It was initially known, after its first chairman, as the Polak Committee and was later more generally referred to as the Restitutions Committee. Before discussing the further consequences of the new restitution policy and the responsibilities of the Restitutions Committee, it is appropriate to first discuss the further recommendations for policy.

After completing the first set of recommendations, the committee proceeded to formulate the recommendations concerning the art trade. To allow the cabinet to form a binding opinion, the State Secretary agreed that this second set of recommendations would be presented before the elections of May 2002, after which the sitting cabinet would only have a de-missionary capacity until a new cabinet was formed. Unfortunately, this intention was made impossible by the fall of the Kok II cabinet in mid-April, a few days before the recommendations were to be formally presented. After the formation of the new Balkenende I cabinet, several months passed before a meeting with the new state secretary could take place. Before this planned appointment, however, that cabinet also fell. The recommendations were nevertheless presented to outgoing State Secretary Cees van Leeuwen on 28 January 2003, nine months later than originally proposed. It was not until December 2003 that his successor Medy van der Laan was able to inform the Lower House that the government was willing to completely adopt the recommendations. This government decision was 18 months later than originally planned. The general tenor regarding this series of recommendations was that the same criteria should also apply to the art trade as to private parties but that sales by art dealer during the occupation could not automatically be categorised as forced. With the first two sets of recommendations adapted into a formal government policy, a framework had been shaped for an extended restitution policy, which had already led to first tangible results in 2002 and 2003 thanks to the efforts of the Restitutions Committee. The Origins Unknown Committee was left with the task of proposing several more general recommendations based on their conducted research. Those recommendations still had the illusion that the flow of claims would quickly dry up and that the expanded policy would therefore only need to have a limited duration. This limitation on the validity of the extended policy was later reversed in 2012. The final recommendations also focused on the question of how to deal with those works of art that could no longer be restituted to their rightful owners, either because the heirs of the former owner could not be traced or because the relevant artworks had been sold at auction in the early 1950s. It was recommended that a calculated countervalue be made available for general Jewish cultural purposes. To this end, it would be prudent to appraise the objects kept in the NK Collection that definitely or most probably could be characterised as looted, confiscated or sold under force and for which no rightful claimants could be found. The equivalent value should then be donated to a Jewish cultural cause. An indexed percentage of the auction proceeds of SNK objects sold off in the 1950s should also be made available for a Jewish cultural purpose. On 14 December 2004, these final recommendations were formally submitted together with a final report by the committee. In a letter to the Lower House on 8 March 2005, the state secretary reported that the government would also adopt the tenor of these recommendations and make the sums available for the Jewish community. This brought an end to the tasks of the Origins Unknown Monitoring Committee, informally referred to as the Ekkart Committee. As of 31 December 2004, the project agency was reduced to two employees to deal with the general current affairs. In November 2005 an additional employee was temporarily hired for in-depth research. This assignment aimed at actively tracing rightful claimants who had not yet come forward themselves. In a few cases, objects certainly or probably were Jewish property but the name of the original owner had yet to be traced. There were also many cases in which the name of the original owner was clear but the heirs of that original owner had not yet been identified or

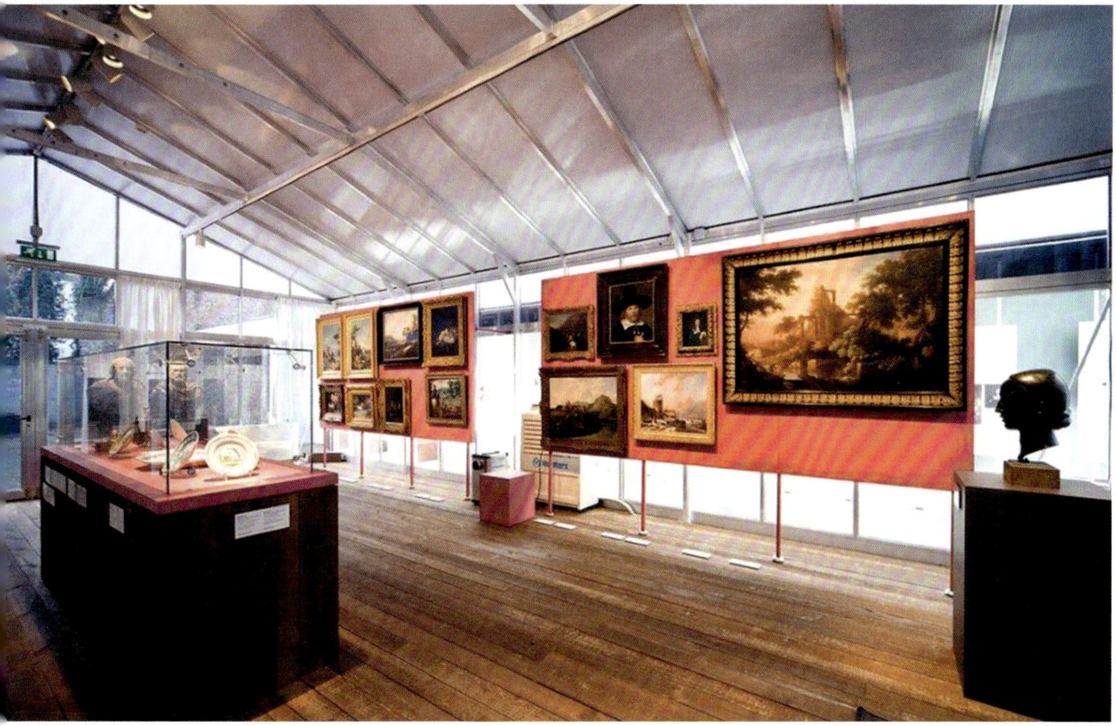

'he exhibition *Looted, but from vhom?* at the Hollandsche ;chouwburg, 2007

n the exhibition *Looted, but from vhom?*, a selection of circa fifty ırtworks from the NK Collection vas on view at the Hollandsche ›chouwburg in Amsterdam from 30 November 2006 to 25 February 2007. All of the pieces on display ›robably had a history of looting, onfiscation or forced sale from ewish property for which the heirs of ıe original owner had not yet been raced. It was partly thanks to this exhibition that several puzzles were olved, which lead to the localisation of the rightful owners of some objects.

located. Within this context, another exhibition was organised, this time in cooperation with the Jewish Historical Museum, at the Hollandsche Schouwburg in Amsterdam. Headed by the title *Geroofd, maar van wie?* (*Looted, but from whom?*) from 30 November 2006 to 25 February 2007, fifty works from the NK Collection were put on view. For all of these works, there were indications for looting, confiscation or forced sale from Jewish property. However, heirs of the original owner still had to be traced (fig. 41-44). The in-depth research and exhibition enabled a series of seemingly insoluble puzzles to be solved, and names and contact details of rightful owners scattered all over the world were dug up. This led to a series of claims that were submitted by the Ministry of Education, Culture and Science to the Restitutions Committee for advice.

THE PROJECT MUSEUM ACQUISITIONS 1940-1948

During the pilot study into the NK Collection, the Dutch museums initiated a second enquiry into their own collections. In March 1998, at the invitation of the Rijksmuseum's chief director, a meeting of museum directors took place in Amsterdam to discuss research into problematic acquisitions by Dutch museums during World War II. The Netherlands Museums Association ('Nederlandse Museumvereniging') was asked to play a fundamental role in the organisation of such a

Carel van Lier (1897-1945) with an *Oliphant* (hunting horn made from elephant ivory), c. 1932-1935
Erwin Blumenfeld (1897-1969)
Photograph, 30.3 x 24 cm,
Stedelijk Museum, Amsterdam
© The Estate of Erwin Blumenfeld

The art gallery Van Lier was a sole proprietorship established in 1927 by Carel van Lier at the Rokin in Amsterdam. It was a renowned centre of modern art and ethnography in the 1930s. During the war, Van Lier was initially given some protection from the persecution of Jews thanks to his marriage to a non-Jewish woman. However, his art gallery was forcedly placed under the administration of the Nazi authorities in 1942. In 1943, Van Lier was arrested by the Germans for his role in the resistance. He died in the Mühlenberg concentration camp in Germany in March 1945.
Carel van Lier had sold this hunting horn to the Frankfurt am Main Ethnographic Museum in 1941. After the war, the horn was returned to the Netherlands from Germany. There are no indications that the Dutch recovery authorities contacted Van Lier's heirs at the time. In 2007, one of Van Lier's grandsons submitted a claim for the hunting horn, after which it was returned to the Van Lier heirs following the advice of the Restitutions Committee. There were enough indications that the horn had not belonged to the gallery's trading stock but to Van Lier's private collection. The committee therefore assessed the claim according to the more lenient standards for private art ownership. According to these more compassionate criteria, sales conducted by Jewish private individuals in the Netherlands from 10 May 1940 were considered involuntary as a principle.

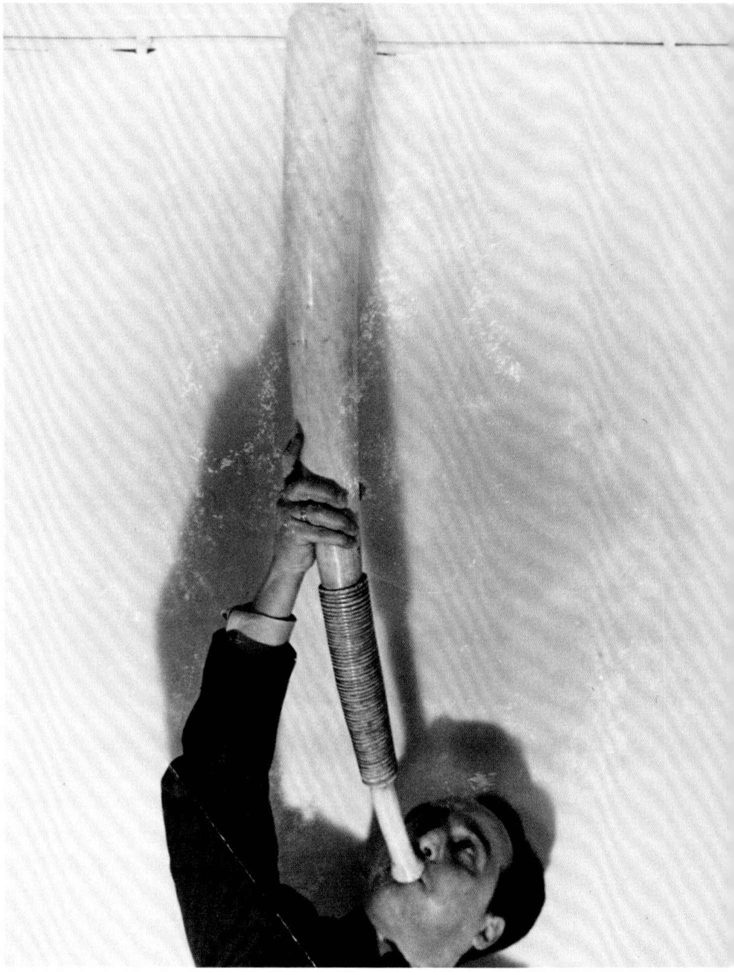

study. All eligible museums were to conduct their own research into their acquisitions during the war years and the first three years after the war, should the acquisitions have been added to the inventory after 1945. Special attention was to given to be to pre-war Jewish loans and museum acquisitions that had been brought into museums during the occupation in order to protect the property of Jewish owners against measures taken by the occupying forces, and which had not been returned to their original owners or their heirs after the war. Also to be considered were the conventional museum acquisitions from the years 1940-1948 with possible suspicious backgrounds. The results of the independent research were to be assembled and analysed by the Museum Acquisitions Committee. Funded by the Ministry of Education, Culture and Science, this committee would be supported by a researcher. The results of the project were published in December 1999 in the Report on Museum Acquisitions 1940-1948, which presented the submissions from all members of the Netherlands Museums Association. Numerous museums responded that the research at hand had not been applicable to them because of establishment after the war but other museums indicated to have found a quantity of pieces with a potentially problematic provenance history.

THE PROJECT MUSEUM ACQUISITIONS FROM 1933 ONWARDS

After completing the research into museum acquisitions from 1940-1948, it was determined that an extension of the research for the entire period from 1933 (the start of the Nazi regime in Germany) was highly desirable. After all, during the time before the occupation, museums could have unwittingly acquired objects that had previously been confiscated or forcibly sold in Germany. Moreover, in the years after 1948, Dutch museums had purchased countless artworks, some of which may have had a suspicious past. The realisation of a new study, however, would be postponed for a few years, partly because research into the NK Collection still required a great deal of attention. A new research project was initiated upon the conclusion of the in-depth research by the Origins Unknown Agency in 2007. As before, the Dutch Museum Association committed itself to providing the organisational framework and in 2008, the Ministry of Education, Culture and Science declared its willingness to subsidize a project agency to be housed at the Netherlands Museums Association and finance the publication of the research results. As was the case with the 1998-1999 study, the museums would be responsible for their own research. However, the size of the project office did take into account that space would be needed to advise and support museums in their own research. An advisory committee was also set up for this particular project. The study began in early 2009, with 162 museum participants, and eventually took five years to complete rather than the originally foreseen four. And, although the majority of the organisations involved had completed their research by the end of 2013, a small number of museums remained with unfinished work due to various circumstances. Special mention should be made of the Rijksmuseum in Amsterdam, which, due to the combination of a thorough ongoing investigation and the enormous number of acquisitions from the period following 1933, will need several more years before the tasks are fully completed.

All suspect or potentially suspicious objects were presented with a clarification on a new website, which also featured the museums' individual reports in summarized form. The website now lists more than 170 objects with a potentially problematic provenance, five of which have in the meantime been returned to their rightful owners or settled with the rightful owners (fig. 45). With the research into acquisitions from 1933 onwards, the Dutch museums have made optimal efforts to trace any looted art in their collections. Nevertheless, new data may still emerge, revealing that objects not signalled by previous systematic research were in fact involuntarily lost by their owners at an earlier stage. Studies in other countries have also shown that even the most scrupulous museum research into a collection's history cannot guarantee a complete and sound reconstruction of every object's provenance.

THE START OF THE RESTITUTIONS COMMITTEE

As already mentioned above, the Restitutions Committee (RC) was established on 22 December 2001 to advise the Minister of Education, Culture and Science on claims for the restitution of works of art from the NK Collection managed by the State and other museum objects belonging to the National Art Collection. Also, at the explicit request of the Lower House, it was made possible for the applicant and the owner of a non-state collection to jointly submit their case to the Restitutions Committee for a binding opinion. This was subject to the condition that all parties agree to implement the advice of the Restitutions Committee in advance. When the committee took office, the ministry had already received several claims for artworks from the NK Collection. In response, the staff of the Cultural Heritage Inspectorate had conducted preliminary investigations into these cases. This was to ensure that the seven-member committee would immediately be able to form an opinion based on the factual material already gathered. Naturally, these exclusively involved cases with losses by private individuals, as the policy on losses by art dealers had yet to be developed and established at the time. The first three recommendations were issued in March and April of 2002. Among them was one of the most extensive claims ever issued: almost 100 objects from Fritz Gutmann's former collection. In this case, the committee recommended granting the heirs' claim in full. The items returned to Gutmann's heirs included important museum artworks, especially objects of applied art (fig. 24). At a later juncture, a few more (minor) requests were submitted by the Gutmann claimants and partly awarded. In December 2003, after the government adopted the recommendations on restitution of artworks from the art trade, the Restitutions Committee also received claims in that area. The first of these regarded the Stodel gallery in Amsterdam, which had already been submitted to the ministry in 2002 but could not be sent to the Restitutions Committee until early 2004, shortly after the new policy was adopted. The latter came up with a recommendation for restitution of the 11 objects in April 2005. An overview of the RC's years makes clear that the committee could not keep up with demand during these first years. The heirs who submitted their claims on their own accord and those who acted as a result of the work of the Origins Unknown Agency created more work than could be realised with a careful working method. Among the completed cases from those early years, there was a clear majority of positive opinions, advocating the return of artworks to the claimants. But soon various negative opinions were given, in which the committee recommended to reject the claims. Some other advices took a differentiated view and recommended refunding some of the claimed pieces and to reject others. The latter was particularly prevalent at the time and also later for claims involving sales by art dealers. Here, after all, the established policy differentiated the question of voluntary or involuntary sale.

THE GOUDSTIKKER CASE

By far the most attention was given to the Goudstikker case. It triggered reactions from around the world, becoming front-page news internationally, and certainly constituted one of the most high-profile restitution cases of the early 21st century. After having had a request for restitution by State Secretary Aad Nuis in the 1990s, the Goudstikker heirs unsuccessfully attempted to win their case through the courts. They then waited for the new art trade policy to be adopted. In April 2004, the heirs filed their first official claim, one that was later slightly extended with a request for several more objects. The Restitutions Committee issued its advice on a total of 267 claimed artworks in late 2005, recommending the restitution for 202 of them (fig. 1-2; 46-48). According to the committee's advice, the other 65 pieces were not eligible for restitution, for various reasons including that several works had been consigned to Goudstikker by other parties, for example. In February of 2006, the Dutch government announced their decision for the restitution of 202 claimed objects. The argumentation for restitution was slightly modified for this case. This was due to the fact that the Minister of Justice feared that a decision that deviated from a previous court ruling could lead to an undesirable precedent. In the Netherlands, the restitution of such a large number of works was widely felt as a heavy loss for the national collection. Iconic paintings disappeared from nearly all of the leading museums in the Netherlands. For some institutions, such as the Maastricht Bonnefantenmuseum, housing a high number of loans from the NK Collection, it even felt like a demolition. Before the handing over of the artworks took place, the Goudstikker heirs and the Dutch state had already agreed on the repurchasing of a few paintings (fig. 2 and 46). As a token of their appreciation, the heirs also donated one work, the portrait of a young boy on his deathbed painted by Bartholomeus van der Helst in 1645 1645 (fig. 47). Later, when the heirs had to sell numerous restituted pieces to meet the high judicial costs, several Dutch museums purchased artworks back from the Goudstikker collection. These included the 1651 *View of Dordrecht* by Jan van Goyen, which returned to the Dordrechts Museum in 2008, partly with the help of a rigorous public campaign. In 2013, the Rijksmuseum acquired Jan Mostaert's *Landscape with an Episode from the Conquest of America* (fig. 48), painted around 1535.

Goudstikker's name was also on the Restitutions Committee's agenda several times after 2005. Relatively straightforward was the binding opinion issued in September 2013 on three paintings that had belonged to the art dealer's stock in May 1940 but had not been recovered from Germany until 2012. Naturally, this advice was also positive. Much more complicated was the issue of the canvas depicting the wedding night of Sarah and Tobias by Jan Steen, for which allocation to the Goudstikker heirs was advised in February 2006. In the distant past, this particular piece was separated from the other half of the original painting but had been reunited with the other section ten years in 1996. The complication was that this other section of the in the meantime reassembled painting had the status of inalienable property of the municipality of The Hague by virtue of Abraham Bredius' testamentary provisions. The Restitutions Committee's advice in October 2008 recommended for the Museum Bredius' piece to be sold to the Goudstikker heirs. However, this required the court's involvement to achieve a necessary dissolution of Bredius' testamentary provisions. It remained a seemingly insolvable problem until it was finally resolved in 2011 by the joint efforts and the financial support from various corners with the sale of the Goudstikker section to the municipality of the city of The Hague.

FURTHER DEVELOPMENTS IN THE WORK OF THE RESTITUTIONS COMMITTEE

In the first fifteen years since its establishment in 2002, the Restitutions Committee has presented approximately 145 recommendations, including a small number on re-submitted restitution requests by previously rejected claimants who hoped to have their case reopened with new arguments. This was usually in vain, but on a few occasions the Restitutions Committee was able to honour new arguments and (partially) amend an earlier advice. The majority of the cases handled still pertained to objects from the national art collection, and then almost always from its NK Collection. However, over the years the number of recommendations on works from other collections grew; these concerned the requests for binding opinions submitted by dual parties. The first of these cases were those regarding the claims made years earlier by the heirs of German collector Ernst Flersheim to two paintings by Jan Toorop in the museums in Middelburg and Rotterdam (fig. 49). In March and April 2008, the RC issued binding opinions that largely met the wishes of Flersheim's heirs. Later advice was also issued on objects that had emerged from the project Museum Acquisitions from 1933 Onwards.

Many of the claims submitted for artworks from the NK Collection involve one or just a few pieces. However, for claims by the heirs of Jewish art dealers, and certainly in the case of claims to objects of applied art, the numbers sometimes run to several dozen. Very extensive claims, apart from those of the Goudstikker and Gutmann heirs, were also those of the Koenigs and Katz heirs. All claims relating to Franz Koenigs' collection were rejected entirely and those for works originating from Kunsthandel Katz were almost entirely denied; the heirs were restituted just one painting. Only in an exceptional case does the RC apply the condition to a restitution that previously received capital for sold artworks should be returned. Such a condition accompanied the RC's 2009 advice to restitute twelve paintings to the heirs of the collector Hans Larsen, provided that the indexed funds from sales during the occupation (€325,000) and later made available to the family would be returned.

In the committee's early years, the majority of positive opinions, i.e. restitution of all or part of the works claimed, was very high. Gradually with time, however, the number of rejections increased. This was not due to a change in direction of the Restitutions Committee, but is probably mainly caused by the gradual change in the nature of the claims submitted and their prior history. During the first decade of the century, a high number of the handled cases derived directly from the

Origins Unknown Agency's efforts. Many claims specifically referred to the letters that had been sent from the agency to heirs of former owners with requests for more information and the following exchange of data. For the majority of the restitution applications made on this basis, it was therefore already clear in advance that there was a good chance of a positive result, although it was of course necessary that a systematic investigation by the RC researchers still had to be carried out first. Moreover, there were also cases where aspirant claimants had been warned in advance by the Origins Unknown Agency that any claim would not stand much of a chance of being successful but who had decided to submit a request for restitution anyway. This usually resulted in a rejection. Over the course of years, however, more and more requests came in, which were not initiated by the claimants themselves, but by an internationally operating commercial research or law firm that had looked for interesting cases on its own accord. That this also increased the likelihood that claims were too weakly founded goes without saying.

THE PROJECT MISSING WORKS OF ART

The recovery and restitution tasks of the SNK was largely based on the declaration forms for artworks lost or sold to Germany. Numerous of the objects described in those forms were recuperated to the Netherlands after the war. However, the SNK's archives still hold about 14,000 declaration forms of pieces that had not yet been recovered or matched with a specific object directly after the war. The information was consulted to a very limited extent due to the poor accessibility and vulnerability of this archival material. During the Museum Acquisitions project, the study of these forms proved to be a time-consuming and inefficient operation, with little guarantee that all relevant data was retrieved in the process. Moreover, the declaration forms were rarely used at all for other purposes, such as research by heirs of the original owners, by art dealers, by auction houses or by collectors. This led to the start-up of a project at Origins Unknown in 2014. It was largely implemented in 2015 and 2016 and aimed to make the declaration forms accessible to the public. Each form was scanned and its basic information was also entered into a database that is searchable in various ways. If such a form also included a photograph of the object at hand, it was added to the digital record as well. This project was funded by the Ministry of OCW and the New York-based Claims Conference (The Conference on Jewish Material Claims Against Germany). The first stage of this project was completed in December 2016, with various tasks still to be carried out. With the project completed, the database of artworks missing from the Netherlands forms an important international research tool, which may lead to the recovery of many more still missing artworks.

NEW DEVELOPMENTS SINCE 2016

With the extended restitution policy implemented in 2001 and the subsequent establishment of the Restitutions Committee, the expectation was that the flow of claims would subside naturally. This explains why a time limit was initially applied to the duration of the extended restitution policy. Over the years, however, it has become evident that restitution applications will continue to be submitted and that the restitution policy still attracts a great deal of international attention as well. Although much had been accomplished, for the time being it was obvious that matters could not be regarded as finalised. A letter to the Lower House from September 2016 conveys that the Dutch government thus opted to make some adjustments to the organisation of activities in the field of restitution. For the Restitutions Committee, measures were taken to allow for a regular succession flow of committee members. A decision was also made to develop a knowledge centre on the subject of restitution. This in order to bundle the fundamental knowledge spread across the RC's research department, the Origins Unknown Agency and the Museum Association and thereby preserve that knowledge for the future. The Expertise Centre for the Restitution of Cultural Property and the Second World War, housed at the NIOD Institute for War, Holocaust and Genocide Studies, was established on 2 July 2018. This centre of expertise was responsible for carrying out both research and public tasks. Researchers from the Restitutions Committee and the Origins Unknown Agency were transferred to the NIOD. Apart from that, it was also determined that the restitution policy would be evaluated in the year 2020.

During the summer of 2017, the exhibition *Looted Art before, during and after World War II* was held on at the Bergkerk Church in Deventer to visualise the exodus and partial return of Dutch art property during and after World War II. The project was the initiative of Eva Kleeman and Daaf Ledeboer of the Ter Borch Foundation. The selection of works was compiled by Rudi Ekkart and Eelke Muller, who also wrote the accompanying publication *Roof & Restitutie*. The exhibition mainly included artworks from the NK Collection and objects that had been returned to their original owners or their heirs shortly after the war or more recently. In addition, in collaboration with Julie-Marthe Cohen, the looting of the Jewish Museum's collection during the war was represented.

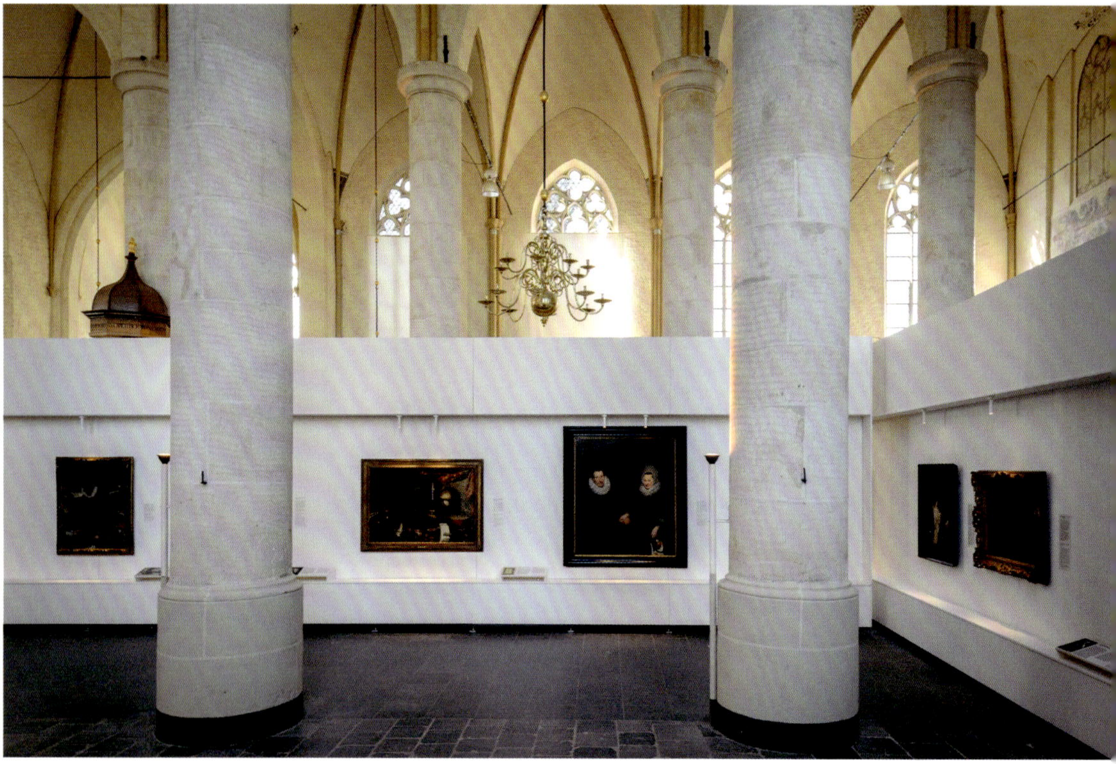

Exhibition *Looted Art before, during and after World War II (Roofkunst voor, tijdens en na WOII)* in the Bergkerk in Deventer, 2017

Studio Koster Van Lienen from Apeldoorn was responsible for the design of the exhibition.

Even before the review that was announced for 2020 took place, negative comments regarding the developments in the Dutch restitution policy emerged. Notorious was the binding opinion issued by the Restitutions Committee on 22 October 2018 concerning the painting *Bild mit Häusern* by Wassily Kandinsky (fig. 50). This canvas with a Jewish provenance had been acquired at an auction by the municipality of Amsterdam in 1940 for the benefit of the city's Stedelijk Museum. In the final conclusion of the advice, the Restitutions Committee stated that the interest of the claimant's artwork in restitution did not outweigh the interest of the municipality of Amsterdam in the preservation of the painting. Such balancing of interests had already been utilized by the committee before but had at the time received little publicity. The ruling on the Kandinsky, however, caused a stir both in the Netherlands and abroad. The widespread publicity was accompanied by other grievances already expressed earlier, such as those regarding the lengthy duration of proceedings. These and other concerns were discussed in the December 2020 report *Streven naar rechtvaardigheid* (Striving for Justice), which was presented by the evaluation committee headed by the former politician Jacob Kohnstamm.

This committee report concluded that the expanded restitution policy originally formulated by the Ekkart Committee should still be the basis for policy today. Due to a limited number of rejected claims, the previously internationally leading Dutch restitution policy had suffered considerable damage in previous years. In particular, the balancing of interests has impaired the restoration of rights in parts. Furthermore, the committee was of the opinion that the procedure applied to restitution applications is often overly formalistic and too insensitive. Another important issue discussed in the report is the observation that structural research into the provenance of Nazi-looted art and into the identification of the heirs of its original owners has been at a standstill since 2007. In connection with this, the Kohnstamm committee strongly recommended resuming structural provenance research and expressed their wish for the existing databases to be updated. It also advocated making adjustments to the assessment framework and the operations of the Restitutions Committee. This included the advice to set up a helpdesk, under ministerial responsibility, to provide others

nstallation representing missing artworks during the exhibition *ooted Art before, during and after World War II (Roofkunst voor, tijdens en na WOII)* in the Bergkerk in Deventer, 2017

n the 2017 exhibition held at the Bergkerk, this installation gave an artistic impression of the enormous umbers of cultural objects that were never found in Germany after he liberation. The design displays a variety of artworks still listed as missing. It was developed by designers Eloi Koster and Jesse van Lienen in ollaboration with researcher Annelies Kool.

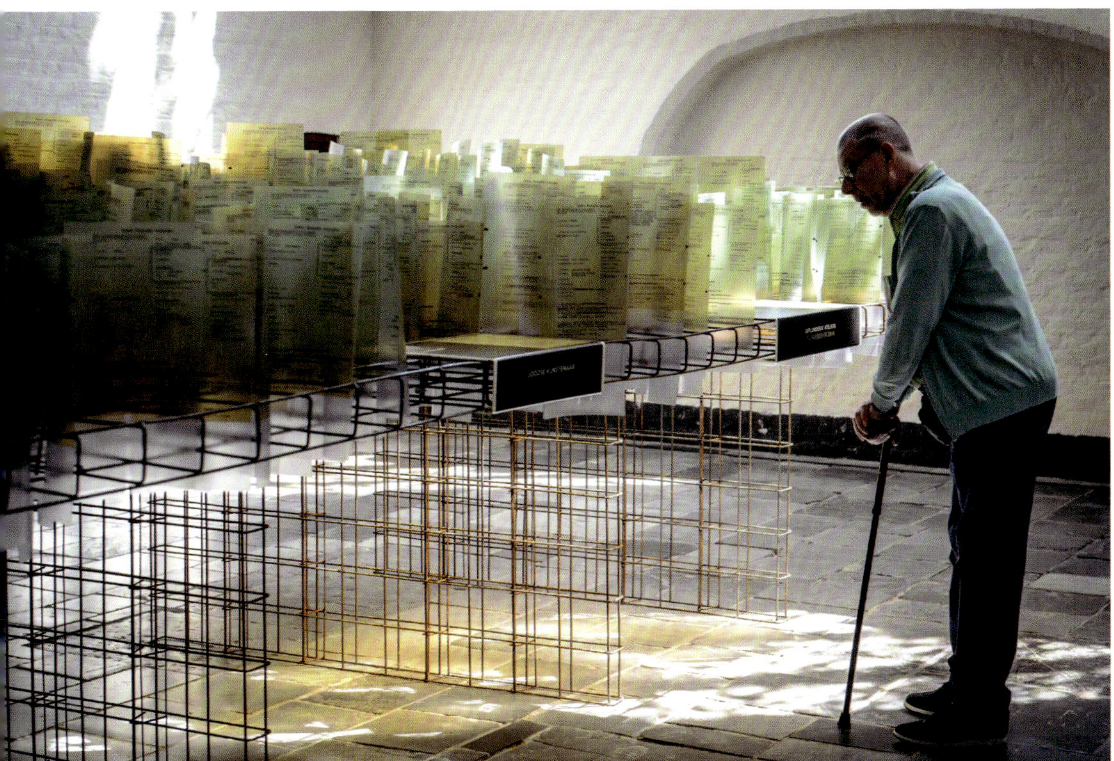

at home and abroad with passive as well as active information about the restitution policy.

As early as March 2021, the Minister of OCW reacted positively in response to the report and approved the recommendation for the assessment framework and the suggestion of a mediating role for the Restitutions Committee. It was announced that the National Cultural Heritage Agency (RCE) would accommodate the proposed helpdesk and that the RCE would also be responsible for a renewed provenance investigation into the NK Collection. The NIOD would continue to be in charge of the research conducted on behalf of the RC for restitution claims. Necessary preparations for the realisation of the plans were in full swing shortly after the announcement. A project organisation was prepared at RCE and a new chairman was appointed to the Restitutions Committee to replace the functionary who had resigned in December 2020.

In 2022, seven researchers were recruited to carry out the renewed provenance investigation so that work could begin that autumn. The helpdesk recommended by the Kohnstamm Committee had already been set up at the beginning of the year. An information and publicity policy was also further developed.

Between December 2021 and November 2022, the Restitutions Committee released a series of new opinions. These included advice on the claims of Emma Budge's heirs, which concerned numerous artworks from the Rijksmuseum, the Amsterdam Museum and the Kunstmuseum The Hague, which had been sold at auction from her estate in Berlin in 1937. These pieces included the four seventeenth-century silver salt vessels by Johannes Lutma kept at the Rijksmuseum and the Amsterdam Museum and the partially gilded silver beaker screw by Andries Grill in the Kunstmuseum The Hague. The RC recommended restitution of the claimed objects to the heirs. The reassessment of the claim on Wassily Kandinsky's *Blick auf Murnau mit Kirche* in the Van Abbemuseum in Eindhoven, rejected in 2018, resulted in an advice that differed from the advice of 2018. The committee now recommended the return of the painting to the heirs of its former owner Johanna Margaretha Stern-Lippmann.

A remarkable development also took place regarding a claim to another work by Kandinsky, which the Restitutions Committee had also rejected in 2018: *Bild mit Häusern* in the collection of the Stedelijk Museum in Amsterdam. At the time, this negative advice caused a whirlwind of reactions worldwide. Following the Kohnstamm report, the municipality of Amsterdam decided to approach the family for mutual consultation, leading to the return of the painting to the heirs in 2022.

As a result of the evaluation report of December 2020, the Dutch restitution policy was given a new impulse, bringing forth positive reactions nationally and internationally.

Following pages:
A hanging rack with paintings in one of the art depots in the The Netherlands Collection Centre in Amersfoort

Although numerous NK objects are currently on loan in Dutch museums and government buildings, a large quantity of the artworks is kept at the Cultural Heritage Agency of the Netherlands. The depots have been housed in The Netherlands Collection Centre in Amersfoort since 2021.

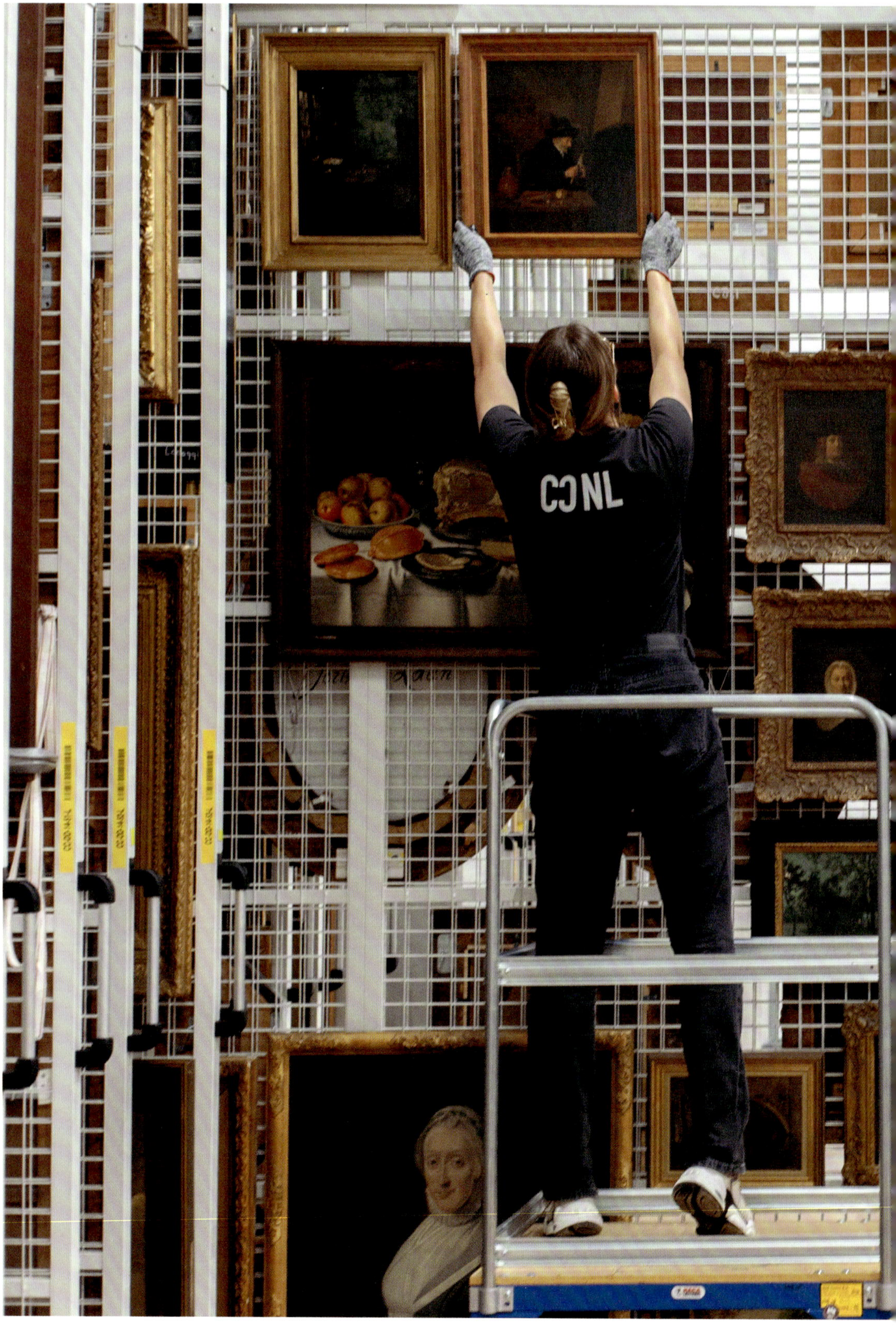
CCNL

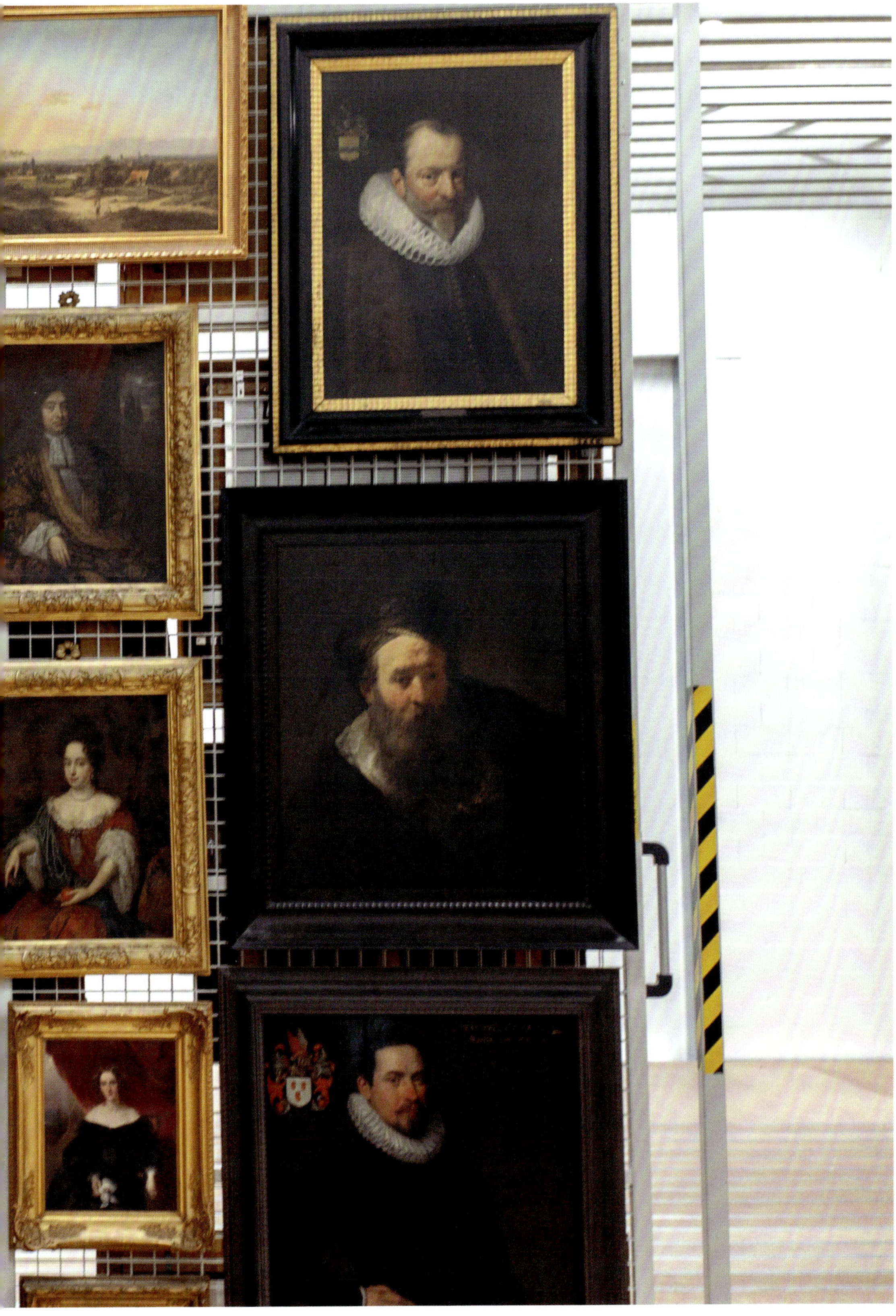

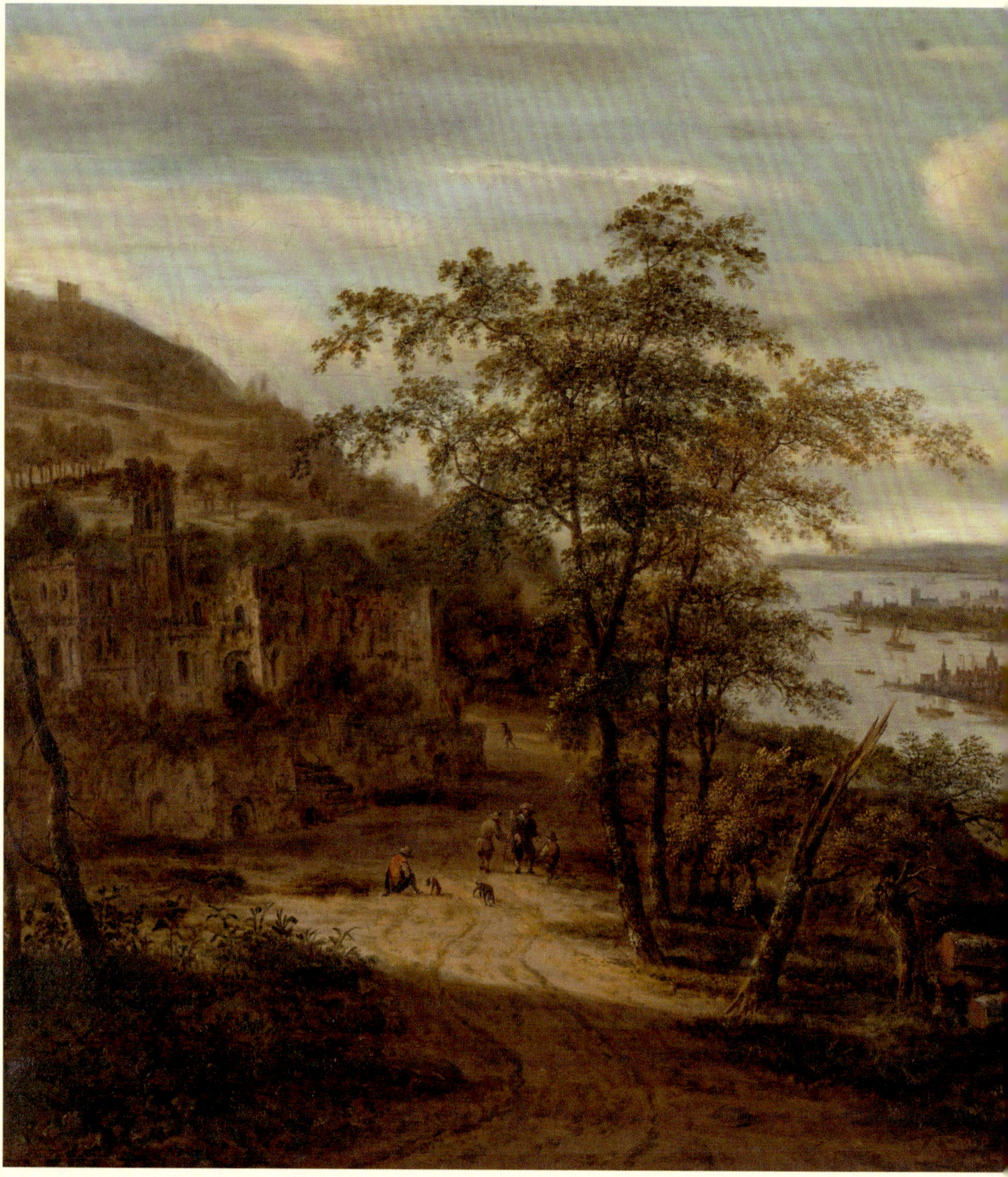

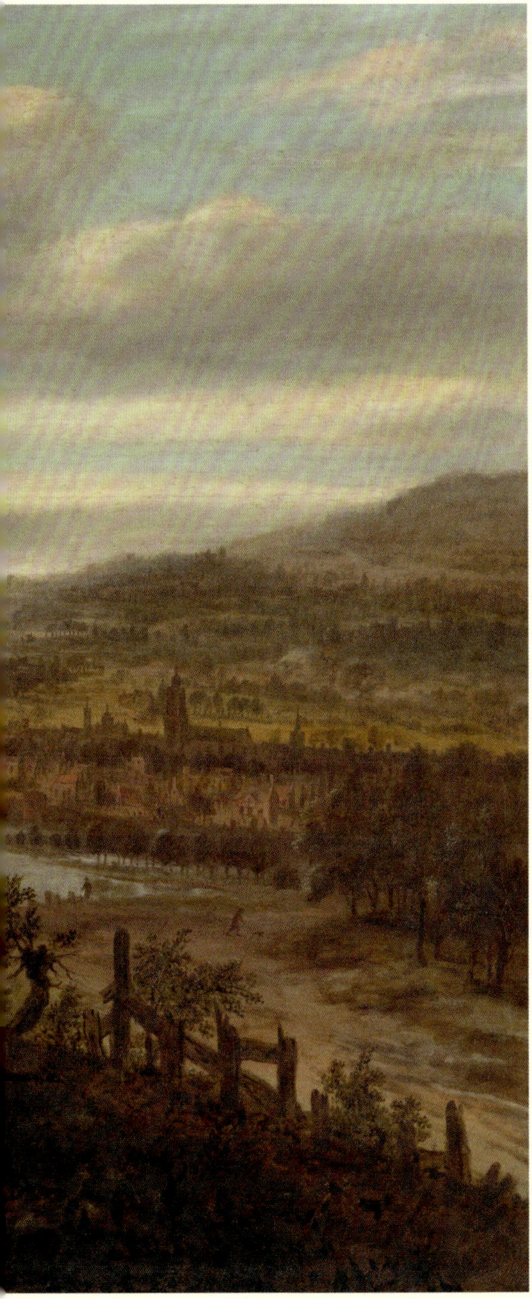

41

River Landscape with Ruin, a Town in the Distance
DIONYS VERBURGH (c. 1655-1722)
Canvas, 80 x 113 cm, Rijksdienst voor het Cultureel Erfgoed, NK2395

During the second World War, many Jewish owners sold their artworks to pay for their livelihood, flight to freedom or to go into hiding. These forced sales necessitated reliable intermediaries, such as the Jewish art dealer Gustav Cramer, who had fled to the Netherlands from Germany in 1938. He himself was granted the protection of Hans Posse, the head of the Sonderauftrag Linz. Cramer stated in 1950 that he had sold a few paintings from a German private collection for a woman who was in hiding during the war. The sale probably included this landscape by the artist Verburgh. For the owner's protection, her name was not recorded in the sale's registration. As a result of this, it is now impossible to identify the rightful owner of the painting.

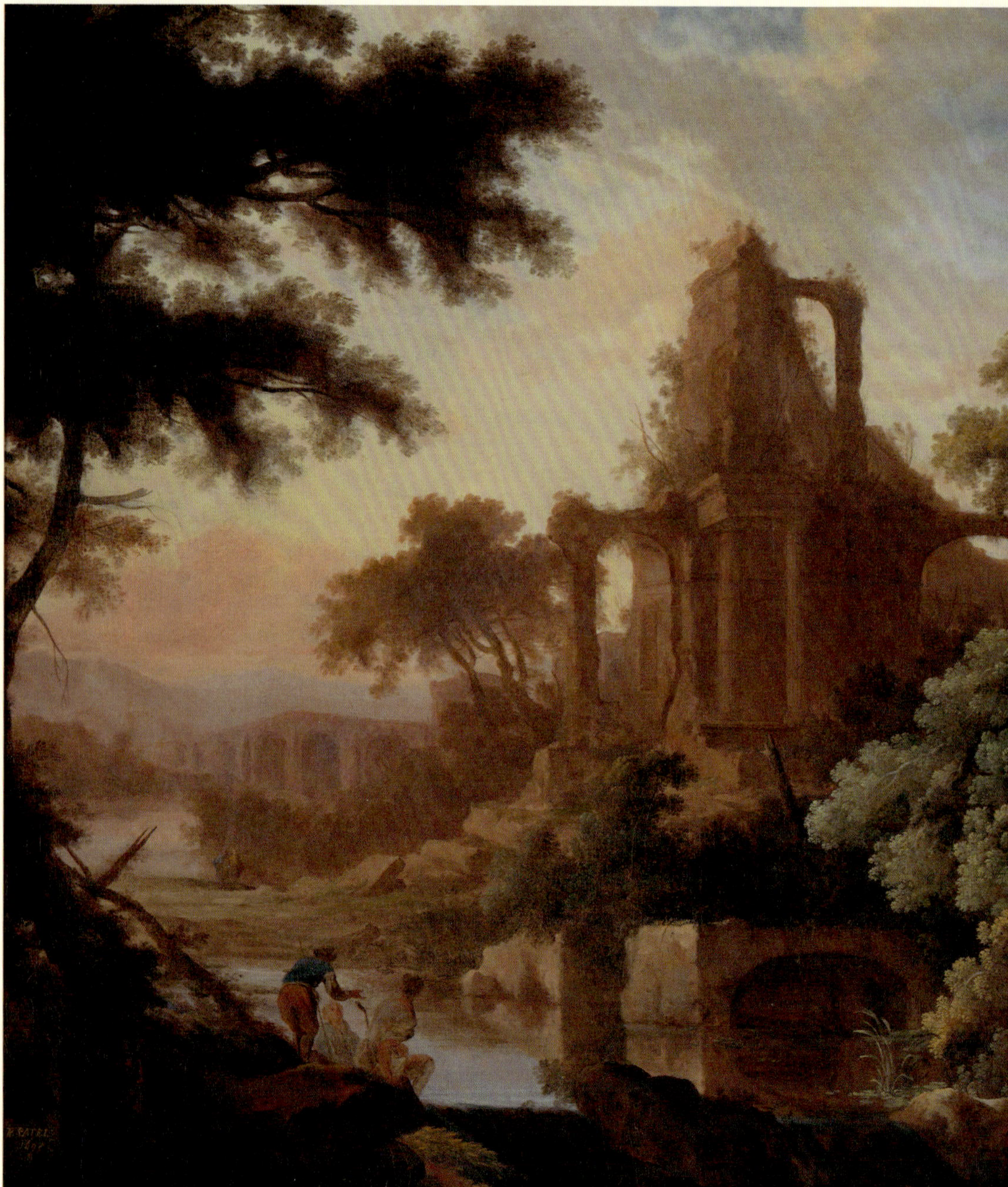

42

Landscape with Classical Ruins, 1695
PIERRE-ANTOINE PATEL II (1648-1707)
Canvas, 91 x 128 cm, Rijksdienst voor het Cultureel Erfgoed, NK2787

This painting was the property of Martin Heidemann and was handed over to the looting bank Liro in Amsterdam during the war. Martin Heidemann lived with his wife on the Sarphatistraat in Amsterdam. In early 1945, the couple fell victim to the persecution of Jews in the Bergen-Belsen concentration camp in Germany. The Liro had the painting auctioned off by S.J. Mak van Waay in Amsterdam in 1943. This auction house sold countless looted Jewish properties for German organisations, particularly the Liro, during the occupation. In 1944, the landscape was sold by its then owner to a German buyer. Marks on the back of a painting can provide valuable clues about its provenance history. The back of the frame of Patel's painting featured a label from a Polish art framer. This offered a further indication that the work was indeed owned by Heidemann, who was born in the Polish town Polczyn. As far as is known, Heidemann had no children. Attempts to trace his heirs remained unsuccessful for years. However, a recent letter requesting information on the landscape may lead to further clarification.

43

Silver Kiddush Cup with Hebrew inscriptions
Silver, 9.7 cm high, Private Collection

This silver kiddush cup was kept in the NK Collection from 1946. In Jewish tradition, Kiddush refers to the blessing recited at the beginning and the end of the Sabbath and other Jewish festivities. For years, the origins of this Kiddush cup and the meaning of the Hebrew inscription remained unknown. Research by the Amsterdam Jewish Museum in 2004 revealed that the object was most probably gifted to Hartog Koopman Sr. (1809/1810-1892) by the Israelite Congregation of Oud-Beijerland in April 1889 as a token of appreciation. In 2006, the Restitutions Committee recommended that the cup be returned to five descendants of Hartog Koopman Sr..

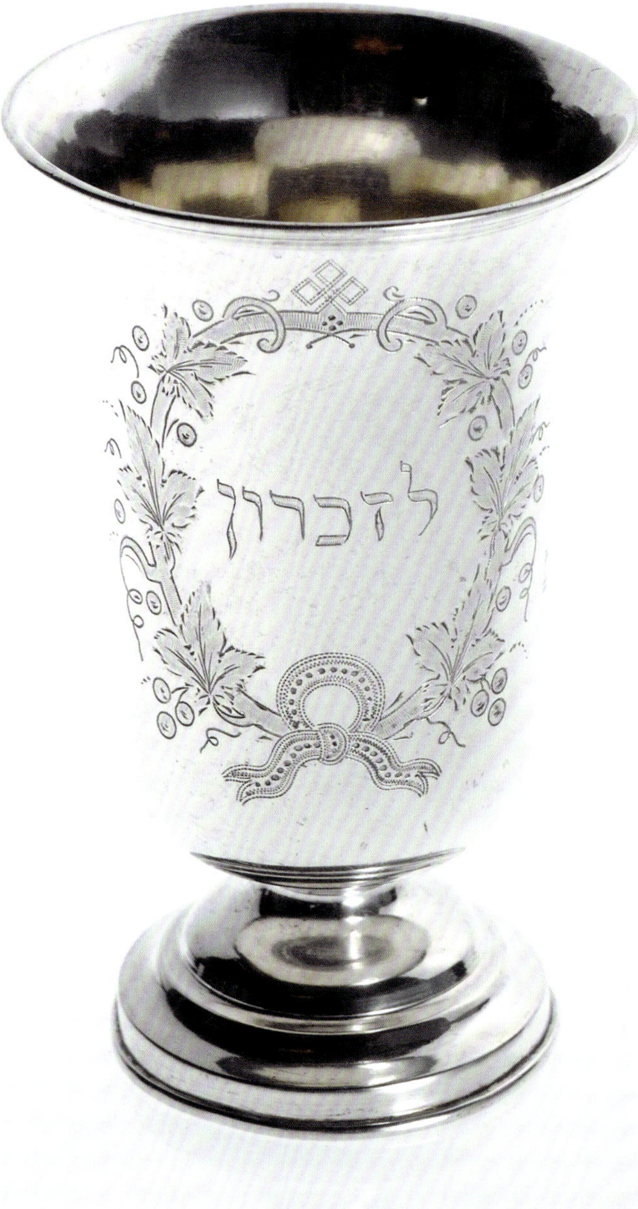
לזכרון

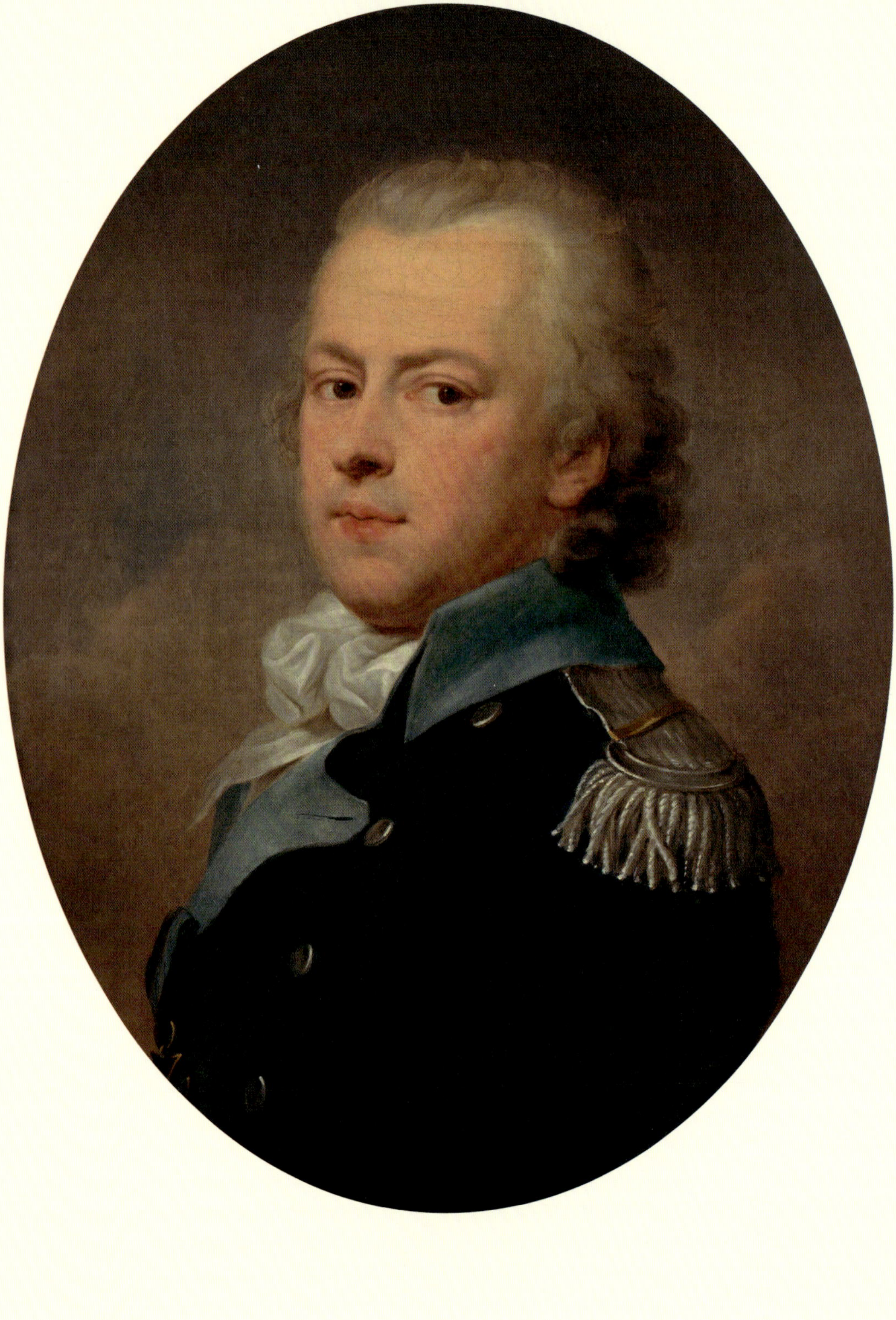

44

Portrait of a Polish Officer
JOHANN FRIEDRICH AUGUST TISCHBEIN (1750-1812)
Canvas, 65.5 x 50.5 cm, Private Collection

The portrait of a Polish officer by the German-Dutch painter J.F.A. Tischbein was sold to the Sonderauftrag Linz in 1944 by the notorious art dealer Pieter Menten (1899-1987). Menten had lived in Poland since 1923 and was active in the art trade there. Because of the advance of the Red Army, he fled Lemberg (now Lviv) in September 1939 and settled in Kraków. When the Germans seized eastern Galicia in 1941, Menten had the opportunity to return to Lemberg, where he was active in the SS and acted as a Verwalter of Jewish art dealers. These activities allowed him to expand his own collection. In 1943, Menten was forced by Himmler to leave Poland. He returned to the Netherlands with four wagonloads filled with artworks and other valuables. The scheduled auction of his painting collection in 1976 prompted the Dutch journalist Hans Knoop to unravel and expose Menten's life history, which led to his arrest. In 1980, he was eventually sentenced to ten years in prison for war crimes, including the involvement in the mass murder of several dozen Jews. When the investigation by the Origins Unknown Agency established that this portrait had been Pieter Menten's, it was unfortunately impossible to reconstruct how he had acquired it. Thanks to a request for restitution by descendants of a Polish noble family, the case was reopened. In 2017, the Restitutions Committee advised for the return of the work to the rightful heirs.

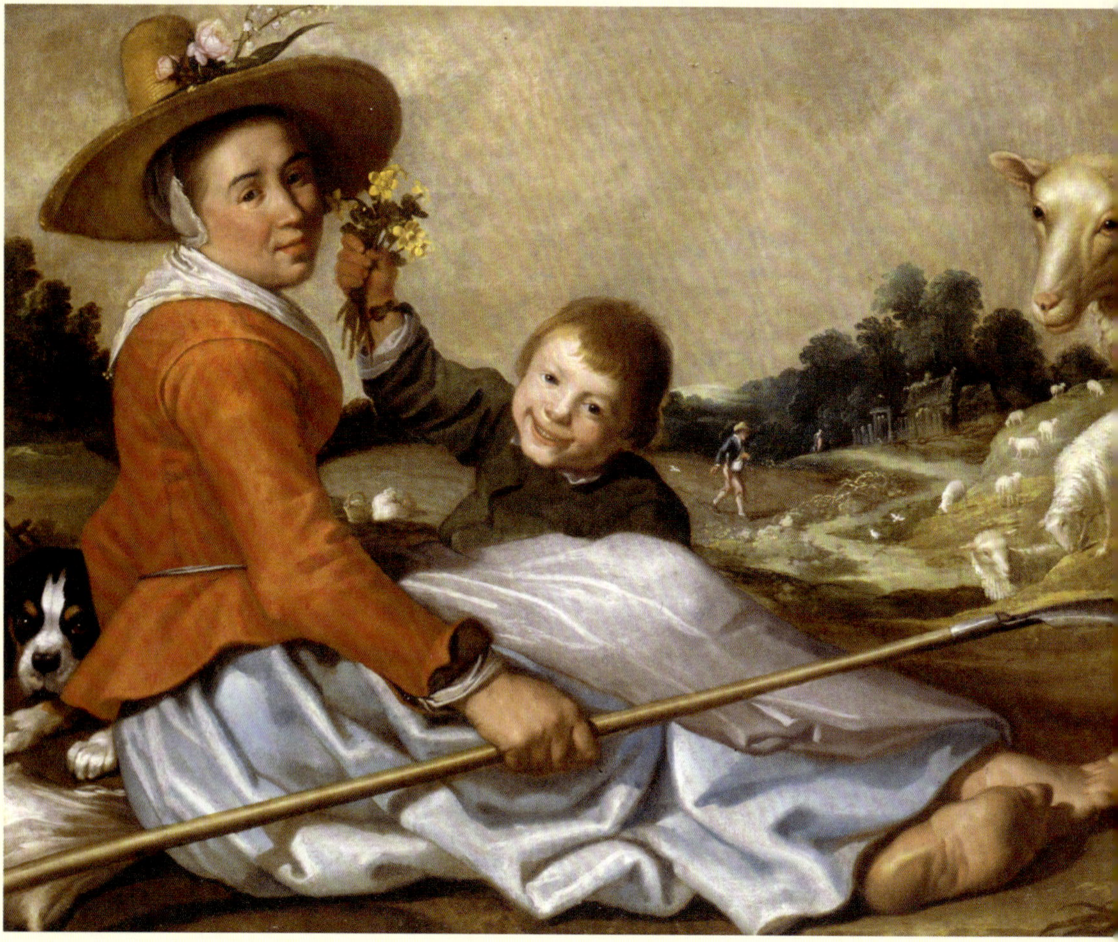

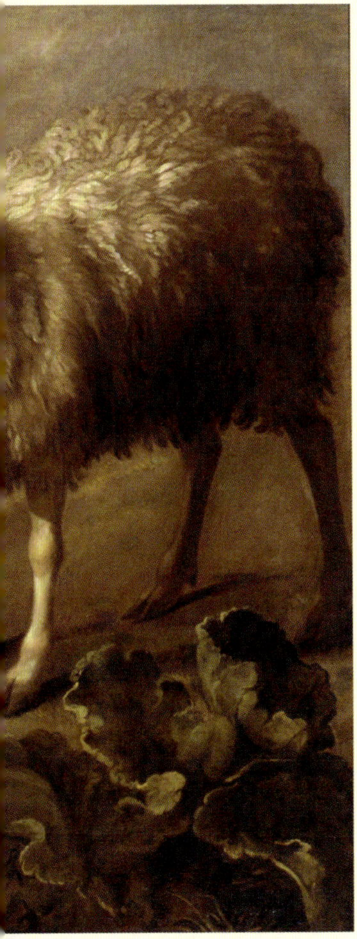

45
Shepherdess with a Child in a Landscape, 1627
JACOB GERRITSZ. CUYP (1594-1652)
Canvas, 112 x 168 cm, Dordrechts Museum, Dordrecht

This painting belonged to the collection of the Jewish textile manufacturer Jacques Hedeman (1879-1948) from Almelo. At the start of the war, Hedeman had stored this painting, along with other artworks from his collection, in a vault of an Amsterdam bank for safekeeping. The collection was then surrendered to the looting bank Liro and sold by the Germans. Hedeman was able to flee to Switzerland and survived the war. In 2002, the Dordrecht Museum acquired the painting from a German private collector, who had lent it out for the exhibition on Jacob Cuyp held at the time. The museum was not aware that it was Hedeman's confiscated property. Research for the national project Museum Acquisitions from 1933 disclosed the artwork's provenance. A vital piece of evidence was formed by the Liro's registration number, which used to be visible on the reverse of the painting. The museum came to an agreement with Hedeman's heirs in 2015. As both preferred the painting to be preserved for the museum, the Dordrechts Museum was able to acquire the landscape by paying an agreed sum to Hedeman's heirs.

46
View of Delft, 1663
DANIËL VOSMAER (1622-after 1666)
Canvas, 90.5 x 113 cm, Prinsenhof, Delft, on loan from RCE

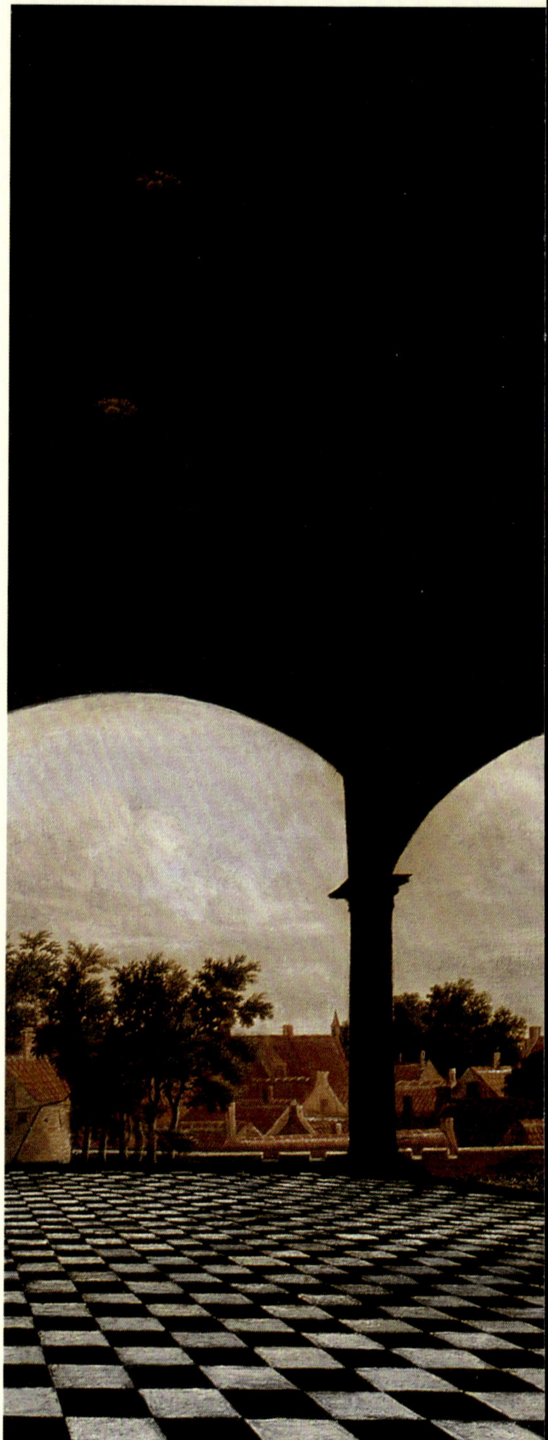

Following the decision in February 2006 to return 202 works of art to the Goudstikker heirs, the possibility of buying back a number of pieces was discussed. At that time, the Von Saher family still intended to keep an extensive core of the collection together and hoped to give it a museum function. As a result, a significant part of the Dutch government's 'wishlist' of the paintings to be bought back was not eligible for acquisition. Ultimately, the government was able to buy back four paintings, which until then had played an important role in the museums where they had been displayed on long-term loan from the NK Collection. These included two portraits by Paulus Moreelse (fig. 11) and this work by Daniël Vosmaer. The *View of Delft* returned to the Prinsenhof, where it forms one of the collection's public favourites.

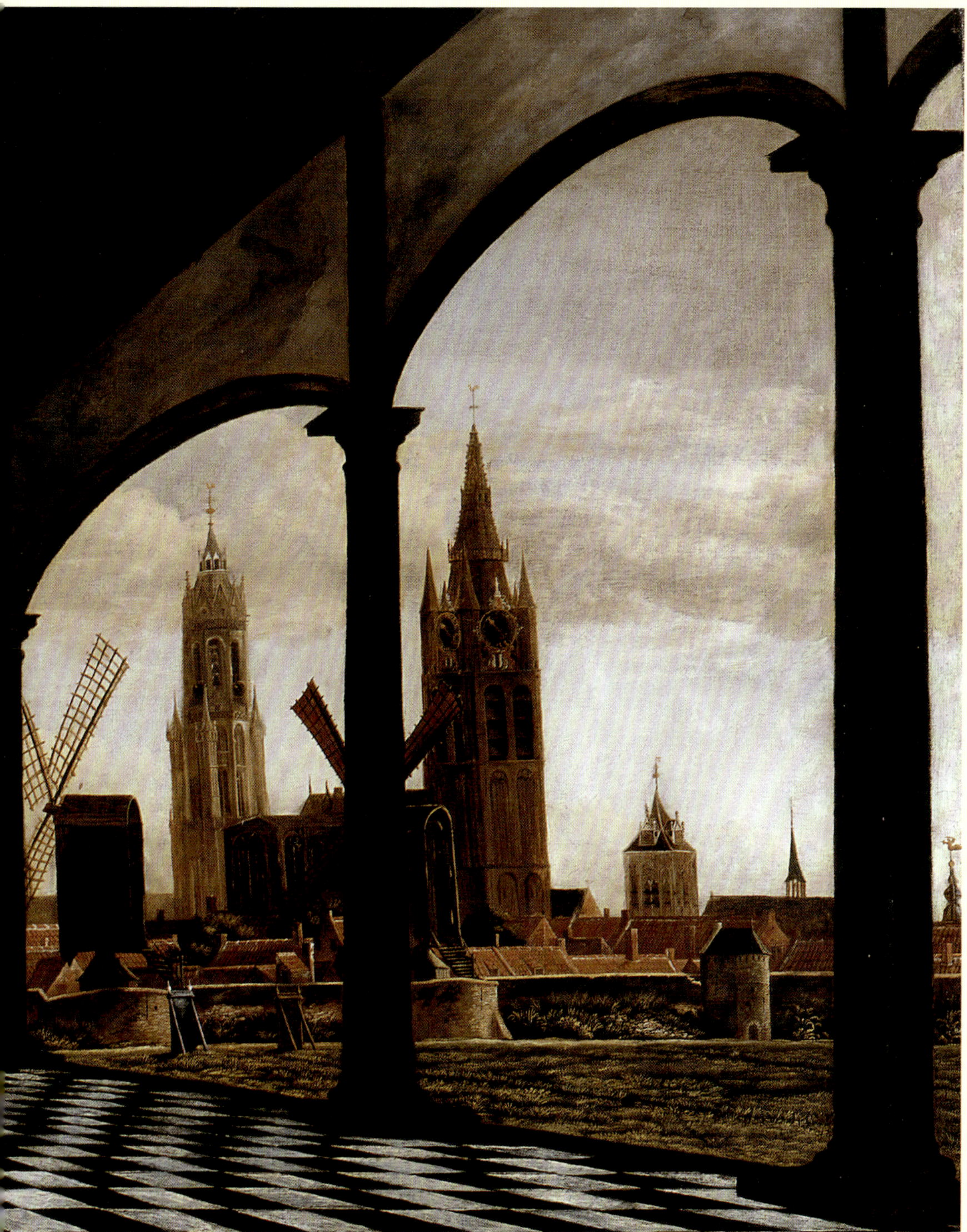

47

A Child on his Deathbed, 1645
BARTHOLOMEUS VAN DER HELST
(c. 1613-1670)
Canvas, 63 x 86.5 cm, Museum Gouda, on loan from RCE

Among the works of art that the Dutch government was keen to buy back from the Goudstikker heirs was the deathbed portrait of a young boy painted by Bartholomeus van der Helst. The painting is one of the best Dutch examples of this genre of portraiture and had been among the museum's public favourites in Gouda for decades. As a token of appreciation for the manner in which the Netherlands had finally honoured the Goudstikker family's old claims by means of the new restitution policy, the heirs gifted this painting to the Dutch government. The deathbed portrait was subsequently returned to Gouda's Catharinagasthuis, the municipal museum.

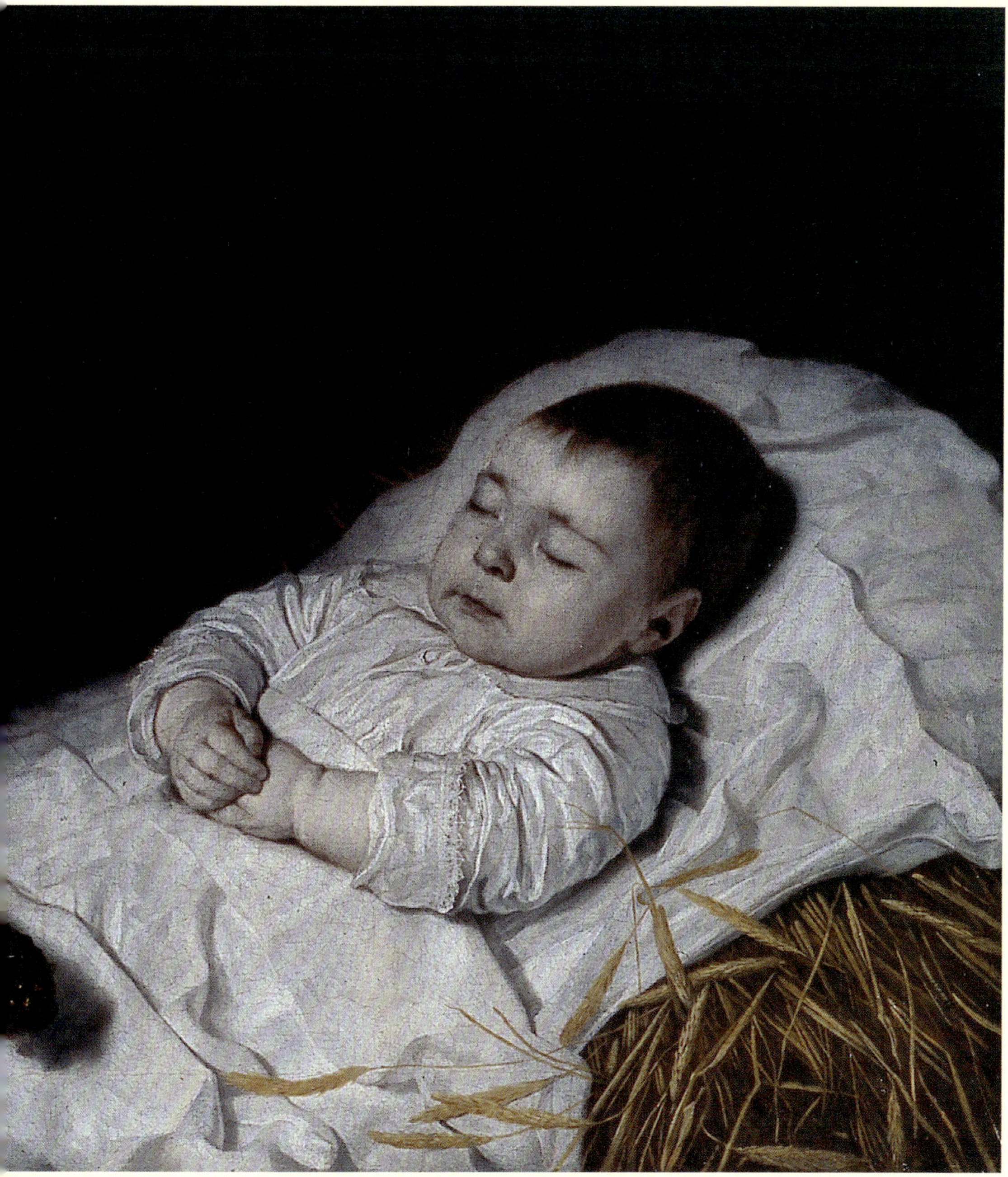

48
Landscape with an Episode from the Conquest of America, c. 1535
JAN MOSTAERT (c. 1475-1552/1553)
Panel, 86.5 x 152.5 cm, Rijkmuseum, Amsterdam

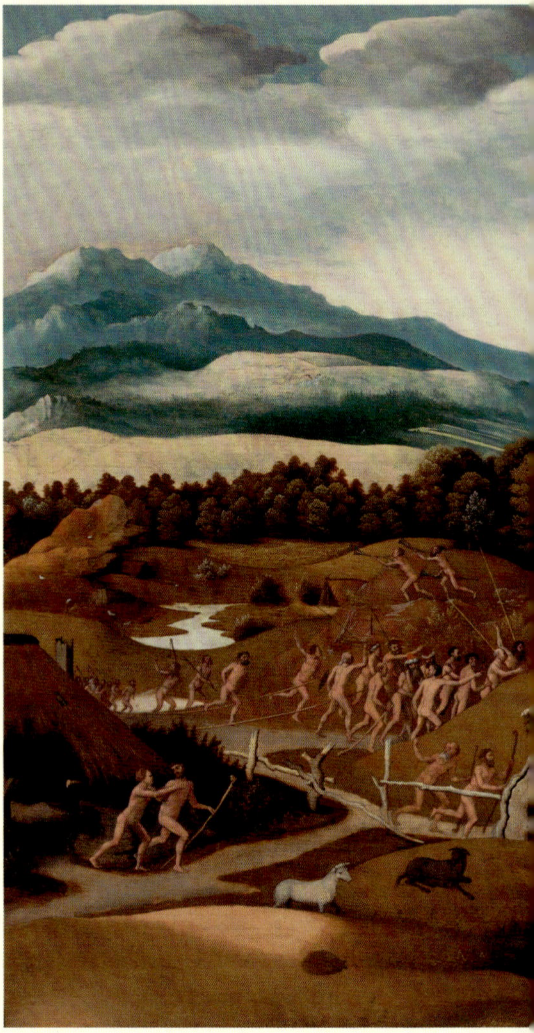

Since the return of over 200 paintings, the Goudstikker heirs have been forced to sell a substantial number of artworks, as the family was faced with high costs for lawyers and researchers who had worked on their behalf. Through purchases at auctions and from art dealers, several Dutch museums have succeeded in the acquisition of several Goudstikker pieces. This painting was purchased by the Dutch State in 2013, thanks in part to the financial support from the Goudstikker family itself, in memory of Jacques Goudstikker.

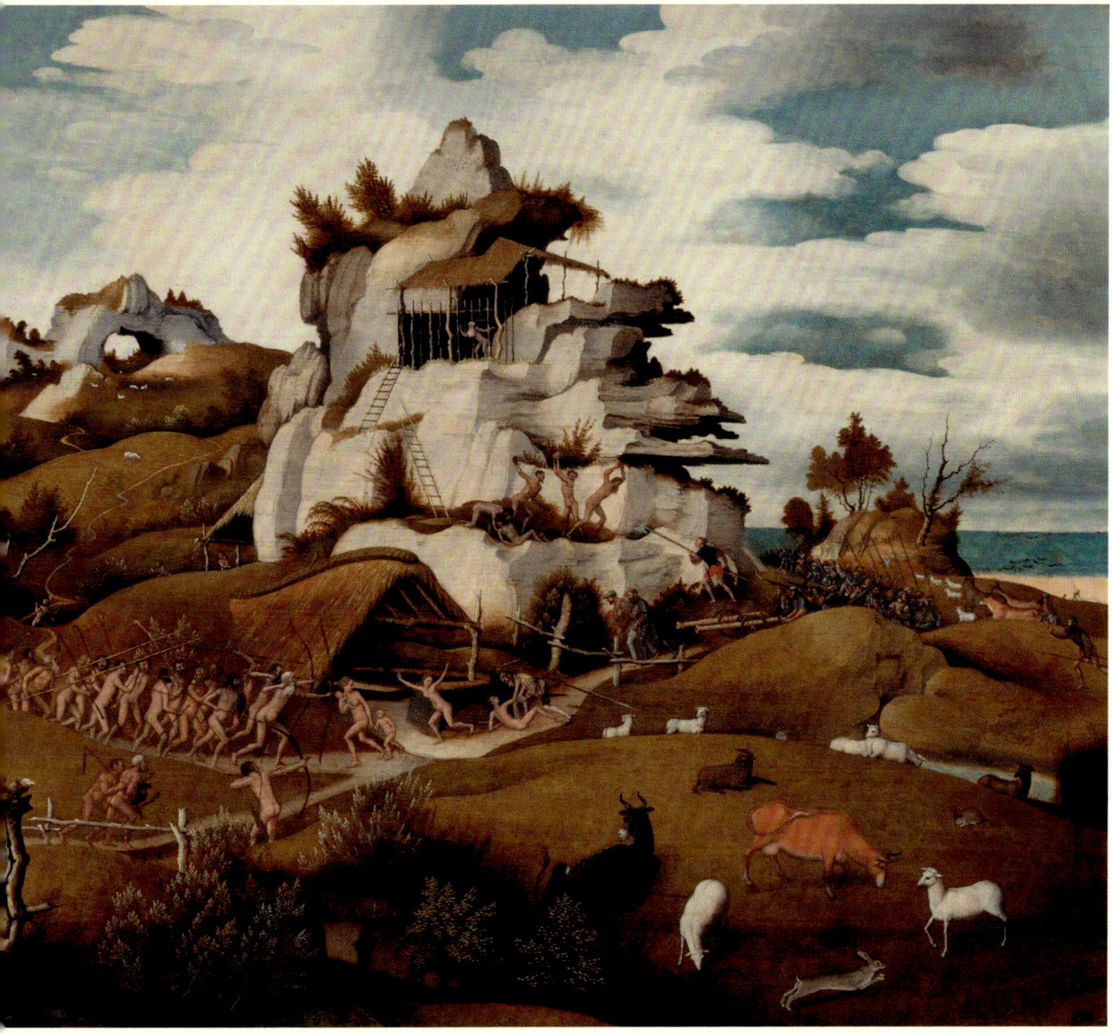

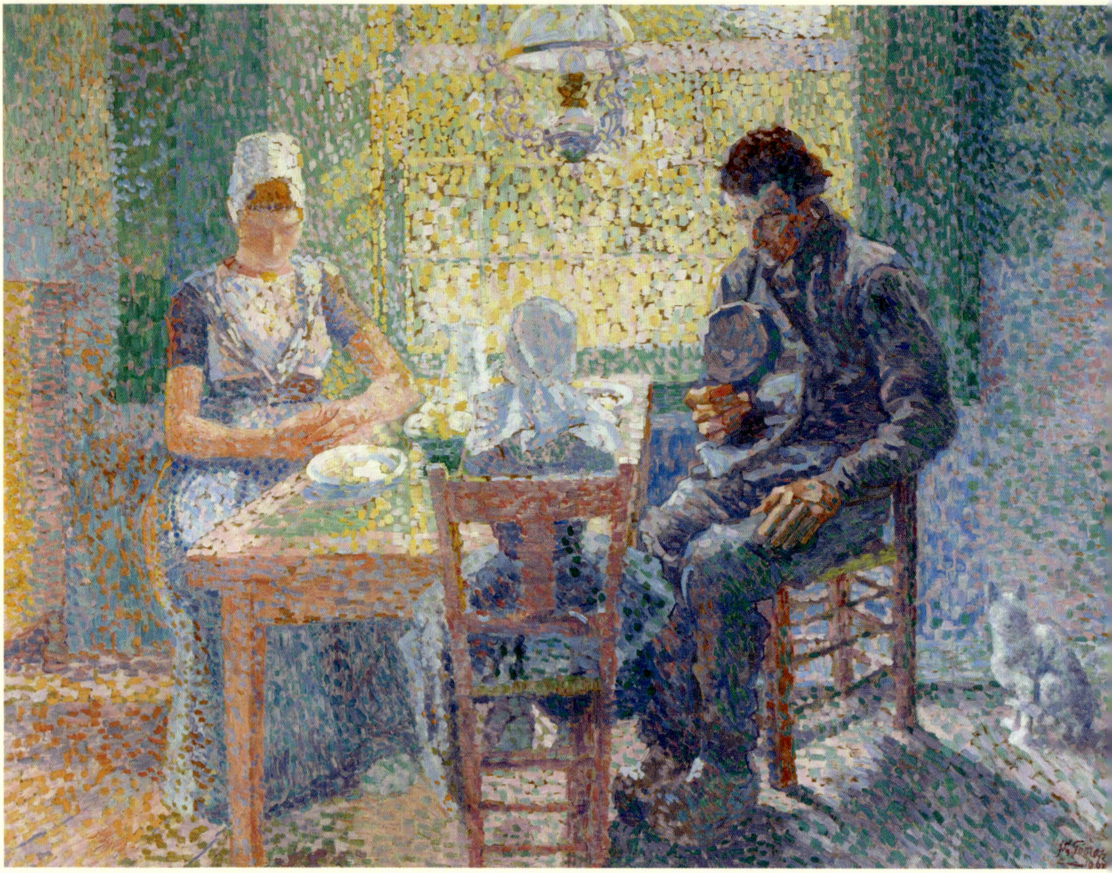

49
Grace before the Meal, 1907
JAN TOOROP (1858-1928)
Cardboard, 74 x 100 cm,
Zeeuws Museum, Middelburg

This painting was the property of the Jewish collector Ernst Flersheim (1862-1944), who fled from Frankfurt am Main to the Netherlands in 1937. The work was left behind in Germany and was reportedly confiscated by the Gestapo around 1938. Flersheim and his wife were murdered by the Germans during the war. No conclusive data on the provenance history of the painting exists but we do know that it passed through the hands of several Dutch art dealers before it was purchased in 1981 by the Zeeuws Museum in Middelburg. In 1999, two of Flersheim's grandchildren requested for the painting to be returned to the family but the appeal was not granted. The claimants and the museum presented the case to the Restitutions Committee for binding advice in 2006. In 2008, the committee ruled that the museum was to return the work to Flersheim's heirs in return for payment of the 1981 purchase price, indexed according to the general price index. The Restitutions Committee also decreed that if the family intended to sell the painting within ten years, it should first be offered for sale to the museum. Following this ruling, the heirs chose to sell the Toorop painting to the museum.

50

Bild mit Häusern, 1909
WASSILY KANDINSKY (1866-1944)
Canvas, 98 x 133 cm, Private Collection

The Russian painter Wassily Kandinsky (1866-1944) was one of the pioneers of abstraction in western modern art. His expressionist painting *Bild mit Häusern* had been part of the Stedelijk Museum's collection since 1940. In 2018, the Restitutions Committee concluded in a binding advice that the city of Amsterdam was not obligated to grant restitution to the heiress of the Jewish original owner, because '...the interest of the applicant in restitution does not outweigh the interest of the City Council in retaining the work.' This binding opinion caused a stir in the Netherlands and abroad.
Following the Kohnstamm Committee's 2020 report, the city of Amsterdam decided to discuss the matter with the family. This resulted in an agreement on the restitution of the piece. In 2022, the Amsterdam returned the Kandinsky to the heiress of the original owner.

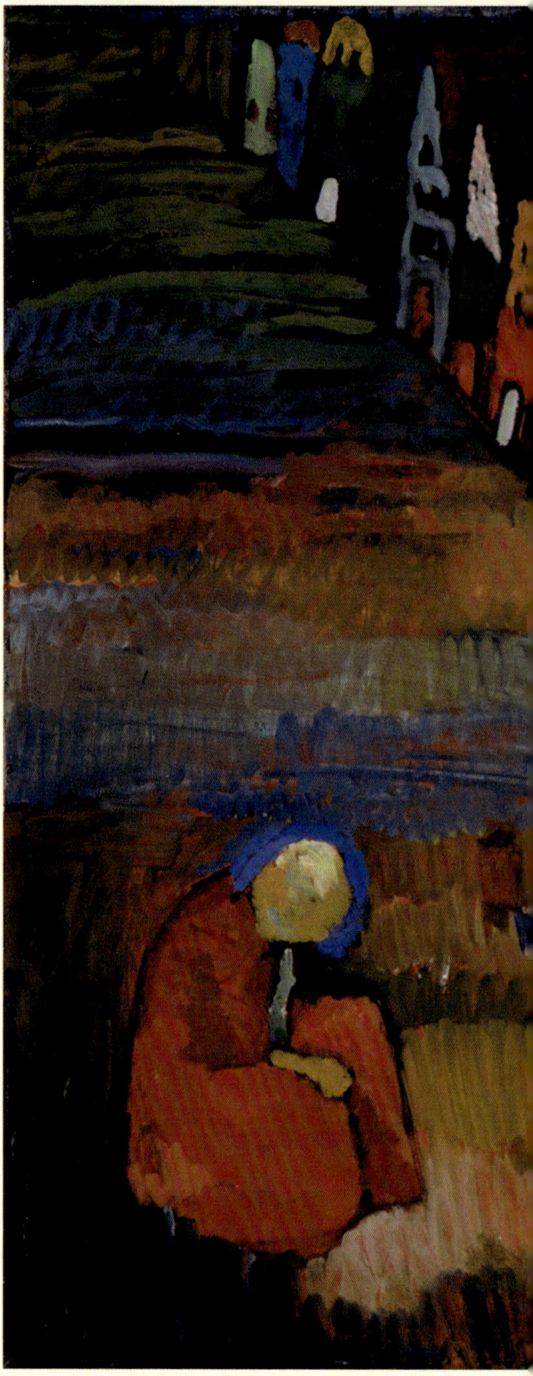

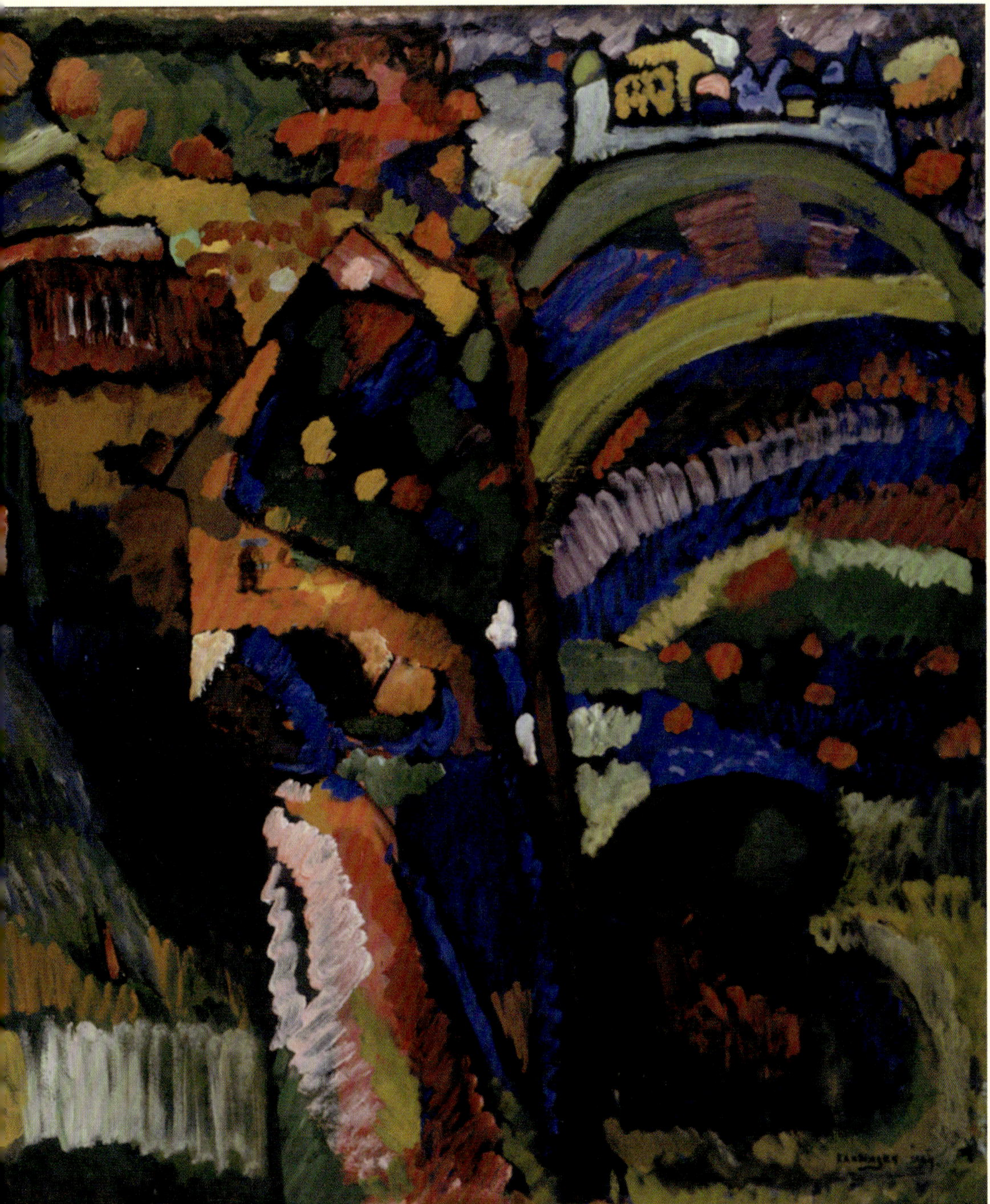

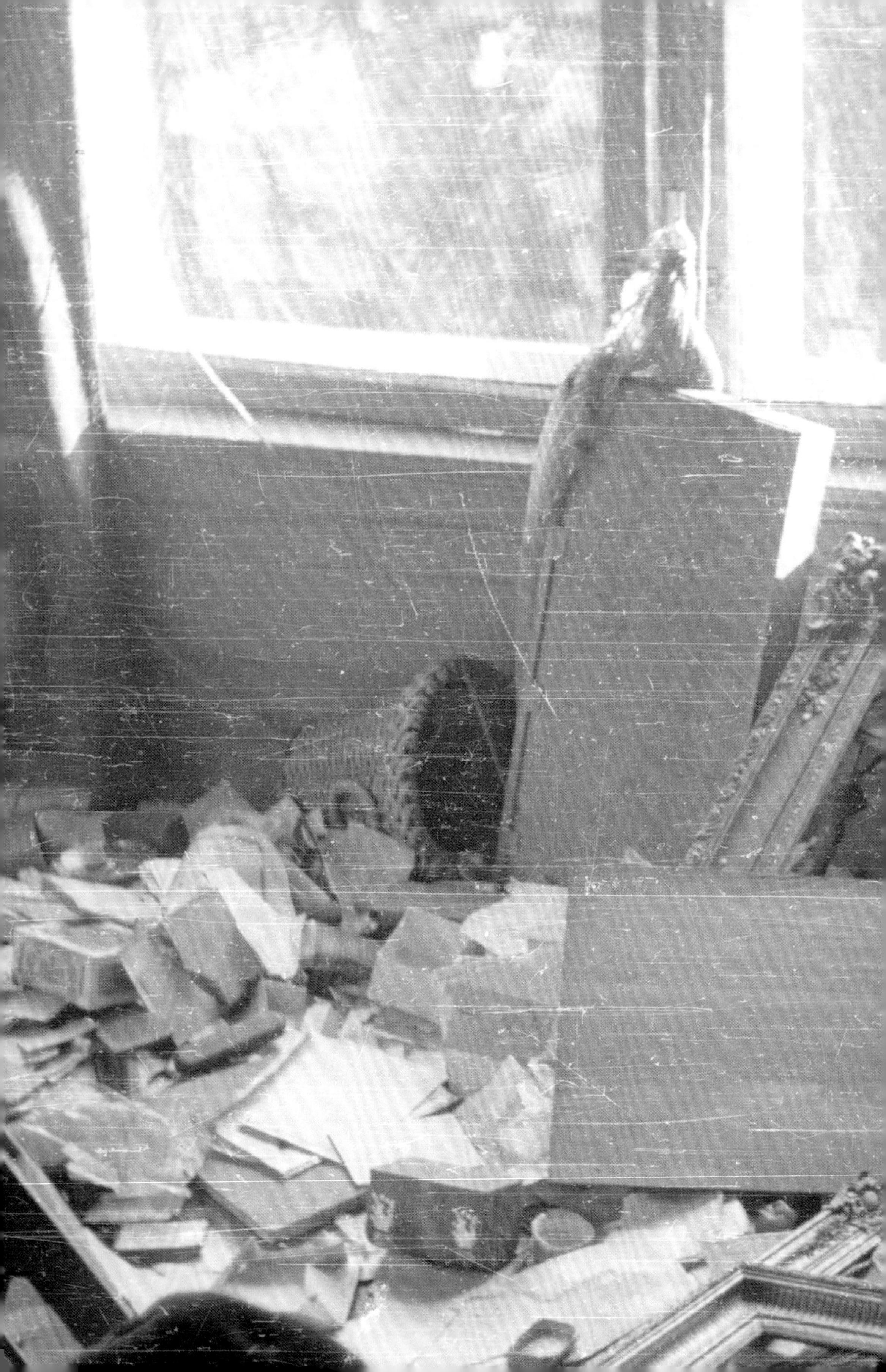

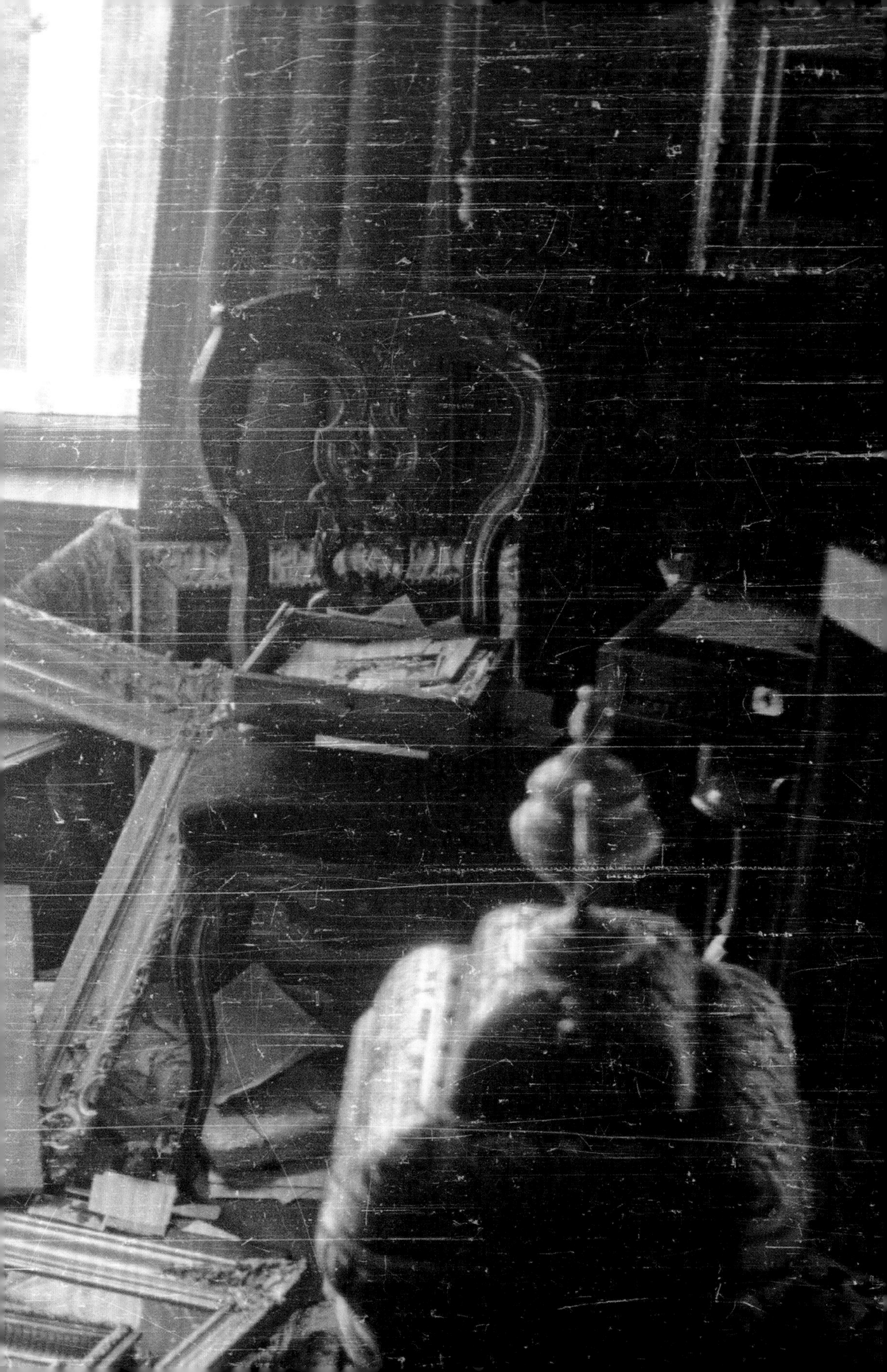

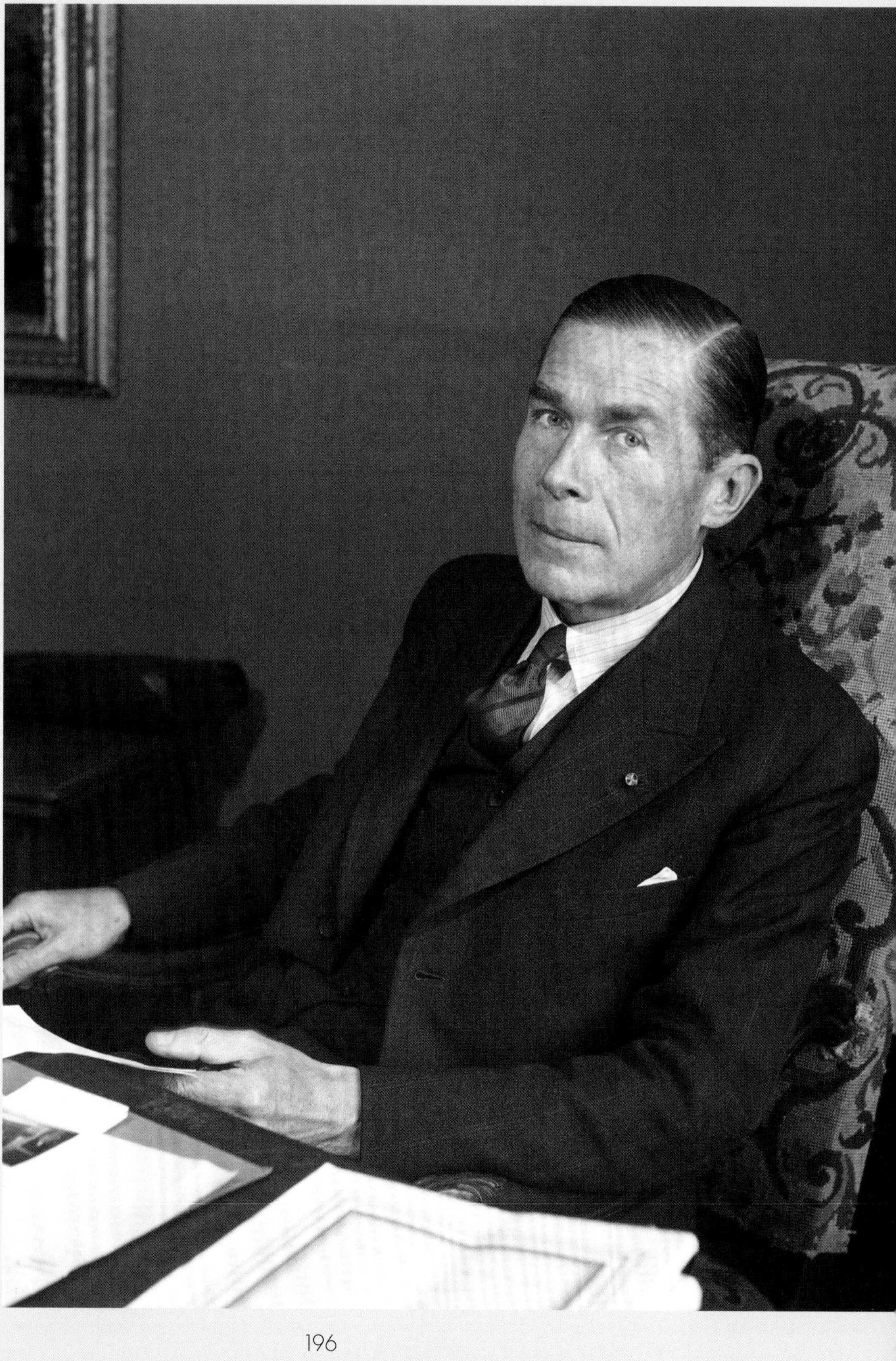

KEY FIGURES IN THE NETHERLANDS ART PROPERTY FOUNDATION (SNK)

JONKHEER DAVID CORNELIS RÖELL

23 November 1894, Utrecht-3 December 1961, Amsterdam

Jonkheer David Cornelis Röell was born 1894 in Utrecht, a son of Jonkheer Johan Hendrik Röell and Jonkvrouw Henriëtte Quirine Hoeufft. He was unmarried.

Leaving school in 1913, Röell read first law and then art history in Utrecht. In 1919 he continued his studies in Paris at the Sorbonne and the Ecole du Louvre. Röell obtained an appointment in the Rijksmuseum in Amsterdam as an assistant, and later as curator of the paintings department, through Frederik Schmidt Degener, who became the museum's director in 1921.

Between 1936 and 1945 Röell was director of the municipal museums in Amsterdam, which included the Stedelijk Museum. One of his tasks during the war was to supervise the municipal art holdings, which for reasons of safety and security had been taken to storage facilities in the sand dunes. He also played a part in the preparations for the post-war return of cultural material that had disappeared to Germany. Röell was a member of the Committee for the Restitution of Dutch Art Holdings, which was established at the end of 1943. Headed by the art historian J.G. van Gelder it issued advice to the Dutch government in London. When the SNK was set up on 11 June 1945, Röell was appointed as chair of the Management Board.

In August 1945 Röell succeeded Schmidt Degener, who had died in 1941, as director of the Rijksmuseum. This museum became linked to the history of the art returned to the Netherlands. It acted as a facilitator for the public-oriented activities of the SNK, including two claim exhibitions staged in 1950. In the post-war years the Rijksmuseum's own collection was supplemented with numerous returned objects, including hundreds of artworks from the collection of the banker and art collector Fritz Mannheimer. When preparations were made in 1949 to wind up the SNK and transfer its tasks to Hergo, Roëll and most of the other members of the Foundation's Management Board resigned with effect from 1 September 1949. In 1959 Röell left the Rijksmuseum on reaching retirement age.

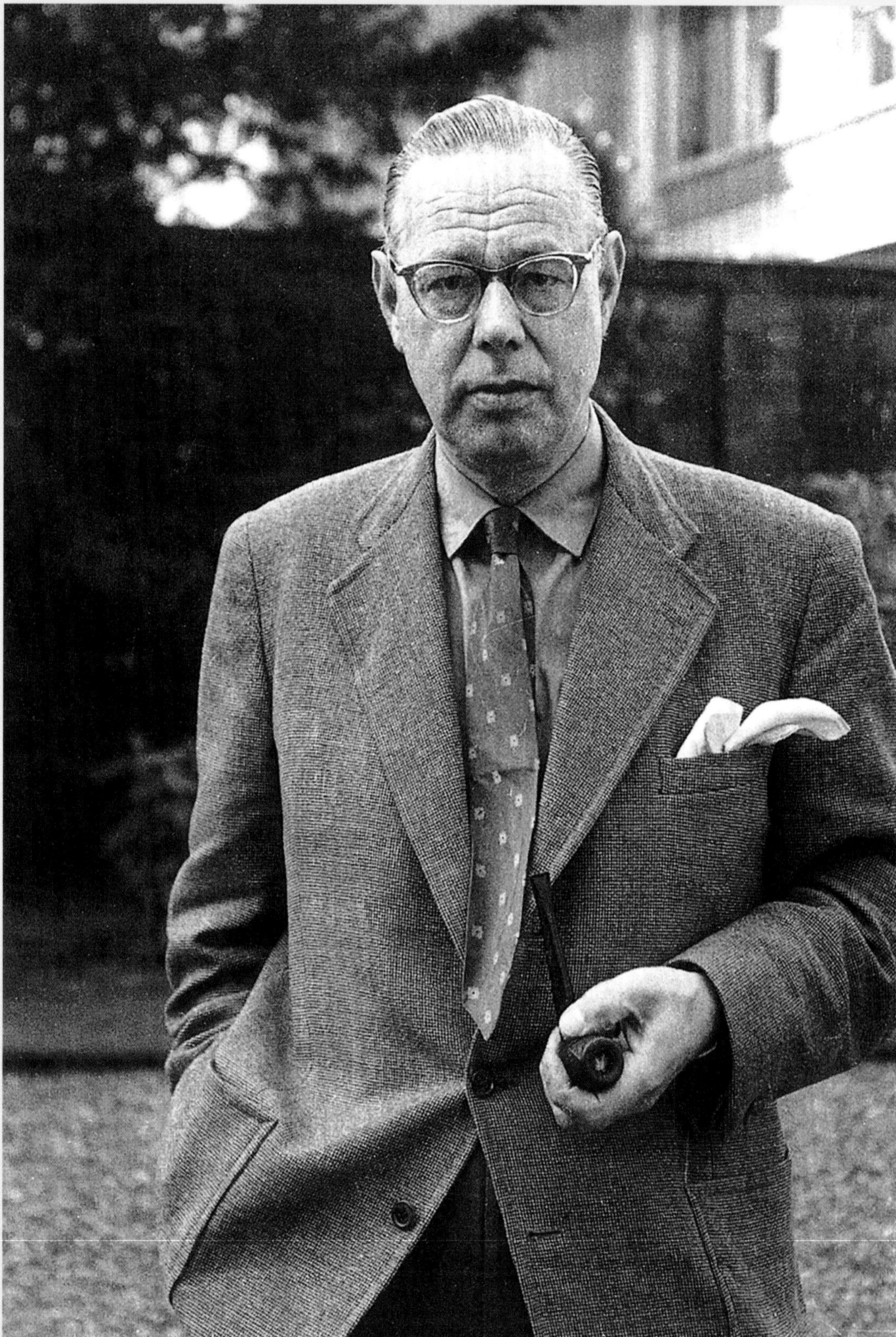

JAN GERRIT VAN GELDER

27 February 1903, Alkmaar-9 December 1980, Utrecht

Jan Gerrit van Gelder was born in Alkmaar in 1903, a son of the archivist and museum director Hendrik Enno van Gelder and Johanna Helena Scalongne. He was married three times and had two children.

Between 1923 and 1927 Van Gelder read art history at Utrecht University under Willem Vogelsang and received his doctorate in 1933 for a thesis on the seventeenth-century draughtsman Jan van de Velde. He also started working in Museum Boijmans in Rotterdam in 1924, initially as a research assistant and later as curator. In December 1940 he became acting director of the RKD in The Hague, where he replaced the Swiss art historian Hans Schneider, who returned to his homeland on sick leave.

During the war Van Gelder became involved in the preparations for the post-war recovery of cultural material that had disappeared to Germany. In 1943 the Dutch government in London asked for his advice about the issue, after which the Committee for the Restitution of Dutch Art Holdings was established. After the liberation, Van Gelder became a member and also secretary of the Management Board of the SNK, which was established in 1945. He was also appointed as director of the Foundation, a post that he shared with the art historian A.B. de Vries. Van Gelder was put in charge of the day-to-day activities in the office in The Hague, which was housed in the RKD at Korte Vijverberg 7, while De Vries was responsible for the office in Amsterdam. It soon became clear that this split was not practical, so the office in The Hague was closed in November 1945 and Van Gelder stood down as director.

In 1945 Van Gelder was appointed director of the RKD and the Mauritshuis, appointments that could not have been made during the Nazi occupation because Van Gelder's father-in-law was Jewish. One of the two exhibitions that he organized in the Mauritshuis was entitled *Art Treasures Regained*. ('Herwonnen Kunstbezit') It ran from March to May 1946 and featured art treasures that had been returned from Germany. That same year the double directorship ended when Van Gelder accepted an appointment as professor of art history in Utrecht. Under his leadership the Utrecht Art History Institute flourished and expanded significantly. In 1966 an internal dispute in the institute resulted in the departure of Van Gelder, who became director of the newly established Centre for Advanced Art Historical Research, which existed until he retired in 1973.

Van Gelder left behind a large scholarly oeuvre. He was also a member of many editorial boards, management boards and committees, and an important source of inspiration and encouragement for students and colleagues. He was a key figure in the Dutch art history world for decades.

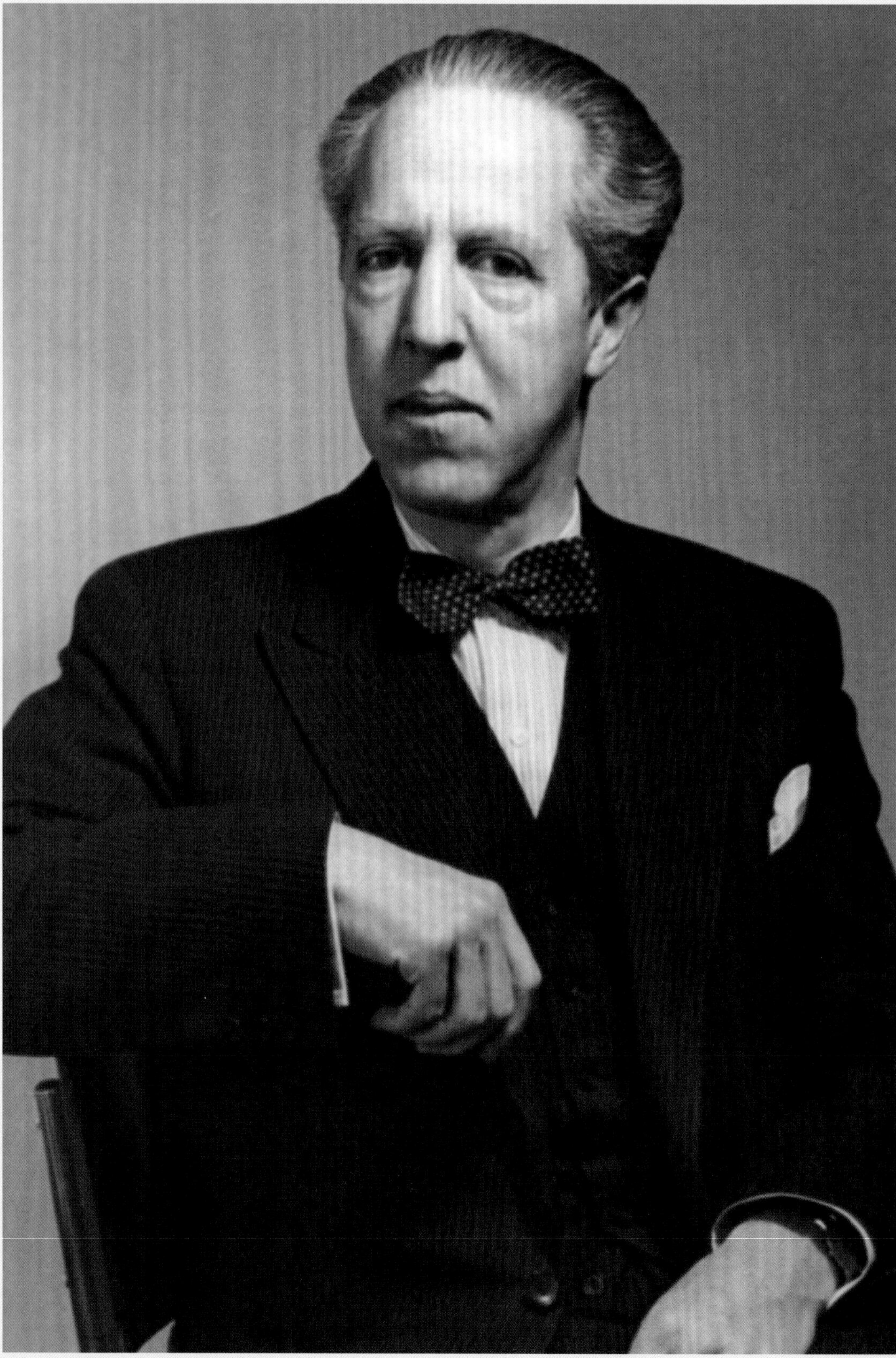

RY BOB DE VRIES

2 May 1905, Amsterdam-10 November 1983, enswoude

ry Bob de Vries was born in 1905 in msterdam, a son of textiles dealer Louis de ries and Clara Dalberg. He was of Jewish escent. In 1936 De Vries married Irène e Gunzburg, a historian and Slavist. She as born in Russia, a daughter of a banker, nd in her youth she became a friend of the msterdam art dealer Jacques Goudstikker. e Vries and his wife had two daughters.

e Vries read art history in Utrecht under rofessor Willem Vogelsang. After studying Paris in 1927 and 1928 he went on to ienna and Rome, returning to Utrecht in 930 to graduate. In 1934 De Vries received is doctorate for a thesis on Northern etherlandish portraiture in the second half f the sixteenth century. That same year e joined the paintings department of the ijksmuseum in Amsterdam. In August 1939, e month that the Netherlands mobilized, e Rijksmuseum was closed to the public r a while. De Vries was one of those who orked on keeping the collections safe by ansferring them to storage facilities outside msterdam.

n November 1940, after the German invasion, e was dismissed from the Rijksmuseum on e grounds of the occupying forces' anti- ewish measures. De Vries, together with is wife and little daughter, succeeded in scaping to Switzerland and settled in Basel the beginning of 1943. From there he sent ports to the Dutch government in London bout art protection and recovery, and he ade himself available to contribute to aving the nation's art holdings' after the war. n December 1944 he went to London, where he worked in the Dutch government's small art recovery department until February 1945. From this period onwards he played a leading role in making preparations for the return of cultural material that had disappeared to Germany.

In June 1945, when the SNK was established, De Vries and fellow art historian Van Gelder were appointed directors. De Vries soon became the only director and not long afterwards was also appointed to succeed Van Gelder as director of the RKD and of the Mauritshuis, responsibilities that he took actually charge of at a later stage. First and foremost, though, De Vries devoted a great deal of energy and dedication to art recovery. Under his leadership, and in collaboration with the allies, thousands of disappeared artworks were brought back to the Netherlands. His knowledge of art history was of great importance here. He was less well equipped for the next task, which was to supervise the further handling of the steadily growing stocks of art treasures. After irregularities had been discovered at the SNK and De Vries's arrest in connection with the Katz affair in July 1948, he was no longer in charge of day-to-day operations, although he remained director in name until 1 July 1950. The charges against De Vries were dropped because of insufficient evidence of guilt, but not until 1951. Meanwhile he had been focusing completely on his tasks at the Mauritshuis and the RKD. In 1954 he exchanged the latter role for the directorship of the Rijksmuseum H.W. Mesdag. He remained in post there and at the Mauritshuis until his retirement in 1970.

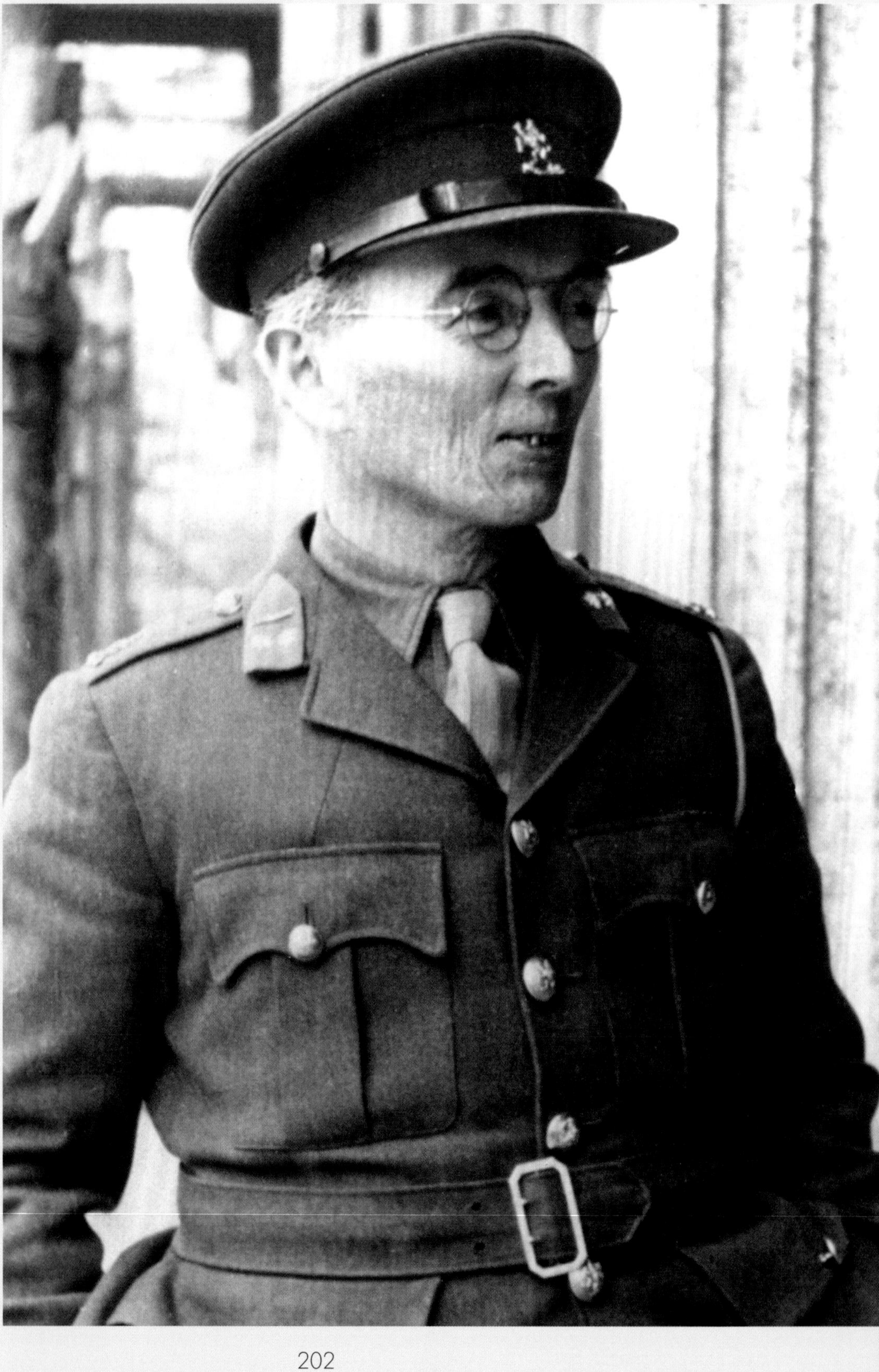

ALPHONSUS PETRUS ANTONIUS VORENKAMP

3 May 1898, Westerlee-18 August 1953, Groningen

Alphonsus Petrus Antonius (Phons) Vorenkamp was born in 1898, a son of the cleric Dr Roelof Vorenkamp and Roelina Harmanna Maria Boerma. He was unmarried.

After secondary school, Vorenkamp read law in Leiden. As soon as the opportunity presented itself, he switched to art history and became a student of Professor Wilhelm Martin. According to the Frisian art historian Abraham Wassenbergh, who became a friend of his, Vorenkamp excelled through initiative, organizational talent and wit. Immediately after he graduated in 1926, Vorenkamp was given a position at Smith College, a women's college in Northampton in the United States. In 1933, during a sabbatical in the Netherlands, he received his doctorate under Martin for a thesis on the Dutch still life in the seventeenth century. In 1942 Vorenkamp enlisted in the American army where, among other things, he gathered information about Dutch monuments, relics and artworks threatened by armed conflict. He retained his Dutch nationality. He returned to Smith College in 1943, but at the end of May 1945, at the request of the Dutch Minister of Foreign Affairs, he went post-haste to the Netherlands, where he was given the rank of lieutenant colonel and assigned to concentrate on the recovery of artworks.

At the invitation of the American authorities, he remained at the Central Collecting Point in Munich from October 1945 to May 1946. During this period he identified thousands of paintings and other works from, for example, the Mannheimer, Koenigs, Lanz and Goudstikker collections. According to Wassenbergh, Vorenkamp flourished in his new work environment. 'This task called for considerable tact and persuasiveness, particularly at the outset when the procedure had not yet been established. And indeed, Vorenkamp did outstanding work in this initial phase thanks to his personality and, needless to say, his excellent relationship with the Americans and understanding of their mentality. His sense of humour also helped to make him popular at an early stage in that extraordinary community'.

There was a celebratory moment in October 1945 when Vorenkamp arrived at Schiphol airport in an American army plane with the first post-war consignment of art transported to the Netherlands. In the summer of 1946 he was made a Knight in the Order of the Netherlands Lion in recognition of his efforts on behalf of Dutch cultural interests. That same year he wrote the catalogue for a travelling exhibition in the United States of forty-six paintings that had been brought back to the Netherlands thanks to the efforts of the American armed forces. Vorenkamp was succeeded in Munich in the spring of 1946 by the art historian R.F.P. de Beaufort. He resumed his work at Smith College, but not for long because in 1947 he returned to the Netherlands to become director of Museum Boijmans in Rotterdam. After only a year he left to be director of the Museum of Antiquities in Groningen. He died in Groningen in 1953.

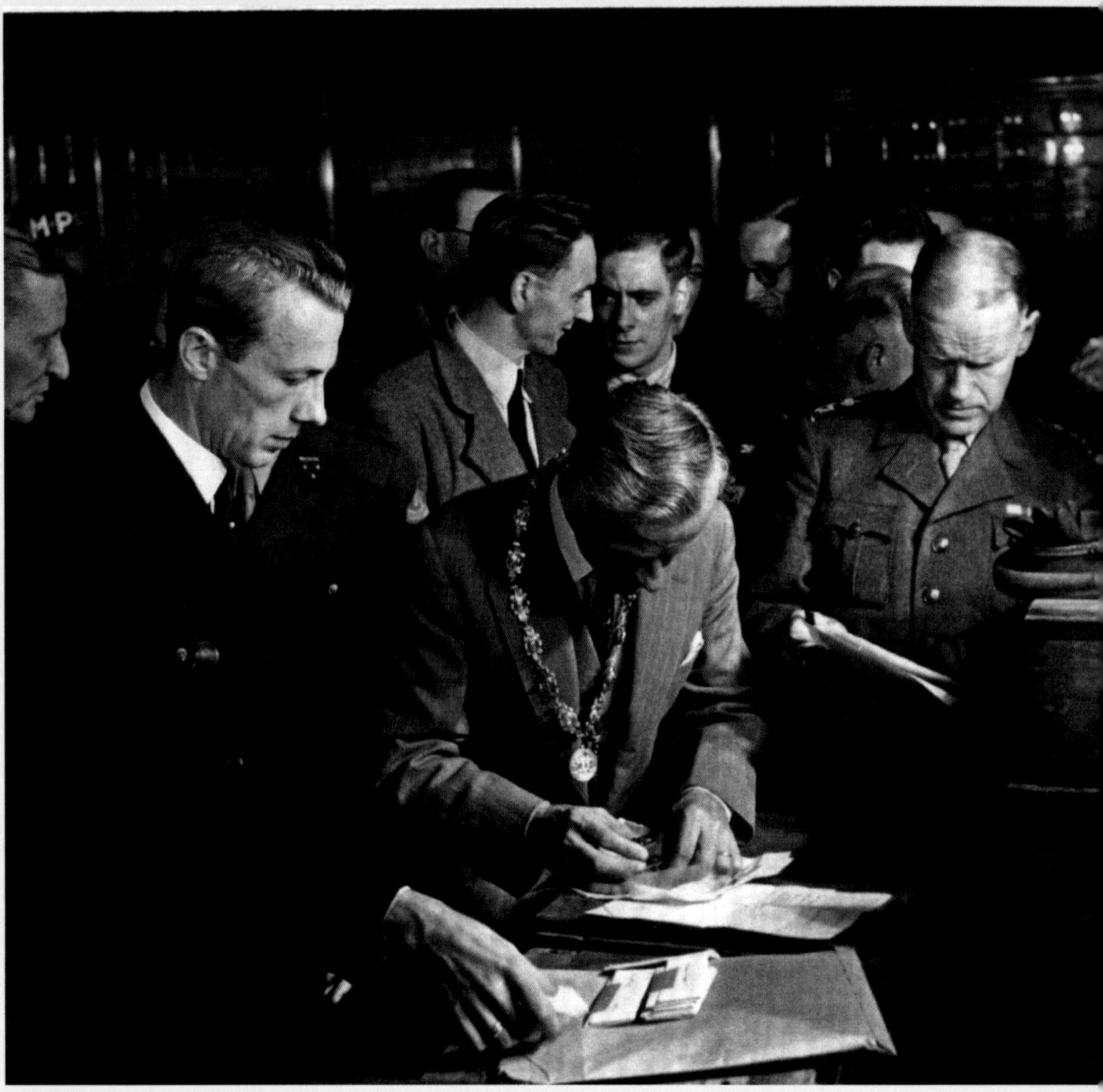
MP

JOLLE JOLLES

13 march 1916, Utrecht-20 August 2004, The Hague

Jolle Jolles was born in 1916 in Utrecht, a son of the medical doctor Willem Hendrik Jolles and Cornelia Johanna Jacoba van de Kasteele. He married Charlotte Gyr and had four children.

During the war Jolles graduated in law in Utrecht and then joined NS Netherlands Railways to work as a trainee inspector in the operations department. When the national railway strike started in September 1944, he went into hiding in Utrecht. At the end of October 1944 Jolles actively supported the organisation of the Binnenlandse Strijdkrachten (BS) union of Dutch resistance groups in Utrecht.

After the war Jolles worked initially in the Political Investigation Department (POD). During the post-war period, when the military authorities administered the Netherlands, this organization was tasked with tracking down and investigating collaborators. At the beginning of 1946 he became head of the War Booty Bureau, a new department of the Ministry of Finance, which was charged with collecting and managing goods left behind by the Germans. As time passed the Bureau was given additional duties, including dealing with goods brought back from Germany. On 26 August 1948, its name was changed to the Bureau for Restoration Payments and the Restoration of Property (Hergo). As the head of Hergo, Jolles's responsibilities included the restitution of diamonds recovered from Germany. When the SNK Netherlands Art Property Foundation was in dire straits as a result of scandals, Jolles was appointed its director in the autumn of 1948. This was an understandable appointment because Hergo and the SNK were involved with recovered goods. Art historian D.F. Lunsingh Scheurleer, State Inspector for Movable Relics, was appointed as acting director. On 1 February 1949 the SNK moved its office from Amsterdam to Mauritskade 37 in The Hague, where Hergo was also located. The SNK's administration was significantly improved under the new management and a more efficient restitution procedure was introduced.

Hergo took over the SNK's activities on 1 July 1950. Hergo's liquidation phase started in that year and ended with its closure on 1 February 1953. The Ministry of Finance's Administration Directorate took over Hergo's tasks. During the years that followed, Jolles became a progressively more senior civil servant in the Ministry of Finance. After a brief interim period in the Ministry of Foreign Affairs, in 1959 he was appointed director of the Dutch News Agency ANP. He continued to work there until his retirement in 1980.

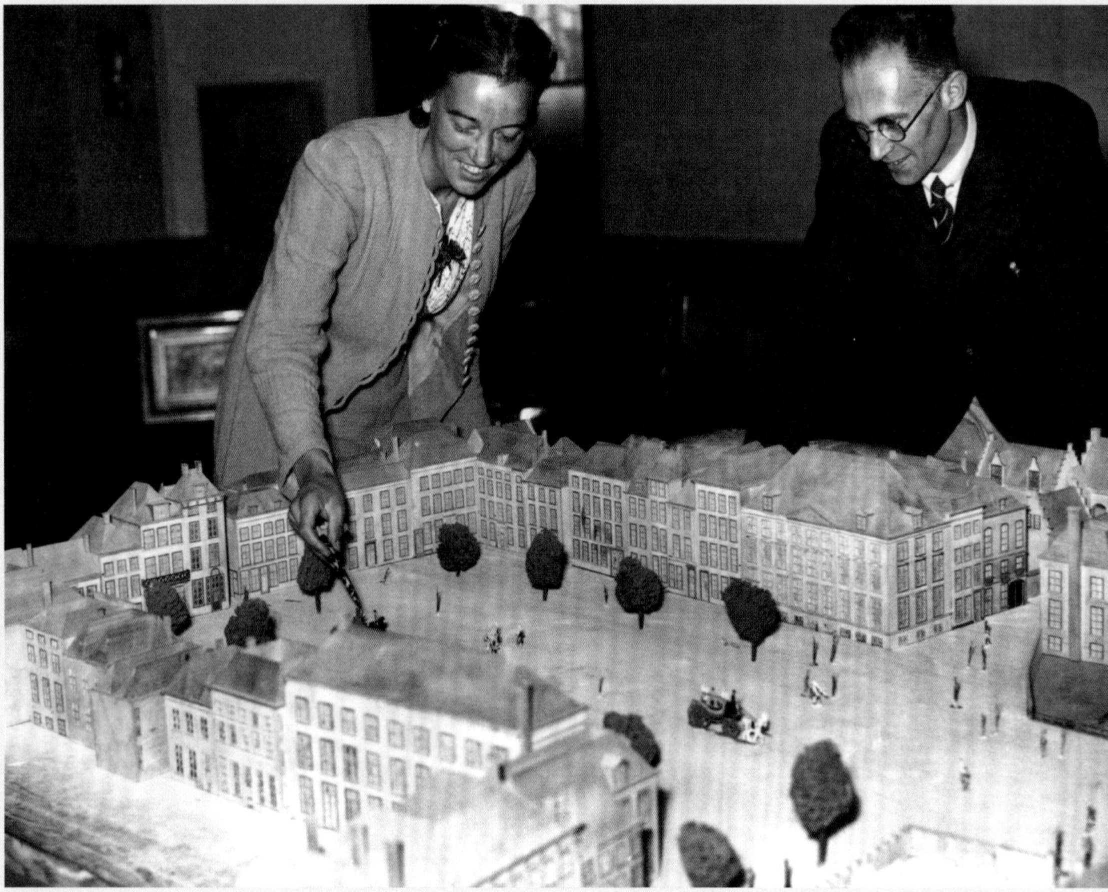

ANIËL FRANÇOIS LUNSINGH CHEURLEER

2 June 1908, The Hague-8 November 1999, ne Hague

aniël François (Daan) Lunsingh Scheurleer vas born in 1908 in The Hague, a son of the anker and archaeologist C.W. Lunsingh cheurleer and J.C.C. de Meester. He was narried three times and fathered three hildren.

unsingh Scheurleer read art history at ne École du Louvre in Paris and then vent to London. After he returned to the letherlands, he joined the Houthakker art allery in Amsterdam. Between 1935 and 1943 e worked at the Haags Gemeentemuseum in he Hague. In 1943 Scheurleer was appointed s an advisor to the State Museums Advisory ommittee. When the lawyer Jolles became ne new director of the SNK in the autumn f 1948, Lunsingh Scheurleer was appointed acting director. This new management brought about improvements in the SNK's chaotic administration. Restitution to original owners also got a new shot in the arm.

In 1949 Lunsingh Scheurleer was made head of the Department for Dispersed Government Artworks (DRVK). This department in the Ministry of Education, Arts and Science was responsible for state-owned works of art that were not in the inventory of a national museum. The DRVK was tasked with the management of recovered art. Lunsingh Scheurleer remained in this post until he retired in 1973. After various name changes, the DRVK was incorporated in the present Netherlands Cultural Heritage Agency.

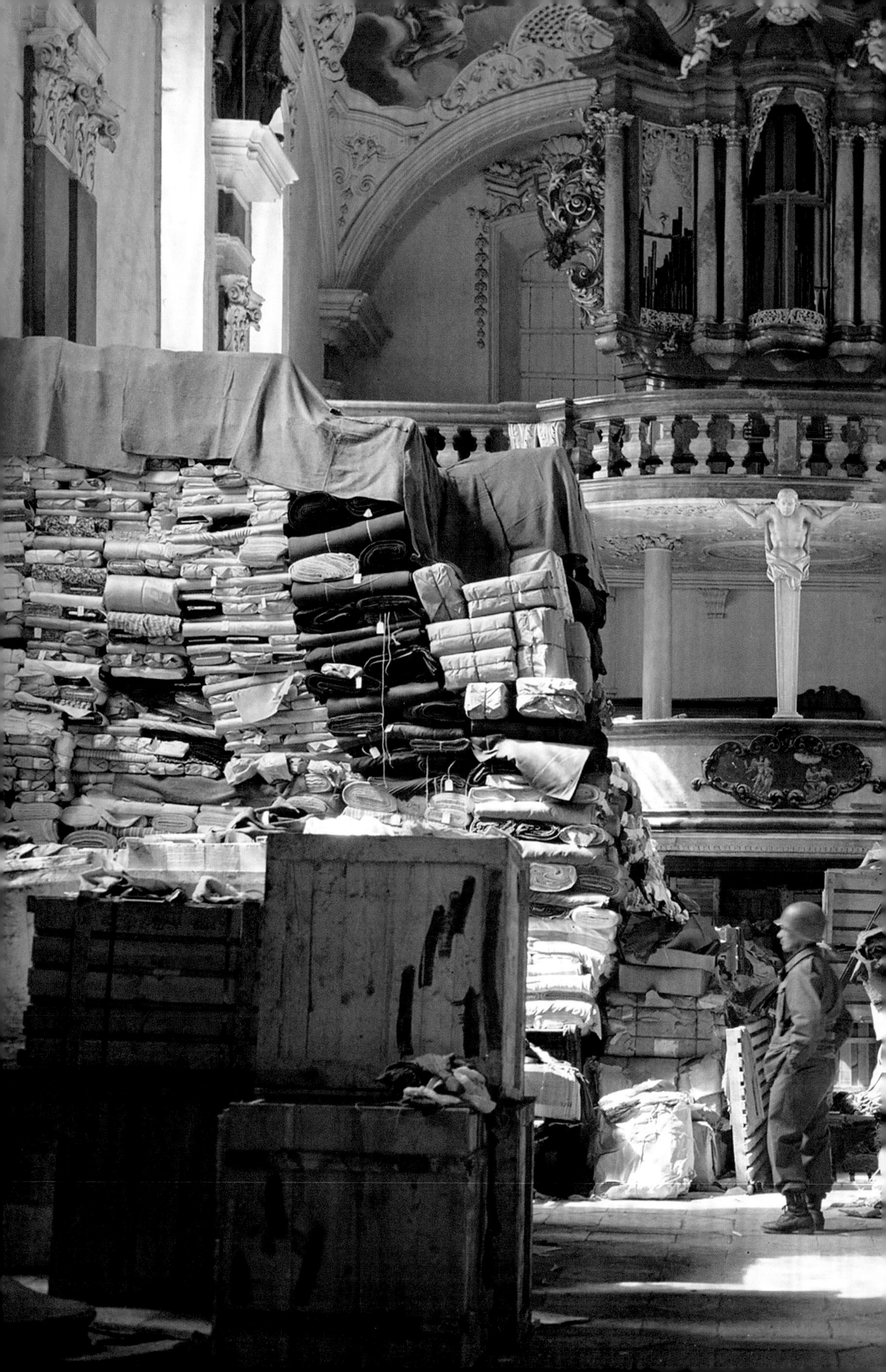

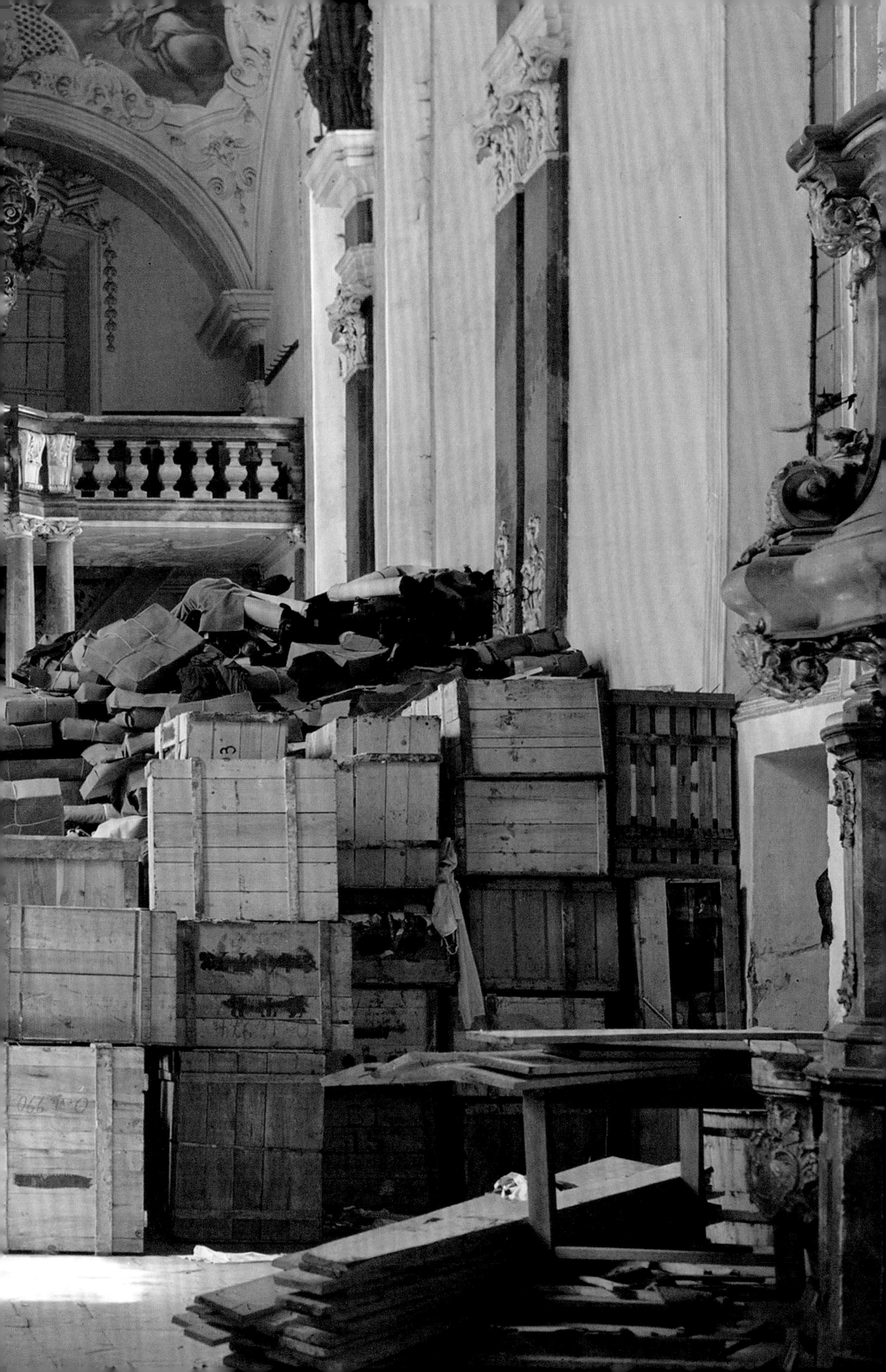

BIBLIOGRAPHICAL REFERENCES

The relevant archives, in particular the archives of the Stichting Nederlands Kunstbezit and the Centraal Archief Bijzondere Rechtspleging in the Nationaal Archief, The Hague, were used to compile the foregoing. Quotations included in the text are, unless otherwise stated, taken from documentation in these archives, including the 1948 Douwes report.

CHAPTER I

Heijbroek and Van Griensven 2007; Van 't Veen 2008; Venema 1986.

CHAPTER II

Euwe 2007; Heijbroek and Van Griensven 2007.

CHAPTER III

Aalders 1999; Boterman 2015; Croes and Tammes 2004; Euwe 2007; Heijbroek and Van Griensven 2007; Hoek and Ten Wolde1999; Jong, De 1969-1994; Kunert and Marck 2012; Michman,Beem and Michman 1999; Moore 1998; Muller and Schretlen 2002; Venema 1986.

CHAPTER IV

Aalders 1999; Croes and Tammes 2004; Dean, Goschler and Ther (eds) 2007; Euwe 2007; Heijbroek and Van Griensven 2007; Hoek and Ten Wolde 1999; Houwink ten Cate 1995; Jong, De 1969-1994; Michman, Beem and Michman 1999; Moore 1998; Muller and Schretlen 2002; Venema 1986.

CHAPTER V

Aalders 1999; Euwe 2007; Löhr 2005 and 2009; Nicholas 1994; Petropoulos 1996 and 2000; Schwarz 2004, 2009 and 2014; Venema 1986; Yeide 2009.

CHAPTER VI

Aalders 2001; Bossenbroek 2001; Cohen and Heimann-Jelinek (eds) 2011; Commission for Looted Art in Europe 2011; Edsel 2010; Hazemeijer 1990 and 2003; Hugh Smyth 1988; Hoogewoud e.a. 1997; Kersten 1999; Muller and Schretlen 2002; Schnabel and Tatzkow 2007; Veraart 2005.

CHAPTER VII

Adviescommissie Restitutieverzoeken, Verslagen; Campfens (ed) 2015; Commissie Ekkart, Proefonderzoek 1998; Commissie Ekkart, Deelrapportages I-VI; Commissie Ekkart, Eindrapportage 2006; Commissie Museale Verwervingen 1999; Ekkart and Schretlen 2014; Hollander, Den 1998.

KEYFIGURES

Bruyn 1981; Duparc 1975; Ekkart 1989; Hoetink 1984; Jolles 2002; Jörg 2000; Muller and Schretlen 2002; Röell 1953; Wassenbergh 1954.

BIBLIOGRAPHY

Aalders, G., *Roof. De ontvreemding van joods bezit tijdens de Tweede Wereldoorlog*, The Hague, 1999.

Aalders, G., *Berooid. De beroofde joden en het Nederlandse restitutiebeleid sinds 1945*, Amsterdam 2001.

Adviescommissie Restitutieverzoeken Cultuurgoederen and Tweede Wereldoorlog (Restitutiecommissie), *Verslagen*, The Hague 2002-2021.

Alford, K.D., *Hermann Göring and the Nazi Art Collection. The Looting of Europe's Art Treasures and Their Dispersal After World War II*, Jefferson NC 2012.

Alford, K.D., *Nazi plunder. Great treasure stories of World War II*, Cambridge 2001.

Armbruster, T., *Rückerstattung der Nazi-Beute, die Suche, Bergung und Restitution von Kulturgütern durch die westlichen Alliierten nach dem Zweiten Weltkrieg*, Berlin 2007.

Baruch, J. and L. van der Horst, *Het Rijksmuseum in oorlogstijd*, Amsterdam 1985.

Bertz, I. and M. Dorrmann (eds), *Raub und Restitution. Kulturgut aus jüdischem Besitz von 1933 bis heute*, Göttingen 2008.

Blom, J.C.H., R.G. Fuks-Mansfeld and I. Schöffer (eds), *Geschiedenis van de joden in Nederland*, Amsterdam 1995.

Boom, B. van der, *'Wij weten niets van hun lot'. Gewone Nederlanders en de Holocaust*, Amsterdam 2012.

Bossenbroek, M., *De meelstreep. Terugkeer en opvang na de Tweede Wereldoorlog*, Amsterdam 2001.

Boterman, F., *Cultuur als macht. Cultuurgeschiedenis van Duitsland, 1800-heden*, Amsterdam 2013.

Boterman, F., *Duitse daders. De Jodenvervolging en de nazificatie van Nederland (1940- 1945)*, Amsterdam 2015.

Bouchoux, C., *Rose Valland. Resistance at the Museum*, Dallas 2013.

Bruyn, J., 'Levensbericht J.G. van Gelder', in: *Koninklijke Nederlandse Akademie van Wetenschappen. Jaarboek 1980*, Amsterdam etc. 1981, 186-191.

Campfens, E. (ed), *Fair and just solutions? Alternatives to litigation in Nazi-looted art disputes: status quo and new developments*, The Hague 2015.

Centrale Archief Selectiedienst, *Inventaris van het archief van het Commissariaat-Generaal voor de Nederlandse Economische Belangen in Duitsland, 1945-1949 (1950)*, Nationaal Archief, The Hague 1988.

Chanel, G., *Saving Mona Lisa. The Battle to protect the Louvre and its treasures from the Nazis*, Poughkeepsie 2014.

Cohen, J.-M. and F. Heimann-Jelinek (eds), *Neglected Witnesses: The Fate of Jewish Ceremonial Objects during the Second World War and After*, Amsterdam 2011.

Commissie Ekkart, *Project Herkomst Gezocht, Aanbevelingen; Aanbevelingen Kunsthandel; Slotaanbevelingen*, The Hague 2001, 2003 and 2004.

Commissie Ekkart, *Project Herkomst Gezocht, Deelrapportages I-VI en Eindrapportage*, The Hague 1999-2004.

Commissie Ekkart, *Project Herkomst Gezocht, Eindrapportage Commissie Ekkart (Origins unknown. Final report Ekkart Committee)*, Zwolle 2006.

Commissie Ekkart, *Project Herkomst Gezocht. Rapport van het proefonderzoek naar de herkomst van de onder beheer van het Rijk gebleven uit Duitsland gerecupereerde kunstwerken*, The Hague 1998.

Commissie Museale Verwervingen 1940-1948, *Rapport museale verwervingen 1940-1948*, Nederlandse Museumvereniging, E. Muller (ed), Amsterdam 1999.

Commissie Van Kemenade, *Tweede Wereldoorlog. Roof en rechtsherstel. Eindrapport van de Contactgroep Tegoeden WOII*, Amsterdam 2000.

Commission for Looted Art in Europe, 'Introduction to The National Archives' records on Nazi-Era Looted Cultural Property', 1939-1961, 2011.

Croes, M.T. and P.J.R. Tammes, *'Gif laten wij niet voortbestaan'. Een onderzoek naar de overlevingskansen van Joden in de Nederlandse gemeenten, 1940-1945*, Amsterdam 2004.

Dean, M., C. Goschler and Ph. Ther (eds), *Robbery and Restitution. The conflict over Jewish property in Europe*, New York etc. 2007.

Dekker, A. e.a., *Omstreden verleden. Museum Boijmans Van Beuningen en de Tweede Wereldoorlog*, Rotterdam 2018.

Douwes, E., 'De kunsthandel in Nederland', 2 October 1948, unpublished report (Nationaal Archief, The Hague).

Duparc, F.J., *Een eeuw strijd voor Nederlands cultureel erfgoed*, The Hague 1975.

Edsel, R.M., *Rescuing Da Vinci. Hitler and the Nazis stole Europe's great art, America and her allies recovered it*, Dallas 2006.

Edsel, R.M. and B. Witter, *De kunstbrigade. Hoe de geallieerden de Europese kunstschatten redden*, Houten 2010.

Ekkart, R. and H. Schretlen, *Museale verwervingen vanaf 1933. Herkomstonderzoek naar museale collecties in verband met roof, confiscatie of gedwongen verkoop in de periode 1933-1945 (investigation into the provenance of museum collections in connection with the theft, confiscation and sale of objects under duress between 1933 and 1945)*, Amsterdam 2014.

Ekkart, R.E.O., 'Gelder, Jan Gerrit van (1903-1980)', in: J. Charité (ed.), *Biografisch Woordenboek van Nederland* 3 (1989), 187-188.

Euwe, J., *De Nederlandse kunstmarkt 1940-1945*, Amsterdam, 2007.

Feliciano, H., *The lost museum. The Nazi conspiracy to steal the world's greatest works of art*, New York 1997.

Goodman, S., *De wolven namen alles mee. Op zoek naar de door de nazi's geroofde kunstverzameling van mijn familie*, Amsterdam 2015.

Hazemeijer, J., *Inventaris van het archief van de Stichting Nederlands Kunstbezit (SNK) en haar taakvoorganger / taakopvolgers, (1930) 1945-1951 (1983)*, Nationaal Archief, The Hague 1990.

Hazemeijer, J., *Inventaris van het archief van de Afdeling Bewindvoering (juni 1945) / Afdeling Juridische Zaken en Bewindvoering (juli 1945) / Directie Bewindvoering (1951) van de Administratie / Algemeen Beheer der Generale Thesaurie, (1940) 1945-1954 (1965)*, Nationaal Archief, The Hague 2003.

Hazemeijer, J., *Inventaris van het archief van het Bureau Herstelbetalings- en Recuperatiegoederen (HERGO) van het Ministerie van Financiën en zijn rechtsvoorgangers, (1945)1946-1953 (1961)*, Nationaal Archief, The Hague 2003.

Heijbroek, J.F. and A.Th.J. van Griensven, *Kunst, kennis en kwaliteit. De Vereeniging van Handelaren in Oude Kunst in Nederland, 1911-heden*, Zwolle 2007.

Hoek, F. and J. ten Wolde, *Roof en restitutie Joods vermogen. Rapport uitgebracht aan de Contactgroep Tegoeden Wereldoorlog II*, 2 dln., 1999.

Hoetink, H. R. 'Ary Bob de Vries (1905-1983)', *Burlington Magazine* 126/981, December 1984, 782.

Hoffmann, M. and N. Kuhn, *Hitlers Kunsthändler. Hildebrand Gurlitt, 1895–1956. Die Biographie*, Munich 2016.

Hollander, P. den, *De zaak Goudstikker*, Amsterdam 1998.

Hoogewoud, F.J. et al (eds), *The return of looted collections (1946-1996). An unfinished chapter: proceedings of an international symposium to mark the 50th anniversary of the return of Dutch book collections from Germany in 1946 (Amsterdam, 15 and 16 April 1996)*, Amsterdam 1997.

Hopp, M., *Kunsthandel im Nationalsozialismus. Adolf Weinmüller in München und Wien*, Cologne 2012.

Hugh Smyth, C., *Repatriation of art from the collecting point in Munich after World War II. Background and beginnings: with reference especially to the Netherlands*, Maarssen 1988.

Huyssen, A., A. Rabinbach and A. Shalem (eds), *Nazi-Looted Art and Its Legacies, an issue of New German Critique* 44/1 (February 2017).

Jolles, J., *'Ha die Jolle'*, unpublished memoirs, Voorschoten 2002.

Jong, L. de, *Het Koninkrijk der Nederlanden in de Tweede Wereldoorlog*, 14 dln., The Hague and Leiden, 1969-1994.

Jörg, C.J.A., 'In memoriam Daan Lunsingh Scheurleer', *Vormen uit vuur* 172 (2000), 2-4.

:ersten, J.W., *Theorie en praktijk van het naoorlogse ɛchtsherstel*, The Hague 1999.

:rul, W.E., *Hannema, museumdirecteur. Over kunst n illusie*, Amsterdam 2018.

:unert, F. and A. Marck, 'The Dutch Art Market 930-1945 and Dutch Restitution Policy Regarding rt Dealers', in: E. Blimlinger and M. Mayer (eds), *:unst sammeln, Kunst handeln: Beiträge des Interationalen Symposiums in Wien*, Vienna 2012.

:urtz, M.J., *America and the Return of Nazi Contraand: The Recovery of Europe's Cultural Treasures*, :ambridge 2006.

angfeld, G., M. Schavemaker and M. Soeting ed.), *Het Stedelijk in de oorlog*, Amsterdam 2015.

auterbach, I., *The Central Collecting Point in Iunich. A new beginning for the restitution and rotection of art*, Los Angeles 2018.

öhr, H.C., *Das Braune Haus der Kunst. Hitler und er 'Sonderauftrag Linz'. Visionen, Verbrechen, 'erluste*, Berlin 2005.

öhr, H.C., *Der eiserne Sammler. Die Kollektion Iermann Göring. Kunst und Korruption im 'Dritten :eich'*, Berlin 2009.

öhr, H.C., *Hitlers Linz. Der 'Heimatgau des 'ührers'*, Berlin 2013.

upfer, G. and T. Rudert, *Kennerschaft zwischen Iacht und Moral. Annäherungen an Hans Posse 1879-1942)*, Cologne 2015.

Ianasse, P.M., *Verdwenen archieven en ibliotheken*, The Hague 1995.

Iarck, A. and E. Muller, 'National Panels advising n Nazi-looted Art in Austria, France, the United :ingdom, the Netherlands and Germany. A brief verview', in: E. Campfens (ed) (2015).

Marck, A. and M. Schoonderwoerd, 'Interviews with Bas van Lier, Ella Andriesse, Robert Sturm and Alfred Jacobsen', in: E. Campfens (ed) (2015), pp. 103-110, 141-152, 223-230.

Mcauley, J., *The House of Fragile Things. Jewish Art Collectors and the Fall of France*, New Haven 2022.

McLaughlin, Jr., A.J., *Art and the Nazis, 1933-1945. Looting, Propaganda and Seizure*, Jefferson NC 2022.

Mellink, G.-J. and Rhijn, L. van, *Museum in de oorlog, kunst in vrijheid. Den Haag 1940-1950*, The Hague 2021.

Moore, B., *Slachtoffers en overlevenden. De nazivervolging van de Joden in Nederland*, Amsterdam 1998.

Muller, E. and H. Schretlen, *Betwist Bezit. De Stichting Nederlands Kunstbezit en de teruggave van roofkunst na 1945*, Zwolle 2002.

Müller, M. and Tatzkow, M., *Verlorene Bilder, verlorene Leben. Jüdische Sammler und was aus ihren Kunstwerken wurde*, Munich 2009.

Nicholas, L.H., *The rape of Europa. The fate of Europe's treasures in the Third Reich and the Second World War*, New York 1994.

Oost, T., *In an Effort to Do Justice? Restitution Policies and the Washington Principles*, Amsterdam 2012.

Palmer, N., *Museums and the Holocaust: Law, Principles and Practice*, 2000.

Petropoulos, J., *Art as politics in the Third Reich*, Chapel Hill 1996.

Petropoulos, J., *Goering's Man in Paris. The Story of a Nazi Art Plunderer and His World*, New Haven 2021.

Petropoulos, J., *The Faustian bargain. The art world in Nazi Germany*, London 2000.

Rijksdienst Beeldende Kunst, *Old master paintings. An illustrated summary catalogue*, Zwolle 1992.

Röell, D.C., 'In memoriam dr. A.P.A. Vorenkamp. Overleden te Groningen 18 augustus 1953', *Nieuws-Bulletin van de Koninklijke Nederlandse Oudheidkundige Bond*, 15 October 1953, kol. 153-176.

Ronald, S., *Hitler's art thief. Hildebrand Gurlitt, the Nazis, and the Looting of Europe's treasures*, New York 2015.

Rydell, A., *De plunderaars. De nazi-obsessie met kunst*, Amsterdam 2015.

Schnabel, G. and M. Tatzkow, *Nazi looted art. Handbuch Kunstrestitution weltweit*, Berlin 2007.

Schwarz, B., *Hitlers Museum. Die Fotoalben 'Gemäldegalerie Linz'. Dokumente zum 'Führermuseum'*, Vienna 2004.

Schwarz, B., *Geniewahn. Hitler und die Kunst*, Vienna 2009.

Schwarz, B., *Auf Befehl des Führers*, Darmstadt 2014.

Sels, G., *Kunst voor das Reich. Op zoek naar naziroofkunst uit België*, Tielt 2022.

Tompkins, A. (ed), *Provenance research today. Principles, practice, problems*, London 2020.

Van 't Veen, F., *Het Nederlandse palazzo. Verzamelingen van vroeg-Italiaanse kunst (The Dutch palazzo: collections of early Italian art)*, Amsterdam 2008.

Venema, A., *Kunsthandel in Nederland 1940-1945*, Amsterdam, 1986.

Veraart, W., *Ontrechting en rechtsherstel in Nederland en Frankrijk in de jaren van bezetting en wederopbouw*, Alphen aan den Rijn 2005.

Wassenbergh, A., 'Alphonsus Petrus Antonius Vorenkamp (Westerlee, 3 May 1898-Groningen, 18 August 1953)', in: *Jaarboek van de Maatschappij der Nederlandsche Letterkunde te Leiden, 1951-1953* Leiden 1954.

Yeide, N.H., *Beyond the dreams of avarice. The Hermann Goering collection*, introd. R.M. Edsel, Dallas 2009.

GLOSSARY

- Rijksdienst voor het Cultureel Erfgoed (RCE) – National Cultural Heritage Agency
- NK-collectie – Netherlands Art Property Collection (NK Collection)
- Stichting Nederlands Kunstbezit (SNK) – Netherlands Art Property Foundation
- Bureau Herkomst Gezocht – Origins Unknown Agency

ABOUT THE AUTHORS

RUDI EKKART is an art historian and was director of the RKD (Netherlands Institute for Art History) from 1990 to 2012 and professor of art history at Utrecht University from 2003 to 2012. From 1997, he has been involved in the research into the fate of works of art during and after World War II as chairman of several successive committees. In that role, Ekkart was jointly responsible for the research of the Origins Unknown Agency and for the realisation of a new Dutch restitution policy. He also contributed to several exhibitions and publications on these issues.

EELKE MULLER is a historian and has worked at the NIOD Institute for War, Holocaust and Genocide Studies since 2018. From 1998 to 2018, she investigated the wartime history of objects from Dutch public art collections for the Ekkart Committee, the Dutch Museums Association and the Restitutions Committee. Muller contributed to several exhibitions and publications on art theft and restitution in the Netherlands. She is, for instance, co-author of a book on post-war restitution policy in the Netherlands: *Betwist bezit. De Stichting Nederlands Kunstbezit en de teruggave van roofkunst na 1945* (Disputed possession. The Netherlands Art Property Foundation and the restitution of looted art after 1945)

The authors would like to thank everyone who helped them with information, photographic material and encouragement. They especially thank Floris Kunert for his critical reading of the manuscript of the original edition.

PHOTO CREDITS

Anne Frank Stiftung, 64
ANP/Polygoon, pagina 206
Archiv der Stadt Linz, 89
Associated Press, 129
Biblioteka Uniwersytecka w Warszawie, 97
Bureau Herkomst Gezocht / Perry Schrier, 155,
Collectie Stedelijk Museum Amsterdam
@The Estate of Erwin Blumenfeld, 160
Photography Liselore Kamping , Amsterdam, 159
Gelders Archief, collection P.J. de Booys, 194/195
Germanisches Nationalmuseum, Deutsches Kunstarchiv, NL Posse, Hans, Neurenberg, 91
Getty Images, Central Press, Hulton Archive, 93
Getty Images, Ullstein Bild, 90
Mike Bink Photography, 168, 169
Nationaal Archief, 134, 138, 196
Nationaal Archief / Collectie Spaarnestad, 15, 16/17, 45, 62, 139, 140
National Archives and Records Administration, 127, 208/ 209,
NIOD, 66/67, 135
Rijksdienst voor het Cultureel Erfgoed, 63
Rijksdienst voor het Cultureel Erfgoed / Adinda van Wely, 172, 173
Rijksmuseum Amsterdam, 10 (for details see p. 13), 13 (top)
RKD – Nederlands Instituut voor Kunstgeschiedenis, 198, 200
Shutterstock, 128
Stadsarchief Amsterdam, 12, 13 (below), 44, 48, 65, 70

Cover
General Dwight D. Eisenhower inspects art treasures looted by the Germans and stored in a salt mine in Germany, 12 April 1945. National Archives and Records Administration, Collage Park
Man with Beard and Turban, follower of REMBRANDT (1606-1669), Panel, 73 x 59.5 cm, Rijksdienst voor het Cultureel Erfgoed, NK1602
German guards of the stolen art treasures stack and inspect the artworks, Hamburg 9 November 1945, Nationaal Archief / collection Spaarnestad/ photographer unknown

CREDITS

PUBLISHER
Waanders Publishers, Zwolle
Rijksdienst voor het Cultureel Erfgoed/National Cultural Heritage Agency

AUTHORS
Rudi Ekkart
Eelke Muller

TRANSLATION
Claire van den Donk
Lynne Richards (Chapter VI & Keyfigures)

DESIGN
Gert Jan Slagter
Frank de Wit

LITHOGRAPHY
Benno Slijkhuis, Wilco Art Books

PRINTING
Wilco Art Books, Amersfoort

This publication is partly based on the Dutch publication *Roof & Restitutie*, published in 2017 to accompany the exhibition of the same name in Deventer, organised by the Ter Borch Foundation.

ISBN 9789462624986
NUR 654

This publication is also available in a Dutch edition: 9789462624979

www.waanders.nl

FSC www.fsc.org MIX Paper | Supporting responsible forestry FSC® C004472